Beyond the Enlightenment

# Beyond the Enlightenment
*Scottish Intellectual Life, 1790–1914*

Edited by Aileen Fyfe and Colin Kidd

EDINBURGH
University Press

Edinburgh University Press is one of the leading university presses in the UK. We publish academic books and journals in our selected subject areas across the humanities and social sciences, combining cutting-edge scholarship with high editorial and production values to produce academic works of lasting importance. For more information visit our website: edinburghuniversitypress.com

© editorial matter and organisation Aileen Fyfe and Colin Kidd, 2023, 2024
© the chapters their several authors, 2023, 2024

Edinburgh University Press Ltd
13 Infirmary Street,
Edinburgh, EH1 1LT

First published in hardback by Edinburgh University Press 2023

Typeset in 10.5/13 GoudyStd by
Cheshire Typesetting Ltd, Cuddington, Cheshire

A CIP record for this book is available from the British Library

ISBN 978 1 4744 9303 1 (hardback)
ISBN 978 1 4744 9304 8 (paperback)
ISBN 978 1 4744 9305 5 (webready PDF)
ISBN 978 1 4744 9306 2 (epub)

The right of Aileen Fyfe and Colin Kidd to be identified as editors of this work has been asserted in accordance with the Copyright, Designs and Patents Act 1988 and the Copyright and Related Rights Regulations 2003 (SI No. 2498).

# Contents

Notes on Contributors     vii
Acknowledgements     xi

1. Introduction: Scotland after Enlightenment     1
   *Aileen Fyfe and Colin Kidd*

2. The Enlightenment Legacy and the Democratic Intellect     18
   *Robert Anderson*

3. Dugald Stewart, William Godwin and the Formation of Political Economy     36
   *Lina Weber*

4. The French Revolution and the Transformation of Moderatism: The Silence of the Scribes     54
   *John S. Warren*

5. James Mackintosh: The Science of Politics after the French Revolution     70
   *Richard Whatmore*

6. Scotland's Freethinking Societies: Debating Natural Theology, 1820–c.1843     89
   *Felicity Loughlin*

7. Christian Isobel Johnstone: Radical Journalism and the Ambiguous Legacy of the Scottish Enlightenment     107
   *Jane Rendall*

8. Robert Mudie: Pioneer Naturalist and Crusading Reformer  126
   *Eva-Charlotta Mebius*

9. Theories of Universal Degeneration in Post-Enlightenment Scotland  137
   *Bill Jenkins*

10. Robert Knox: The Embittered Scottish Anatomist and his Controversial Race Science in Mid-Nineteenth-Century Britain  151
    *Efram Sera-Shriar*

11. Thomas Carlyle and the Scottish Enlightenment Concept of Sympathy  168
    *Joanna Malecka*

12. Covenanting and Enlightenment in Nineteenth-Century Reformed Presbyterian Political Theory  187
    *Valerie Wallace*

13. Andrew Lang and the Cosmopolitan Condition  205
    *Catriona M. M. Macdonald*

14. Criticism and Freethought, 1880–1914  223
    *Colin Kidd*

15. Epilogue: The Afterlife of the Enlightenment in Scottish Criticism  241
    *Gerard Carruthers*

Index  258

# Notes on Contributors

**Robert Anderson** is Emeritus Professor of History at the University of Edinburgh. He has written extensively on the history of education in Scotland, Britain and Europe. His books include *Education and Opportunity in Victorian Scotland: Schools and Universities* (1983), *Education and the Scottish People 1750–1918* (1995), *European Universities from the Enlightenment to 1914* (2004) and *British Universities Past and Present* (2006). He is joint editor of *The Edinburgh History of Education in Scotland* (2015).

**Gerard Carruthers** is Francis Hutcheson Professor of Literature at the University of Glasgow. He is general editor of the multi-volume Oxford University Press edition of the *Collected Works of Robert Burns*, for which he is currently editing correspondence and poetry volumes.

**Aileen Fyfe** is Professor of Modern History at the University of St Andrews. She is a social and cultural historian of science and technology, and has written extensively about the communication of science, and the history of academic publishing more broadly. Her books include *A History of Scientific Journals: Publishing at the Royal Society, 1665–2015* (2022), *Steam-Powered Knowledge: William Chambers and the Business of Publishing 1820–1860* (2012) and *Science and Salvation: Evangelicals and Popular Science Publishing in Victorian Britain* (2004).

**Bill Jenkins** is a temporary Lecturer in the School of History at the University of St Andrews, where he was previously a postdoctoral fellow on the Leverhulme-Trust-funded project 'After the Enlightenment: Scottish Intellectual Life, 1790–1843'. He is the author of *Evolution before Darwin: Theories of the Transmutation of Species*, published by Edinburgh University Press in 2019, and several articles.

**Colin Kidd** is Wardlaw Professor of Modern History at the University of St Andrews. A former editor of the *Scottish Historical Review*, his books include *Subverting Scotland's Past* (1993) and *Union and Unionisms* (2008). He co-edited the *International Companion to John Galt* (2017) and *Literature and Union: Scottish Texts, British Contexts* (2018).

**Felicity Loughlin** is a Lecturer in the History of Modern Christianity at the University of Edinburgh. She was previously an Early Career Fellow at Edinburgh, and before that a Leverhulme-funded postdoctoral research fellow at the University of St Andrews. A revised version of her thesis will be published as *The Scottish Enlightenment Confronts the Gods: Paganism and the Birth of Religion*. She has also co-edited *Antiquity and Enlightenment Culture: New Approaches and Perspectives* (2020).

**Catriona M. M. Macdonald** is Reader in Late Modern Scottish History at the University of Glasgow. She is the author of *Whaur Extremes Meet: Scotland's Twentieth Century* (2009) and *The Radical Thread* (2000), and edited *Scotland and the Great War* (1999) and *Unionist Scotland* (1998). She is Director of the Centre for Scottish and Celtic Studies at the University of Glasgow, President of the Scottish History Society, and a former editor of the *Scottish Historical Review*.

**Joanna Malecka** is Lecturer in English Literature at the Open University. Her doctorate was on Thomas Carlyle's *The French Revolution: A History*, and she has subsequently published articles on Carlyle in *History of European Ideas*, *Global Intellectual History* and *Studies in Scottish Literature*.

**Eva-Charlotta Mebius** is a Postdoctoral Researcher within the Bernadotte Programme at Uppsala University, where she is running the project 'Embroidered Landscapes'. She is also an Honorary Research Associate at the University of London. Her interests are interdisciplinary but centre on literature in its broadest definition and art history.

**Jane Rendall** is an Honorary Fellow of the History Department and the Centre for Eighteenth Century Studies at the University of York. She has published extensively on the history of the Enlightenment, and on women's and feminist history, especially in Scotland in the eighteenth and nineteenth centuries. Most recently, she is a co-editor of *The New Biographical Disctionary of Scottish Women* (2018), and of *Association and Enlightenment: Scottish Clubs and Societies, 1700–1830* (2020).

**Efram Sera-Shriar** is a Copenhagen-based historian and writer. He received his PhD from the University of Leeds and has worked in higher education and the museum sector for nearly twenty years. He is Associate Director of Research for the Centre for Nineteenth-Century Studies International at Durham University. Sera-Shriar has published extensively on the history of science and belief. His books include *The Making of British Anthropology, 1813–1871* (2013), and *Historicizing Humans: Deep Time, Evolution, and Race in Nineteenth-Century British Sciences* (2018). Since 2006 he has also been a senior editor for *The Correspondence of John Tyndall*. His new book, *Psychic Investigators*, explores British anthropology's engagement with modern spiritualism during the late Victorian era.

**Valerie Wallace** is Lecturer in the History of Scotland and the Wider World at the University of St Andrews. Formerly a senior lecturer in History at Te Herenga Waka–Victoria University of Wellington, Aotearoa New Zealand, she is the author of *Scottish Presbyterianism and Settler Colonial Politics: Empire of Dissent* (2018), which won the Frank Watson book prize for best first book in Scottish history, awarded by the University of Guelph. She has also authored articles on interrelated topics in ecclesiastical, intellectual and radical history in various journals including the *Scottish Historical Review*, the *Journal of Imperial and Commonwealth History* and *Utilitas*. She is currently co-editor of the *Journal of Scottish Historical Studies*.

**John S. Warren** was until recently an Honorary Research Fellow in Intellectual History at the University of St Andrews. A retired businessman who worked for STV and various other companies, he has published articles on the history of nineteenth-century science in *History of European Ideas*.

**Lina Weber** is Associate Director of the St Andrews Institute of Intellectual History and Dugald Stewart project fellow at the Institute for Advanced Studies in the Humanities, University of Edinburgh. She has edited the economic writings of the Swiss philosopher Isaak Iselin (2016) and the lectures on political economy of Dugald Stewart (Edinburgh University Press, forthcoming). Her articles on the history of European political and economic thought in the long eighteenth century have been published in various collections and journals including *History of Political Economy* and *The Historical Journal*.

**Richard Whatmore** is Professor of Modern History at the University of St Andrews and co-director of the St Andrews Institute of Intellectual History. He is the author of *Republicanism and the French Revolution* (2000), *Against War and Empire* (2012), *What is Intellectual History?* (2015), *Terrorists, Anarchists and Republicans* (2019) and *The History of Political Thought. A Very Short Introduction* (2021).

# Acknowledgements

The editors would like to thank the Leverhulme Trust (RPG-2018-017) for its support of this project as a whole, and particularly of Chapters 1, 3, 5, 6, 9 and 14. They would also like to thank Andy Eccles for his help with the final preparation of the text.

# 1

# Introduction: Scotland after Enlightenment

## Aileen Fyfe and Colin Kidd

Nineteenth-century Scotland lacks a compelling descriptor of cultural and intellectual life, by contrast with the well-understood significance of 'Renaissance', 'Reformation' and 'Enlightenment'. Perhaps this absence goes some way towards explaining why intellectual historians have difficulty gaining a purchase on the period. Of course, we sometimes label the era 'Victorian', but the term carries pejorative overtones, an association with a prim and stifling conformity which is especially misleading in the context of intellectual enquiry. Strictly speaking, moreover, the term 'Victorian' is chronologically limited to the period of Victoria's reign, 1837–1901. Instead, this volume tackles a more extended period – a long nineteenth century – between the French Revolution and the First World War as the most potentially insightful means of understanding post-Enlightenment Scotland. It focuses attention in the first instance on the legacy of the Enlightenment at the very end of the eighteenth century, but also takes note of those influences which persisted as late the Edwardian era – which saw the zenith in the reputations of figures such as Sir James Frazer and the dominant figure in British freethought, the rationalist J. M. Robertson.

Our knowledge of Scotland's post-Enlightenment is surprisingly sketchy. Whereas the Scottish Enlightenment has been studied in extraordinary detail over the past fifty years, by a huge army of scholars from across the world who have analysed it with vitality, nuance and authority, we have only a patchy and disjointed understanding of Scottish intellectual life in the century that followed. The priorities of nineteenth-century Scottish historians have been very different, and there has been very little attention paid to the legacy of the Enlightenment for succeeding generations.

Our histories of Scotland in the long nineteenth century have been dominated by industrialisation, ecclesiastical Disruption, and accounts of migration to and from Scotland. This is understandable: the consequences of industrialisation spread far beyond the stereotypical factories and shipyards, and affected the provision of everything from teapots, ribbons and buttons, to education, religion and healthcare. Similarly, the drama of the Disruption of 1843 stands out amidst the competitive tensions between denominations, church schisms and reunions that preceded (and succeeded) it. Migration too was a dominant theme in nineteenth-century Scottish life: emigration to North America and Australasia had its counterpoint in the arrival in Scotland's cities and coalfields of Irish immigrants. These patterns of migration – and the ways in which their supposed causes and consequences were mythologised and distorted – have played a major role in how modern Scotland sees itself.

Historians have properly devoted attention to these topics, but what has been overlooked? Many things, no doubt, but intellectual life is clearly one of them. We know about several aspects of nineteenth-century Scottish intellectual life, though often in isolation: studies of individual authors, scholars and thinkers, and of particular fields and controversies. We know little about how they relate to each other, or to the achievements and concerns of earlier periods. This volume aims to sketch a map of Scottish intellectual life from the French Revolution to the First World War, not only identifying some of its major features and characteristic personalities, but also attempting to highlight over the course of a long post-Enlightenment the efforts of the eighteenth-century Enlightenment's posthumous continuators and critics, revisionists and debunkers.

The essays here attempt across a broad front to link the nineteenth century to the achievements of the previous century. What became of the Scottish Enlightenment after 1790? How far did anti-radical reaction in the wake of the French Revolution inhibit – or reshape – intellectual activity? Did the conservative reaction to Jacobinism lead to the constraining, self-censoring or submersion of enlightened provocation? On the other hand, how far did trends in eighteenth-century Scottish intellectual life continue into the nineteenth? How conscious were nineteenth-century Scottish intellectuals of the Scottish Enlightenment? (Not that they gave it that name, the term was only coined in 1900 by the economist and historian W. R. Scott; but is that coinage itself significant?)[1] Or did the social, ecclesiastical and economic concerns of nineteenth-century Scotland come to overshadow the intellectual legacy of the Enlightenment? Indeed, how much did indigenous Scottish trends – such as changes in religion or in publishing and communications – contribute to creeping provincialisation? For, certainly, by 1914 Edinburgh was not the 'metropolis' of intellect it had been in 1790. Indeed, it is striking how many Scottish intellectuals covered in this volume – Carlyle, Mudie, Knox, Lang, Robertson, Archer and others – spent at least part of their careers in London. This raises the further question, whether it was publishing opportunities in London or the stifling fug of religiosity back in Scotland – or both (or indeed individual circumstances that defy any general pattern of interpretation) – which drew Scottish thinkers to the English capital.

Furthermore, did the rising tide of evangelicalism wash away all traces of Humean freethinking? Certainly, sectarian and denominational tensions have obscured tensions between orthodoxy and forms of irreligion. Popular unbelief is just as much an absence in the historiography as the crisis of faith, the higher agnosticism, anticlericalism, indifferentism and philosophical materialism. Moreover, if the dissolution of the unity of knowledge was the fruit of the Enlightenment through the establishment of specialist professorships, was this a process which continued throughout the nineteenth century? While universities became the home of increasingly specialised fields of knowledge, where could bigger, wider, cross-cutting questions be discussed? How did the landscape of Scottish intellectual life shift? These are challenging questions, but all the more important for it. This volume is a call to arms that we hope will encourage historians of the nineteenth century to pay more attention to intellectual culture, and might encourage intellectual historians to look beyond the Enlightenment.

In the remainder of this introduction, we consider some of the reasons why a study of Scottish intellectual life in the long nineteenth century might seem more challenging than that of the eighteenth century – the fragmentation of knowledge, and the changed position of Scotland (and Edinburgh, and their cultural institutions) in the wider British establishment – and then survey the current state of the literature. We also highlight some of the big themes arising from the contributions to this volume, which offer both continuities and discontinuities from the Enlightenment.

The dissolution of the unity of knowledge is widely regarded as a fruit of the Enlightenment. The early decades of the nineteenth century saw a proliferation of specialist learned societies, scholarly journals and university professorships, with the old 'natural philosophy' and 'natural history' giving way not just to 'chemistry', 'geology' and 'botany' but, as the century wore on, to even newer fields such as 'physiology', 'physics' and 'organic chemistry'. By the end of the century, these scientific specialisms had been joined by 'modern history' (rather than 'ancient', classical history), 'English literature', 'economics' and 'sociology', along with many other now-familiar academic disciplines.[2]

This fragmentation was both epistemological and sociological: just as textbooks and encyclopaedias suggested that knowledge was divided into increasingly smaller chunks, so too the communities of people who studied these areas became more divided from each other. By the early twentieth century, Dundee and St Andrews professor D'Arcy Thompson (1860–1948) was a rare example of a scholar equally at home in classical studies, mathematics and natural history. This specialisation was not confined to university life, but also characterised the professionalisation of older occupations and the emergence of new ones.[3] For instance, by the late nineteenth century, it had become rare to find lawyers and doctors who were also expert in geology or philosophy, while busy ministers were equally unlikely to have time to become noted classical scholars or entomologists.

Many years ago, R. M. Young described a 'common context' of intellectual debate in the early nineteenth century, and its subsequent fragmentation. His interest in the origins of evolutionary theory had led him to observe that debates about economics, social theory, theology and natural history had once taken place within the pages of the same periodicals – in a 'common context' of shared understanding and interest – but that, by the mid-late nineteenth century, scholars could not – or did not – communicate with those outside their immediate fields.[4] He was not writing particularly about Scotland, but his insight is useful for thinking about the changes in intellectual life over the course of the nineteenth century.

At the start of the century, the intellectual community of Scotland was a relatively small proportion of its population, and its members tended to have many things in common: usually a shared upbringing within Scottish Presbyterianism; a social background that was sufficiently affluent to permit an extended education and attention to intellectual pursuits; a standardised educational experience; and an intellectual life that revolved around Edinburgh and its institutions, including the Royal Society of Edinburgh and the dominant cultural arbiter of the early nineteenth century, the *Edinburgh Review* (established 1802). By the end of the century, the proliferation of periodicals for every denomination, interest or social group meant that university professors were not the only ones who could be so immersed in a particular interest to be oblivious of developments in other fields.

The old 'common context' had been a relatively elite, and heavily masculine, affair. The effects of its fragmentation were exacerbated by the entry of new and diverse voices into intellectual debates. Scotland's famed provision for elementary education was strained by urbanisation in the early decades of the century, but philanthropic action (by mostly evangelical charities), followed by government intervention, ensured that literacy and basic education became even more widespread among the working classes, although that only rarely translated into access to university. The second half of the century saw the creation of a wave of girls' schools across Scotland that ensured middle-class girls could get access to advanced secondary education; and in the 1890s, they were eventually permitted to matriculate at the universities.[5]

For those who, for reasons of class or gender, could not attend the universities, there were nonetheless many more ways to keep up to date with – and perhaps participate in – the debates of the day. Scottish publishers, such as W. & R. Chambers and William Collins, pioneered the provision of cheap informative and educational print for newly literate audiences.[6] At the same time, there were new venues for education and debate, from Mechanics' Institutes and athenaeums to Chartist organisations and freethinking societies. All this meant that the fragmentation of elite scholarly culture due to specialisation was accompanied by the growing participation of new voices, whose concerns and approaches reflected their different socio-economic, political, religious, geographic and gendered perspectives.

By the end of our period, Scotland had become home to many diverse and different intellectual communities. Perhaps it no longer makes sense to talk about 'Scottish intellectual culture' in the singular. That said, there are questions yet to be asked about what else was going on, despite – or because of – the fragmentation, specialisation and diversification of intellectual cultures. Were there still venues where the big, cross-cutting questions could be discussed? Were there hidden connections and commonalities beneath the fragmentation of knowledge and of communities?

These questions also need to be set against the changing place of Scotland within Britain and the British Empire. Railways, steamships and telegraphs all helped connect the disparate parts of Britain together. The Scottish economy became increasingly integrated into a national British market, enabling Edinburgh publishers and Glasgow manufacturers to sell their wares in London, Liverpool and Cork, with Scottish shops stocked with goods from across the United Kingdom. These improvements in communications enabled the participation of people in the remotest corners of Britain in national communities of interest – magazines for every hobby from gardening to astronomy – and yet they simultaneously extended the influence of London and its organisations over intellectual life in Scotland and the rest of the kingdom.

In the early nineteenth century, Edinburgh was a vibrant publishing centre, home of the *Encyclopaedia Britannica*, the *Edinburgh Review*, *Blackwood's Magazine* and the poems and novels of Walter Scott. Co-publishing agreements enabled London and Edinburgh publishers to cooperate to share the works of their authors with readers far away. By the late nineteenth century, such agreements had faded away. London publishers no longer needed an Edinburgh partner to target the Scottish market, and though Scottish publishers could also, in principle, reach readers throughout Britain, in practice, establishing a London branch – or, even, moving operations to London – became common. Scottish-based authors could just as easily choose to work with a publisher in London, if they wished. Edinburgh remained the second largest publishing city in Britain, but it was no longer what it had been.[7] The last decades of the century saw a flourishing of local newspapers across Britain, facilitating the formation of local and regional identities beyond the metropolis.[8] Yet at the same time, railway delivery was extending the reach of London-based daily newspapers, enabling them to aspire to a new role as national newspapers.

It was a similar story in other (non-printed) aspects of intellectual life. The old 'Literary and Philosophical Societies' were joined by 'Scientific and Literary Societies', 'Mechanics' Institutes', 'Athenaeums' and any number of more specialised reading clubs, debating societies and natural history field clubs. All of this suggests a widening of access to, and participation in, intellectual culture across the nineteenth century.[9] But those aspiring to make original contributions to scholarly and intellectual debates increasingly looked to London. Local clubs and societies might spark an interest, and provide a congenial social space for its development – but it was to London-based organisations –the Astronomical, Geological, Chemical, Linnean and Zoological societies – that new species of lichen or sightings of comets were reported. The Royal Society of Edinburgh's literary section dwindled, but its scientific section continued to meet and provided a valuable social setting for scholarly discussions (albeit one dominated by Edinburgh university professors).[10] But its most active scholars were also contributing to the specialist learned societies in London; and they aspired to fellowship of the Royal Society in London.

It is thus perhaps not surprising that those who have investigated the intellectual cultures of nineteenth-century Britain have tended to focus on the thoughts and actions of those in London, or those associated with the two ancient English universities. There is clearly a need for a fuller and more diverse understanding of other parts of Britain including (but not limited to) Scotland. In some areas of scholarship, this enterprise is well underway: literary scholars have explored the richness of both provincial fiction and provincial newspapers (where 'provincial' typically seems to mean 'England-outside-London');[11] and historical geographers have investigated the scholarly activities and communities of particular regions, from Cornwall to Perth and Edinburgh.[12]

But is Scotland's role in this enterprise destined to be nothing more than another region within the British world, to be studied in the same way as one might study Lancashire, Cornwall or Ontario? While we fully support the ambition of a study of the connections and comparisons of the different parts of the nineteenth-century British world, we suggest that Scotland is worthy of study in its own right. Its history as a separate kingdom has left a cultural and institutional legacy than endures to this day, and marks it as different both from the English provinces and the colonies. Despite the Union of 1707, Scotland's church, legal system and educational provision – higher education explicitly so – remained distinct from that of England. But how important was that, in the increasingly interconnected nation that was nineteenth-century Britain? We do not currently know.

The towns and cities of nineteenth-century Scotland acquired the same kinds of reading clubs and public libraries that were being founded by civic-minded Victorians across Britain – but in the case of Scotland, these new institutions for widening participation in knowledge were layered on to a core of mature and well-established institutions. There were centuries-old universities in four towns, and the College of Physicians and Surgeons of Glasgow (f. 1599); the Royal College of Physicians of Edinburgh (f. 1681), Society of Antiquaries of Scotland (f. 1780, royal charter 1783), Royal Society of Edinburgh (f. 1783). Other than the 'golden triangle' of London, Oxford and Cambridge, few parts of the British world had such mature institutional provision for scholarship and intellectual debate (though the colonies were certainly in the process of establishing such institutions). These learned institutions provided education and professional accreditation, and could act as venues for intellectual debate and scholarly socialising. But to what extent were these vestiges of an older time able to retain a meaningful role? We can think of various reasons why we might *expect* scholars and intellectuals based in Scotland to have a distinctive approach to the big issues of their day, but, as with the long-term legacy of the Enlightenment, whether – or to what extent – they did, remains to be seen. We are conscious that the intellectual hinterland outside Edinburgh is still to be mapped.

The best routes into nineteenth-century Scottish intellectual life are Douglas Gifford's splendid nineteenth-century volume in the 4-volume *History of Scottish Literature*, under the general editorship of Cairns Craig;[13] Craig's own interventions on literature, philosophy and science;[14] and works that are primarily ecclesiastical in their orientation, such as S. J. Brown's magnificent *Thomas Chalmers and the Godly Commonwealth*.[15] This is not to say that the ecclesiastical was in any way peripheral to nineteenth-century Scottish intellectual life. It was inescapable; but it was not the whole story, by any means.

The history of science has enjoyed better coverage than other aspects of intellectual life, though again rarely in a holistic way. We know vastly more about early nineteenth-century Edinburgh than about anywhere else, thanks to scholarly interest in debates about brain function, the differences between animal species, the immateriality of the soul, or the possibility of developmental links between species.[16] Much of the work in the history of Victorian science has been set in a British (or at best North British) framework, and its fruits have not been obviously visible to Scottish historians.[17] While the historiography of North British science has been well integrated with social, economic and religious developments, there has been less articulation with Scottish intellectual culture more generally.

Having said all that, there have been some advances in certain aspects of Scottish intellectual history. No longer are we confronted with the notion of a bald transition from the Enlightenment to its Romantic antithesis. In particular, a whole generation of scholars working on Walter Scott has established the ways in which enlightened sociology and jurisprudence underpinned Scott's hitherto supposed anti-modern medievalism.[18] This has been a useful corrective. Moreover, late nineteenth- and early twentieth-century 'kailyard' literature has been pruned of some of its more egregious myths, and we now have a greater sensitivity, through the work of Philip Waller, Andrew Nash and Keith Ives, to the role of William Robertson Nicholl as a cultural entrepreneur within the publishing world of British Nonconformity.[19] There have also been isolated studies of particular linkages between past and present in Scottish intellectual life, particularly among historians of anthropology who note the influence of Hume's philosophy on Frazer, the author of the monumental *Golden Bough*.[20] Yet, notwithstanding the puncturing of certain myths and the correction of certain assumptions in areas such as literary history and anthropology, the broader field of nineteenth-century Scottish intellectual history remains woefully underappreciated by contrast with our knowledge of the eighteenth century. For example, the attention of nineteenth-century scholars has been fixed on interdenominational jostling to the exclusion of tensions between religious orthodoxy and freethinking.

We identify where relevant continuing currents of intellectual life from the Enlightenment (as well as addressing adaptations and reinventions, declensions and gaps); we recover some intellectual controversies which have become submerged or invisible in historical memory, not least given a selective and sometimes near-vestigial historiography; and we interrogate afresh four key themes that have dominated the historiographical debates about nineteenth-century Scotland. These are the ongoing prominence of religion, as well as questions about its status and authority, in an evangelically tinged post-Enlightenment Scotland; the extent to which the French Revolution and the conservative reaction that ensued smothered intellectual innovation; the implications of the perceived provincialisation or marginalisation of Scotland and Scottish forms of intellectual life relative to London as the metropolitan core of Britain and its Empire; and, implicitly, the intriguing question of how we might identify the end of the Enlightenment, if nineteenth-century Scotland was indeed 'beyond' it.

Religion – including its obverse, the challenge of freethinking irreligion – inevitably, occupies a prominent place in our collection. Its importance was recognised as early as the mid-nineteenth century by the pioneering English sociologist, Henry

Buckle (1821–62), who identified a hulking, elephantine puzzle at the centre of Scottish intellectual history. Buckle died young, and did not live to complete his projected multi-volume *History of Civilization in England* (1857–61). However, what he did publish included comparative studies of the relative long-term stagnation of intellectual life in Scotland and Spain. In the case of Scotland, there was the difficulty of reconciling the achievements of its eighteenth-century intelligentsia with the stultifying clerical orthodoxy which preceded it, and – significantly – also came after. Buckle gnawed over the central 'paradox' of Scottish history: 'that knowledge should not have produced the effects which have elsewhere followed it; that a bold and inquisitive literature should be found in a grossly superstitious country, without diminishing its superstition', and that the Scottish people should be liberal in politics yet under the illiberal thrall of their clergy. Moreover, this 'anomaly' continued into the present. Such was the 'peculiarity of Scotland' that during the eighteenth century and down to the mid-nineteenth 'industrial and intellectual progress [had] continued without materially shaking the authority of the priesthood'. Why, Buckle asked, did the country of Hume and Adam Smith remain 'awed by a few noisy and ignorant preachers'? Why did a 'very advanced' people holding 'enlightened views' on politics, display on 'all religious subjects' such a 'littleness of mind, an illiberality of sentiment, a heat of temper, and a love of persecuting others'?[21]

Part of the answer, according to Buckle, was the continuity in Scottish intellectual life – the baton passed from clergy to enlightened literati and then back to clerics – of 'deductive' modes of reasoning: something at odds with our own appreciation of the inductive methods that seemed to predominate during the Scottish Enlightenment. Indeed, this aspect of Buckle's thesis is clearly mistaken, deriving, it seems, from an assumption that anything smacking of psychology was *ipso facto* deductive. Nonetheless, the vital marrow of Buckle's overall analysis endures, and continues to prompt searching questions. Was the Enlightenment no more than erratic blip which was soon corrected by a return to religious norms? Did evangelicalism utterly overwhelm the remnants of Enlightenment culture – Moderatism in the Kirk, a liberal tolerance of free enquiry, the secularising stamp of the emergent social sciences? Alternatively, was an evangelical outlook surprisingly compatible with many of the key developments of the Scottish Enlightenment, especially the physical sciences and political economy? Or was there perhaps a division of spheres, with some areas of the natural and social sciences more easily aligned with Calvinist orthodoxy than others? Yet the evidence of the daring forms of biblical criticism, sometimes anthropologically inflected, found in the late nineteenth-century Free Church – of all unlikely places – suggests that ingenuity was not so easily stifled by orthodoxy, and sometimes flourished at the frontiers of theological enquiry. Of course, the rash of heresy trials which preoccupied the Free Church during the 1880s and 1890s shows that the story is more complex and convoluted still,[22] and that Buckle's insights retain some purchase. Notwithstanding the fixation of Scottish ecclesiastical historians with interdenominational wrangling, there were other battles being waged: between the churches and an avant-garde of freethinkers who rejected Christianity outright, between advanced theologians and their more stolid colleagues, and an internal conflict within the minds and consciences of a highly educated clergy, aware of the intractable tensions between the disturbing findings of biblical scholarship and the hoary seventeenth-century doctrinal standard – the Westminster Confession of Faith – that they were still pledged to uphold.

But did Buckle's emphasis on the nineteenth-century resurgence of religiosity serve to deflect attention away from other significant changes? Emma Rothschild, in particular, has shown how in the febrile environment engendered by the French Revolution the vigorous political economy of the Smithian Enlightenment shrivelled into a more narrowly technical discipline: foregrounding economics as a science of constraints meant downplaying the open-ended possibilities inherent in Smith's science of the legislator.[23] To what extent is the French Revolution or the rise of evangelicalism the pivot between Enlightenment and post-Enlightenment? Or are these two phenomena inseparable? Yet the decades of the French Revolution arguably marked not a post-Enlightenment moment, but the apogee of Enlightenment. This was the era when three future British prime ministers came to study at the Scottish universities: William Lamb, Lord Melbourne under John Millar at Glasgow between 1799 and 1801, Henry Temple, Viscount Palmerston at Edinburgh under Dugald Stewart between 1800 and 1803, and Lord John Russell under John Playfair at Edinburgh between 1809 and 1812. At this point too, the Athens of the North was arguably the arbiter of British taste, through the cultural authority embodied in the *Edinburgh Review*. Edinburgh and London were for a matter of decades twin cultural capitals, though in the medium term, London and a reformed Oxbridge regained their pre-eminence.

Nineteenth-century Scottish intellectual history is in part a story of dwindling cultural authority and a slow retreat into provinciality. Yet as Nicholas Phillipson, building upon the insights of John Clive and Bernard Bailyn,[24] demonstrated in a series of remarkable essays, provincialism had been an energising force during the eighteenth-century Enlightenment: then provincial life had been refreshingly rich in possibilities, fostering an openness to both the metropolitan and the cosmopolitan. Indeed, Phillipson's renowned interpretation of the Scottish Enlightenment celebrates a self-conscious provincialism as a means of reorientating the Scots intelligentsia from merely national horizons.[25] However, by the mid-nineteenth century, the tension between core and periphery was impoverishing rather than enriching, relegating Edinburgh to a satellite of London. But how long did the process take? When did the Athens of the North cease to be a major cultural citadel? It was, after all, only in 1890 that A & C Black, which owned the *Encyclopaedia Britannica*, shifted its operations to London.

Nor should we overlook other signs of provincialisation. Marinell Ash drew attention to a marked lowering of ambitions in nineteenth-century Scottish historical writing. The historiographical revolution forged by Scott – itself as we know a fusion of a Romanticism with the sociological perspectives of the Scottish Enlightenment – gave way to exercises in textual editing, a sub-Romantic escapism and a lack of confidence in grand narrative.[26] But there is another way to view this: as a retreat from confident nationhood certainly, but also as the emergence of a more technical historical discipline which prioritised sources at the expense of the stories the nation told about itself.[27]

More controversially, George Davie examined the long-term crisis of confidence in the nineteenth-century universities.[28] Why did Scotland's academic leaders manifest such scant pride in the achievements of the Scottish Enlightenment? Why instead was there such a cowed acceptance of anglicising interference, Oxbridge norms and the supposed superiority of mandarin exercises in the classical languages to the roundedness of a generalist curriculum? The Davie thesis has attracted considerable criticism from historical specialists,[29] but some of its overall contours remain compelling. The long transition from Enlightenment generalism to the specialisation of the twentieth-century university occurred against a backdrop of marginalisation, the denigration of indigenous educational traditions and – at least implicitly – a devaluation of the multidisciplinary ethos which had underpinned the Scottish Enlightenment.

More recently, Cairns Craig – one of Davie's most attentive readers – has invited us to see the supposed post-Enlightenment anew. Craig asks a question which turns out to produce far-from-obvious answers: 'When was the Scottish Enlightenment?' Why, Craig asks, should we view James Clerk Maxwell's physics as a post-Enlightenment sequel rather than as the triumphant 'fulfilment' of the Scottish Enlightenment? The major intellectual achievements of late nineteenth-century Scotland were not 'isolated afterthoughts' to the Enlightenment, but a culmination of its possibilities. Not only does Craig point to the markedly Humean psychologising of Frazer's *Golden Bough*, he also perceives the influence of eighteenth-century Scottish stadialist and conjectural histories on the pioneering anthropology of J. F. McLennan and William Robertson Smith. Why *do* we put Adam Smith and Robertson Smith in different pigeonholes? Admittedly, there were differences of tone and context between the two moments. Craig shows how for Henry Calderwood, a nineteenth-century Scots philosopher and theologian, Hume loomed larger as a doubting agnostic than as a proponent of sceptical raillery. Yet why did Scotland give rise to two such notable galaxies of genius, first in the mid to late eighteenth century and then again a century later?

And why are they studied in such splendid isolation from one another?[30]

Our collection combines a measure of necessary eclecticism – given the range of Scottish intellectual endeavour – and a synoptic coherence. While most of the chapters deal directly with individuals, themes and episodes from Scotland's long nineteenth century, these are bracketed by the essays of Robert Anderson and Gerard Carruthers which both address the Davie thesis and provide longer perspectives on the legacy of the Enlightenment from the vantage points, respectively, of historiography and literary criticism. The volume gives access to the particular flavours of Scottish intellectual life in certain contexts and also provides a sense of the whole. It is our hope that these essays individually provide a series of cutting-edge interventions in a neglected but important area of Scottish studies, but also collectively a pioneering overview of Scottish intellectual life during the long nineteenth century.

## Notes

1. W. R. Scott, *Francis Hutcheson* (Cambridge, 1900).
2. Martin Daunton, *The Organisation of Knowledge in Victorian Britain*, British Academy Centenary Monographs (Oxford, 2005); Bennett Zon and Bernard Lightman (eds), *Victorian Culture and the Origin of Disciplines* (London, 2019).
3. Harold Perkin, *The Rise of Professional Society: England since 1880* (London, 1989).
4. Robert M. Young, 'Malthus and the Evolutionists: The Common Context of Biological and Social Theory', *Past & Present* no. 43 (1969), 109–45; 'Natural Theology, Victorian Periodicals and the Fragmentation of a Common Context', in *Darwin to Einstein: Historical Studies on Science and Belief*, ed. Colin Chant and John Fauvel (Harlow, 1980). See also Jonathan R. Topham, 'Beyond the "Common Context": The Production and Reading of the *Bridgewater Treatises*', *Isis* 89 (1998), 233–62.
5. Robert Anderson, *Education and Opportunity in Victorian Scotland: Schools & Universities* (Oxford, 1983); Carol Dyhouse, *No Distinction of Sex?: Women in British Universities, 1870–1939* (London, 1995).
6. Aileen Fyfe, *Steam-Powered Knowledge: William Chambers and the Business of Publishing, 1820–1860* (Chicago, 2012).
7. Bill Bell (ed.), *Edinburgh History of the Book in Scotland, Volume 3: Ambition and Industry 1800–1880* (Edinburgh, 2007).
8. Martin Hewitt, *The Dawn of the Cheap Press in Victorian Britain: The End*

of the 'Taxes on Knowledge', 1849–1869 (London, 2013); Andrew Hobbs, *A Fleet Street in Every Town: The Provincial Press in England, 1855–1900* (Cambridge, 2018).

9. Jonathan Rose, *The Intellectual Life of the British Working Classes* (New Haven, CT, 2001); Diarmid A. Finnegan, *Natural History Societies and Civic Culture in Victorian Scotland* (London, 2009).
10. N. Campbell and R. M. S. Smellie, *The Royal Society of Edinburgh (1783–1983): The First Two Hundred Years* (Edinburgh, 1983).
11. Hobbs, *Fleet Street in Every Town*.
12. Simon Naylor, 'The Field, the Museum, and the Lecture Hall: The Spaces of Natural History in Victorian Cornwall', *Transactions of the Institute of British Geographers* 27, no. 4 (2002), 494–513; 'Collecting Quoits: Field Cultures in the History of Cornish Antiquarianism', *Cultural Geographies* 10 (2003), 309–33; David N. Livingstone, 'Science, Region, and Religion: The Reception of Darwinism in Princeton, Belfast and Edinburgh', in *Disseminating Darwinism: The Role of Place, Race, Religion, and Gender*, ed. Ronald L. Numbers and John Stenhouse (Cambridge, 1999), pp. 7–38; David N. Livingstone and Charles W. J. Withers, *Geographies of Nineteenth-Century Science* (Chicago, 2011).
13. Douglas Gifford (ed.), *History of Scottish Literature*, volume III (Aberdeen, 1987).
14. See especially Cairns Craig, 'Nineteenth-Century Scottish Thought', in Susan Manning (ed.), *Edinburgh History of Scottish Literature Volume Two: Enlightenment, Britain and Empire (1707–1918)* (Edinburgh, 2007), pp. 267–76; Craig, *Intending Scotland: Explorations in Scottish Culture since the Enlightenment* (Edinburgh, 2009).
15. S. J. Brown, *Thomas Chalmers and the Godly Commonwealth* (Oxford, 1982).
16. Jack B. Morrell, 'Professors Robison and Playfair, and the Theophobia Gallica: Natural Philosophy, Religion and Politics in Edinburgh, 1789–1815', *Notes and Records of the Royal Society* 26 (1971), 43–63; Geoffrey N. Cantor, 'The Edinburgh Phrenology Debate: 1803–1828,' *Annals of Science* 32, no. 3 (1975), 195–218; James A. Secord, 'Edinburgh Lamarckians: Robert Jameson and Robert E. Grant', *Journal of the History of Biology* 24 (1991), 1–18; Bill Jenkins, *Evolution before Darwin: Theories of the Transmutation of Species in Edinburgh, 1804–1834* (Edinburgh, 2019).
17. Crosbie Smith and M. Norton Wise, *Energy and Empire: A Biographical Study of Lord Kelvin* (Cambridge, 1989); Crosbie Smith, *The Science of Energy: A Cultural History of Energy Physics in Victorian Britain* (London, 1998); Ben Marsden, '"A Most Important Trespass": Lewis Gordon and the Glasgow Chair of Civil Engineering and Mechanics, 1840–1855', in *Making Space: Territorial Themes in the History of Science*, ed. Crosbie W. Smith and Jon Agar (London, 1998), pp. 87–117.

18. Duncan Forbes, 'The Rationalism of Sir Walter Scott', *Cambridge Journal* 7 (1953), 20–35; David Daiches, 'Sir Walter Scott and History', *Etudes Anglaises* 24 (1971), 458–77; Peter D. Garside, 'Scott and the "Philosophical" Historians', *Journal of the History of Ideas* 36 (1975), 497–512; George Dekker, *The American Historical Romance* (Cambridge, 1987).
19. Philip Waller, *Writers, Readers and Reputations: Literary Life in Britain 1870–1918* (Oxford, 2006); Andrew Nash, *Kailyard and Scottish Literature* (Amsterdam, 2007); Keith Ives, *Voices of Nonconformity: William Robertson Nicoll and the British Weekly* (Cambridge, 2011).
20. Robert Ackerman, *J. G. Frazer: His Life and Work* (Cambridge, 1987), p. 184; Robert Fraser, 'The Face Beneath the Text: Sir James Frazer in his Time' and David Richards, 'A Tour of Babel: Frazer and Theories of Language', both in Robert Fraser (ed.), *Sir James Frazer and the Literary Imagination* (Basingstoke, 1990), pp. 8–9, 93–4.
21. Henry Thomas Buckle, *On Scotland and the Scotch Intellect*, ed. H. J. Hanham (Chicago, 1970), pp. 26–7, 156.
22. Colin Kidd and Valerie Wallace, 'Biblical Criticism and Scots Presbyterian Dissent in the Age of Robertson Smith', in Scott Mandelbrote and Michael Ledger-Lomas (eds), *Dissent and the Bible in Britain, c. 1650–1950* (Oxford, 2013), pp. 233–55.
23. Emma Rothschild, *Economic Sentiments* (Cambridge, MA, 2001).
24. John Clive and Bernard Bailyn, 'England's Cultural Provinces: Scotland and America', *William and Mary Quarterly* 3rd ser. 11 (1954), 200–13.
25. See especially Nicholas Phillipson, 'Culture and society in the eighteenth-century province: the case of Edinburgh and the Scottish Enlightenment', in Lawrence Stone (ed.), *The University in Society* (2 vols, Princeton, 1975), II, pp. 407–48; Phillipson, 'Adam Smith as civic moralist', in Istvan Hont and Michael Ignatieff (eds), *Wealth and Virtue: the shaping of political economy in the Scottish Enlightenment* (Cambridge, 1983), pp. 179–202.
26. Marinell Ash, *The Strange Death of Scottish History* (Edinburgh, 1980).
27. Colin Kidd, 'The Strange Death of Scottish History Revisited: Constructions of the Past in Scotland, c. 1790–1914', *Scottish Historical Review* 76 (1997), 86–102.
28. George E. Davie, *The Democratic Intellect* (Edinburgh, 1961); Davie, *The Crisis of the Democratic Intellect* (Edinburgh, 1986)
29. See, for example, Jennifer Carter and Donald Withrington (eds), *Scottish Universities: Distinctiveness and Diversity* (Edinburgh, 1992); Withrington, 'Ideas and Ideals in University Reform in Early Nineteenth-Century Britain: A Scottish Perspective', *The European Legacy* 4 (1999), 7–19; Anderson, *Education and Opportunity*.
30. Craig, *Intending Scotland*, ch. 2 'When was the Scottish Enlightenment?'

# 2

# The Enlightenment Legacy and the Democratic Intellect

*Robert Anderson*

On and around Calton Hill in Edinburgh are monuments to David Hume (1777), the mathematician and geologist John Playfair (1825), Robert Burns (1830) and the philosopher Dugald Stewart (1831). But tributes to Enlightenment figures are rare in later years. Victorian Scots had a mania for monuments: they commemorated literary figures like Burns and Scott, national heroes like Bruce and Wallace, and contemporary politicians, generals and religious leaders.[1] But the principal thinkers of the Scottish Enlightenment seemed to be forgotten. Today, it is true, there are statues of Hume and Adam Smith on Edinburgh's Royal Mile, and since they are sculpted in classical style, the unwary visitor may think they are contemporary; but they were erected in 1995 and 2008 respectively.[2] This story illustrates two points. First, the Enlightenment has in recent years become a mark of Scottish identity and pride, as the older identification with Protestantism has become unusable – and in Edinburgh (the 'hotbed of genius') an icon of civic boosterism. Second, the nineteenth century lost a sense of the Enlightenment as a movement, and of its leading thinkers like Hume, Smith, Adam Ferguson and William Robertson as a cohesive group. For a time, the Enlightenment's direct influence was still alive – Dugald Stewart was a significant figure here – but by mid-century its achievements were absorbed into the general movement of ideas.

In the nineteenth century there was a common view of the past which saw Reformation and Enlightenment as episodes in the progressive unfolding of rationalism, individualism and 'freedom of thought', along with the Renaissance and the scientific advances of the seventeenth century. This historiography was liberal and Protestant, but not specifically Scottish. H. T. Buckle was not Scottish, but the last part of his widely read *History of Civilization in England* was devoted (despite the book's title) to Scotland. Buckle did not see the Reformation as progressive, but denounced the Presbyterian clergy for enforcing a rigid theocratic tyranny; even the 'free and sceptical literature' of the eighteenth century was unable to defeat religious illiberality and 'superstition', which were still alive in Buckle's own day. For this he blamed the Scottish habit of deductive argument rather than the inductive scientific approach which Buckle used in trying to discover laws of history. In a long chapter on 'the Scotch intellect during the eighteenth century', Buckle examined the leading thinkers of the period, including its medical pioneers and men of science. Whatever Buckle's prejudices and questionable generalisations, this was one of the fullest treatments of the subject available in its time.[3]

The European Enlightenment is often seen as an anti-religious movement, which sought to place politics and ethics on a rational, secular basis and to demolish priestcraft and superstition. Nineteenth-century France had a 'Voltairean' bourgeoisie which saw Enlightenment rationalism as a national inheritance, but there was nothing like this in Scotland, where the Enlightenment was closer to Germany, Holland and other northern European countries, in seeking to reconcile religion with reason, and the state with the church, while secularising areas of life like education.

In this context the scepticism of David Hume had been exceptional, and the mainstream thinkers of the eighteenth century took their distance from him. Their spirit was embodied in the Moderate Party in the church, led by the historian William Robertson, which preached a rational morality, endorsed the existing social order, and maintained its influence through the discipline of the 'parish state'.[4] But this sober harmony was challenged by the growth of frequent dissenting factions, and by a broader evangelicalism, which sought to base religion on personal feelings of salvation, emotional rather than rational, and to emancipate the church from subordination to the state and the control of aristocratic patrons. The Disruption of 1843 is a convenient date for identifying the end of the Scottish Enlightenment, though it was only the culmination of long-standing religious tensions.

Another striking feature of the Scottish Enlightenment, which contrasted with France and England, though less so with Germany or Italy, was the centrality of the universities, which trained a large part of the Scottish elite, including ministers. Many of the leading thinkers were university professors, whose lectures led on to books. The development of university teaching in the nineteenth century, especially the arts degree and the philosophy classes, is therefore a natural focus of any attempt to evaluate the later legacy of the Enlightenment. The eighteenth-century universities also established long-lasting traditions in science, medicine and law which are outside the scope of this essay. Chemistry in particular, originally seen as an auxiliary of medicine, contributed to the early progress of industry in Scotland, and one strain of the Enlightenment, emanating from mercantile Glasgow rather than professional Edinburgh, supported 'useful knowledge' alongside traditional university education.[5] The college established in Glasgow in 1796 by John Anderson (later a leading technical college, and today Strathclyde University), the Mechanics' Institutes created in many towns in the early nineteenth century, and the various forms of self-improvement and mutual instruction adopted by working men, inherited this strain.

It is generally agreed that the phrase 'Scottish Enlightenment' was first used by William Scott in his 1900 study of Francis Hutcheson: Hutcheson was 'the prototype of the Scottish Enlightenment'. This was reported, and the phrase used, in Peter Hume Brown's contemporary *History of Scotland*, and since this remained the standard university textbook of Scottish history until the 1960s, the phrase was perhaps not as unfamiliar as is sometimes said. Hume Brown's history itself discussed Scottish philosophers mainly in the context of the Moderate Party in the church, and he saw the 'common sense' philosopher Thomas Reid as the best representative of the 'Scottish philosophy' because of his influence abroad. Adam Smith was mentioned only in passing, Adam Ferguson not at all.[6] Another widely read work of the period, Henry Grey Graham's *Social Life of Scotland in the Eighteenth Century*, had much the same approach. Scottish thinkers like Hume, Smith and Robertson were praised for their contribution to 'literature', especially as part of the 'town life' of Edinburgh, but only mentioned very briefly, while three chapters were devoted to religion.[7]

Modern scholarship on the Scottish Enlightenment began in the 1950s and has since flourished, much of it the work of the 'Cambridge school' of intellectual history. One key event was the second International Congress on the Enlightenment held at St Andrews and Edinburgh in 1967, at which Hugh Trevor-Roper gave an influential lecture.[8] His approach saw the Scottish Enlightenment as the local expression of a European movement, stimulated by Scotland's political situation after 1707, and by the priorities of its landed and urban elites. Politically, according to scholars drawing on the concept of civic humanism, the Enlightenment sought to instil 'virtue' into the elite, part of a broader project of a 'science of man'. From this point of view, the movement came to an end when its leading thinkers departed from the scene. For Richard Sher, who saw the heart of the movement in the group of Moderate clergy who dominated the church and the universities, the death of William Robertson in 1793 symbolised 'the end of the Moderate age and the Scottish Enlightenment'.[9] Enlightenment scholarship has tended to put firm chronological limits on the movement, and has been more willing to seek earlier Scottish roots than to extend its approach forward.

In the later nineteenth century the histories of Hume and Robertson were still read, and Adam Smith celebrated as the founder of political economy, but there was little continuing memory of the Enlightenment as a movement. This can perhaps be explained by two different but related factors: first, Scottish public life in the nineteenth century was dominated by religious divisions and disputes, and it was to the legacy of the Reformation and John Knox, rather than to Hume and Smith, that Scots looked for the roots of the present in the past.

Second, the nineteenth century created problems to which the Enlightenment had no answers. That movement played out in a Scotland which was still largely pre-industrial and dominated by the landed classes.[10] But the nineteenth century saw the transformation of Scotland into a leading industrial and urbanised country, and the growth of both middle and working classes. It was religious energy and idealism which tackled problems like poverty, crime, working-class housing and the extension of elementary education. The religious life of Victorian Scotland had a richness and diversity which the twenty-first century is perhaps ill-equipped to appreciate. Ultimately, however, sectarianism led to secularisation. Once the Disruption destroyed the ability of the Established church to speak for the nation as the natural partner of the state – as it had during the Moderate dominance – functions such as the poor law (1846), civil registration (1855), and school education (1861 and 1872) became the province of national legislation, usually administered by local elites. The universities were also affected, as legislation in 1853 and 1858 laicised appointments and governance.

Politically, mainstream liberalism looked back to the revolution of 1688 and the growth of parliamentary government. But the American and French revolutions made the Enlightenment vocabulary of civic virtue obsolete, and created new causes like manhood suffrage, and new methods of extra-parliamentary agitation, as with the Scottish Jacobins of the 1790s or the Chartists. Robert Owen, in his factory community at New Lanark, can be seen as an heir to the Enlightenment in his Lockean belief that society could be changed through education and environment; but the wider Owenite movement, and its appeal to working men, were the product of a new political climate.

Scotland was a liberal society in the nineteenth century, both in the sense that the Liberal Party was politically dominant after the 1832 Reform Act, and because of the prevalence of what are today called 'Enlightenment values' (especially when they are felt to be threatened): belief in rational and critical argument, toleration of different creeds and cultures, a society open to social mobility, and so on.[11] This liberal order had many deficiencies – including the refusal of political rights to women, patriarchal ideas about the family, reluctance to see Roman Catholics as full members of the national community, the emphasis on property as the basis of political rights, and belief in racial hierarchy as the basis of Britain's position in the world. These negative features might not have been repudiated by the original Enlightenment thinkers, who were generally supporters of the existing order, but have mostly been removed by the long-term working out of 'Enlightenment values'.

Social change also brought Scotland and England closer together, in ways which are familiar: the unifying effect of railways, telegraphs and postal services, the expansion of a national and regional press, Scotland's significant partnership with England in the enterprise of empire, the growing dominance of intellectual life by the great Victorian reviews and London publishing houses. Political parties and pressure groups now operated on a British stage, and national 'public opinion' superseded the face-to-face 'public sphere' of urban clubs, taverns and coffee-houses. In the academic world, expanding subjects, especially medicine and the natural sciences, were national or international in their scope rather than particularly Scottish, and the growth of the universities created an academic profession which thought in British or imperial terms, as did students contemplating their careers after graduation.

These changes relate to a problem which has preoccupied historians in recent years, as part of a general interest in questions of identity, and in the position of Scotland within Britain: why was there no national movement, on European lines, in the nineteenth century? One answer was given by Tom Nairn. Following Ernest Gellner's modernist theory of nationalism, he saw its mainspring in 'uneven development': the middle classes created by capitalist growth, frustrated at being ruled by archaic agrarian empires, sought national independence. But in Scotland the union of 1707 preceded the modernising revolutions, political and economic, of the late eighteenth century. The Scottish elite gained a share in the economically advanced English state, and made a distinctive contribution to modern ideas through the Enlightenment. This was not sustained, however, as the Scottish intelligentsia collapsed into 'provinciality', or migrated to London.[12] Though it is questionable to identify the Enlightenment with the middle classes, by the nineteenth century the Scottish elite did identify with progress and liberalism, and saw themselves as successful partners in the British state, feeling no need for nationalist assertion.

At the 1967 Enlightenment conference, the St Andrews historian Ronald Cant gave a paper on 'Scottish universities and Scottish society in the eighteenth century' which contrasted with Trevor-Roper, seeing the Scottish Enlightenment as an expression of permanent Scottish traits and intellectual habits. The 'broad scope and philosophical emphasis' of the arts curriculum reflected an 'integrated society' which 'had long been permeated by libertarian ideas and democratic attitudes that blunted the inequalities of rank and influence'. For the Enlightenment was the 'fulfilment . . . of certain deeply cherished aspirations of the Scottish people, above all a desire for liberty'. Moreover, 'the low cost of university education ensured that any pupil of reasonable ability – the "lad o' pairts" of Scottish tradition – could proceed to a university without undue difficulty'.[13]

Cant's emphasis on democracy reflected the influence of George Davie's book of 1961, *The Democratic Intellect: Scotland and her Universities in the Nineteenth Century*, a book which had a key influence on the growth of cultural nationalism in the 1960s and 1970s.[14] It combined a historical account of university reform in the nineteenth century (which has been heavily criticised by historians) with a survey of Scottish academic thought in various fields, in which Davie discerned a common philosophical approach stressing generalism rather than specialisation. The advance of specialisation was deplored by Davie, and explained as the work of an 'anglicising' party.

Behind Davie's book lay a view of the Enlightenment derived from his study of the Common Sense school of philosophy, and linking it both with the university question in the nineteenth century and with the problems of his own day. There is, he said, a perpetual tension between the demands of specialised expertise and those of the common interest, a tension already present in the intellectualism of the Presbyterian pulpit and the willingness of congregations to argue with their ministers. Common Sense philosophy was able to bridge the gap between the university-educated elite and 'ordinary people'. After 1707 there was unity in politics between England and Scotland, but diversity in 'social ethics'. Scotland maintained a balance in which the potentially theocratic inclinations of the church were countered by the rationalism of the philosophers, forming 'a distinctive blend of the secular and of the sacred'. Although Enlightenment scholarship has not paid much attention to Davie, he anticipated its recent stress – including its reinterpretation of Adam Smith – on the movement's vision of society as a moral community, rather than an individualist, market-based arena of competition.

In the early nineteenth century, for Davie, Scottish philosophy still provided a check on the growth of material wealth. But this balance was threatened on one side by utilitarian philosophy (despite its own roots in the Scottish Enlightenment), with its uncritical welcome of economic progress, and on the other by the rise of evangelicalism, based on emotion rather than reason. Evangelicalism is often seen as part of the Romantic reaction against Enlightenment rationalism, yet Thomas Chalmers's vision of a 'godly commonwealth' could also be related to the common-sense ideal of a harmonious society. So too the post-1843 established church might be seen as inheriting the Moderate ideal of a national community bound by the alliance of church and state.

For Davie, the Disruption was a cultural disaster, as religious sectarianism came to dominate contests for professorial chairs, which play a key role in his story. The appointment of Evangelical candidates to philosophy chairs marked the triumph of 'provincialising philistinism ... The classic age of common sense had ended.' Scots turned their back on the national philosophical heritage, and denominational squabbles paralysed Scottish intellectual vitality into the twentieth century.

Davie's view that the Enlightenment legacy was betrayed and forgotten has been widely accepted, but some otherwise sympathetic commentators have rejected his pessimism. Alexander Broadie, the historian of the Scottish philosophical tradition, traces its roots back to the Middle Ages, and its influence forward into the nineteenth and twentieth centuries. Philosophy was 'a principle of unity of Scottish culture for centuries', not based on a single doctrine, but on 'libertarianism, a strong doctrine of moral freedom'. Enlightenment, in both eighteenth and nineteenth centuries, was 'a period of intellectual progress made through the exercise of autonomous reason in circumstances in which people may put their ideas into the public domain without risk of persecution by the authorities, whether political or religious'.[15] This, of course, could be said of many nineteenth-century states with liberal constitutions.

While Broadie sees continuity between eighteenth and nineteenth centuries, Cairns Craig prefers to identify a 'second Scottish Enlightenment' in the nineteenth. He stresses the vitality of Scottish thought in many fields apart from philosophy – science, theology, classical studies or sociology. The Scottish pioneers of social anthropology, for example, such as J. F. McLennan and James Frazer, drew on the Enlightenment concepts of a science of man and historical sociology. Craig argues that Davie's concentration on the common-sense school was too narrow, not least because it excluded David Hume, who continued to be influential in England (through James and John Stuart Mill) as well as Scotland (including the Aberdeen philosopher Alexander Bain). Scottish art and literature also reflected a distinctive national tradition with roots in the Enlightenment.[16] It has to be admitted, however, that many of the scientists and scholars mentioned by Craig either had no academic positions in Scotland, or began their careers there but moved later to England, like the scientist James Clerk Maxwell, or the theologian and student of comparative religions William Robertson Smith.

Common Sense doctrines were transmitted to the nineteenth century by Dugald Stewart, who held the moral philosophy chair at Edinburgh between 1785 and 1810 (though he lived until 1828). Stewart's lectures had a profound influence on a generation of Whig politicians and intellectuals, including the founders of the *Edinburgh Review* – though many of these Whigs transferred their political activity to London.[17] Stewart has attracted more scholarly attention than later Scottish philosophers. He has been credited with defending university independence at a time when conservative politicians and ecclesiastics, in the backlash against the French Revolution, were suspicious of all liberal and radical ideas.[18] As a professor, it has been claimed, Stewart synthesised the ideas of the Scottish Enlightenment to teach an ethics in harmony with students' religious upbringings, to create a practical and unthreatening pedagogy suitable for future ministers and teachers, and to define the 'Scottish philosophy' which became influential in France and other countries.[19]

In 1901 Henry Craik, the powerful secretary of the Scotch Education Department, surveyed a 'century of Scottish history'. He argued that Stewart was the last true representative of the 'Scottish school of philosophy'. In the eighteenth century, this had a 'firm hold upon the intellectual growth of the nation', but lost this position through its embroilment in political controversy. After Stewart, there were still distinguished philosophers in the Scottish universities, but 'their influence was confined to an academic clique'; William Hamilton, for example, the Edinburgh professor of Logic from 1836 to 1856, 'never guided the nation's thought, and never attempted to mould her history'.[20]

Leaving aside the question of anglicisation, the universities continued to have a central position in Scottish life, with student enrolments much greater than in English universities. Down to the 1890s, the Master of Arts degree, which was normally taken as a preliminary to studying law and divinity, as well as by prospective teachers and as part of a general liberal education, consisted of seven or eight compulsory subjects, including Logic and Moral Philosophy. Philosophy was thus part of the training of a significant part of the Scottish elite – though not all: a separate science degree developed from the 1860s. The idea of a 'Scottish philosophy' continued to be held, and there was debate about who belonged to it.[21] Nevertheless, by the end of the century the predominant school was neo-Hegelian idealism, derived from Germany via Oxford, which was strongest at Glasgow. This taught an ethic of public service and community which was not so different from the common-sense view that expertise needed to be tempered by a social conscience. Perhaps more important than the doctrines of individual professors was their personal influence and example, and the stimulus of the generalist lectures which arts students had to attend. But as philosophy became professionalised, along with other academic subjects, it became more difficult for professors to reconcile their role as 'social educators' seeking to shape the minds of future professional men with the scholarly demands of their discipline.[22]

Whatever the virtues of the uniform MA curriculum, it had a negative side, by inhibiting the introduction of new subjects. English literature was admitted to the programme in the 1860s, though it could trace its lineage to the chair of Rhetoric founded at Edinburgh in 1760 and first occupied by the prominent Moderate Hugh Blair. A chair of Political Economy, supporting the free trade orthodoxies of Adam Smith, was founded at Edinburgh in 1871, without being included in the degree curriculum, but at commercial Glasgow there was no chair until 1896. Other disciplines such as general history, geography, archaeology and modern languages had no place in the universities until the 1890s or later, meaning that the Scottish contribution to these subjects was limited. While the BSc degree and the central position of medicine in the Scottish universities gave institutional support to science, the new arts subjects might have been more distinctively Scottish if they had been admitted to the universities before English influences took hold.

History provides a particularly clear case of intellectual discontinuity. The Scottish Enlightenment made two contributions to historical understanding. Its leading historians, Hume and Robertson, wrote philosophical histories (Hume on England, Robertson on Scotland, America and Europe) in which grand narratives surveyed long-term development, with political history at the core but tied also to social and religious factors. Secondly, Scottish thinkers, notably Smith and Ferguson, developed the 'stadial' theory of history (Dugald Stewart called it 'conjectural history'), which traced human development through four stages – from hunter-gatherers to pastoral, agricultural and commercial societies.

Edinburgh University had a chair of 'civil history' founded in 1719, and its occupant between 1780 and 1801, Alexander Fraser Tytler, gave lectures in the philosophical tradition, covering the whole of civilised history since the ancient Egyptians. This chair later became ineffective, and when it was revived in the 1860s it became a chair of constitutional history, reflecting the new English scholarship which celebrated the development of British liberties over the centuries through the rise of Parliament.[23] But this was more than a piece of anglicisation: Colin Kidd has argued that 'Whig constitutionalism' was well established in eighteenth-century Scotland, as part of an 'Anglo-British identity' among the elite.[24]

The stadial theory of history was influential in the long run on the development of social science in the later nineteenth century, but was not taken up by academic historians. It did influence Walter Scott, whose Scottish novels, like *Waverley* and *Rob Roy*, contrasted the pastoral and patriarchal Highlands with the commercial society of the Lowlands.[25] Later, however, stadial interpretations gave way to racial ones, and the contrast between Highlands and Lowlands was interpreted as one between Celts and Teutons.[26] Like Whig constitutionalism, the idea of a common Teutonic identity between lowland Scots and English supported unionist interpretations of history.

Scott illustrates how one cannot draw a clear line between Enlightenment and Romanticism. Despite his enormous influence on the European Romantic movement, many now see Scott as a modern-minded figure for whom the past recreated in his fiction was no longer usable in the present. But his influence directed attention to daily life and customs, landscapes and buildings, and other material or folkloric aspects of history, rather than to the analysis of historical change. Marinell Ash showed how Scott inspired a period of active interest in Scottish history, reflected notably in the publication of historical texts. This might have formed the basis for new syntheses of Scottish historical development, but without a place in the university curriculum the subject failed to develop.

Ash claimed that Scott created a historical movement on a level with other European countries, but by the 1860s, after a collective 'failure of nerve', the historical edifice reared by Scott was 'shattered into many pieces'. The religious partisanship which beset interpretations of the past was a major reason for this fragmentation, and the Disruption destroyed the uniformity of the nation's culture.[27] There is a clear parallel with George Davie's picture of how the Scottish elite turned their back on their philosophical traditions.

What of the democratic side of the democratic intellect? Davie argued that the anglicisation of the universities restricted the opportunities given to lads o' pairts, but this does not seem to have been the case. The nineteenth century saw great changes in education, especially after the Education Act of 1872, as a centrally administered state system, with compulsory primary education, replaced the rural parish schools and the additional elementary schools created by the efforts of the churches. The parish school, though it had been unable to cope with the changing demography of industrial Scotland, became the object of sentiment, and the link between schools and universities was much debated. Scots were very conscious of having a tradition of broad education and literacy reaching well down into society. But they attributed this to the Reformation and Presbyterianism, rather than the Enlightenment.

The Scottish Enlightenment, unlike some of its European equivalents, did not produce a significant body of pedagogic theory, or have much to say about education in Scotland, though Adam Smith praised the parish schools as a justifiable use of public funding. If the parish schools were a legacy of the Reformation, the Enlightenment inspired the foundation and reorganisation of secondary schools in Scottish burghs, often called academies, to give a modern education in tune with the times.[28] This movement continued in the first decades of the nineteenth century, but secondary education remained underdeveloped until knitted into a national system after 1872 under the aegis of the state.

It was not just Scotland's advanced education, but the general democratic and egalitarian features of Scottish society which were attributed to the Reformation, thanks to which Scotland had become a country where a sense of community and common humanity overrode class and wealth. As Andrew Carnegie put it succinctly in 1904, John Knox 'made Scotland a democracy while England remains a nation of caste'.[29] Innumerable speeches celebrated how Presbyterianism had moulded the Scottish national character, along with the poverty of the soil and a harsh climate, and had nurtured individualist and enterprising Scots. The Reformers' emphasis on reading the Bible had encouraged the achievement of widespread literacy, helping to form an enlightened and peaceable peasantry. The Presbyterian system of church government was itself democratic, and the First Book of Discipline of 1560 had projected a national system of education, with organic links between schools and universities, which had opened the path to higher education for boys from poor rural backgrounds.

It was also a common idea that Calvinism had created the 'metaphysical' Scot, alive to philosophical and religious debate, and inclined to reduce all issues to first principles. In 1932, the Conservative politician Walter Elliot claimed that 'the essentials of Church government in Scotland were a fierce egalitarianism, and a respect for intellectual pre-eminence, and a lust for argument on abstract issues, and these are the traditions of Scotland to-day'.[30] Davie took over Elliot's phrase 'democratic intellectualism', and also his view that after flourishing for centuries, it was challenged by the Disruption and the Industrial Revolution.

However, the Scottish propensity for abstract speculation and first principles could equally be attributed to Enlightenment philosophy, and had long been commented on – often satirically, as in the character of Mr Mac Quedy in Thomas Love Peacock's novel *Crotchet Castle* (1831). Versions of Elliot's idea were often found in pronouncements on the Scottish 'national character'. James Bryce, for example, thought that William Gladstone inherited from his 'Scottish blood' the 'love for abstractions and refinements and dialectical analysis which characterises the Scotch intellect'.[31] And in 1860 the Edinburgh jurist and university reformer James Lorimer published an essay on 'Scottish nationality – social and intellectual', which argued that if Scottish 'individuality' was to be preserved, it must be 'not political, or even institutional, but social, and, above all, intellectual' – for which the philosophy-centred MA must be preserved. Lorimer was a unionist who generally welcomed the convergence of Scotland and England: after all, the two nations were originally identical offshoots from 'the great Teutonic stem'. But Scots tended more than the English to generalise, to think logically and to appeal to principle. They had more affinity with Continental intellectual habits, and though Lorimer did not have a conception of the Enlightenment, he attributed this affinity to the long-standing links between Scotland and France.[32]

If statues give one clue to the later fate of the Enlightenment, other visual clues may be sought in architecture. The New Town in Edinburgh is rightly seen as a major achievement of the Enlightenment, reflecting the principles of classical order, harmony and social segregation. There were similar but smaller developments in Glasgow, Aberdeen, Perth and other towns. Enlightenment modernity also saw classicism as suitable for confining and disciplining the masses in prisons, poorhouses and schools.[33] The construction of Edinburgh's New Town, and the use of classical styles for churches and public buildings, continued into the 1840s: the new buildings of Edinburgh University, often seen as a symbol of the Enlightenment, were only started to Robert Adam's design in 1789 (arguably after the university's golden age), and completed much later.

Classicism in architecture was eventually superseded by a variety of historical styles – Gothic, 'collegiate' or baronial – which were more distinctively Scottish, and which were a clearer expression of national identity: the cosmopolitan taste of the Enlightenment – in painting, sculpture or poetry as well as architecture – conformed to standard European patterns, whereas that of the Romantic era was more reflective of national consciousness. In moving forward from the Enlightenment after the middle of the nineteenth century Scotland also moved, within the political union, towards a greater sense of its historic past.

## Notes

1. James J. Coleman, *Remembering the Past in Nineteenth-Century Scotland: Commemoration, Nationality, and Memory* (Edinburgh, 2014).
2. The sculptor is Alexander Stoddart.
3. Henry Thomas Buckle, *History of Civilization in England* (1861: 3 vols, London, 1891), III, pp. ix–xvi, 281–482. See N. T. Phillipson, 'Henry Thomas Buckle on Scottish History and the Scottish Mind', *History of Education Quarterly* 14 (1974), 407–17.
4. T. M. Devine, *The Scottish Nation, 1700–2000* (London, 2000), pp. 84–102.
5. R. B. Sher, 'Commerce, Religion and the Enlightenment in Eighteenth-Century Glasgow', in T. M. Devine and Gordon Jackson (eds), *Glasgow. Vol. I. Beginnings to 1830* (Manchester, 1995), pp. 312–59.
6. P. Hume Brown, *History of Scotland. Vol. III. From the Revolution of 1689 to the Disruption, 1843* (Cambridge, 1909), pp. 264, 371–5. On historians, see also Christopher Harvie, 'Enlightenment to Renaissance: Scottish Cultural Life in the Nineteenth Century', in C. Bjørn and

others (eds), *Social and Political Identities in Western History* (Copenhagen, 1994), pp. 214–43.
7. Henry Grey Graham, *The Social Life of Scotland in the Eighteenth Century* (1899: London, 1969), p. 114.
8. Reprinted as 'The Scottish Enlightenment', in Hugh Trevor-Roper, *History and the Enlightenment* (New Haven, CT, 2010), pp. 17–33.
9. Richard B. Sher, *Church and University in the Scottish Enlightenment: The Moderate Literati of Edinburgh* (1985: Edinburgh, 2015), p. 322.
10. T. C. Smout, *A History of the Scottish People, 1560–1830* (London, 1972), pp. 470–83.
11. Ritchie Robertson, *The Enlightenment: The Pursuit of Happiness, 1680–1790* (London, 2020), pp. xvi, 41.
12. Tom Nairn, *The Break-Up of Britain: Crisis and Neo-Nationalism* (London, 1977), esp. pp. 92–125, 148–69.
13. Ronald G. Cant, 'The Scottish Universities and Scottish Society in the Eighteenth Century', *Studies on Voltaire and the Eighteenth Century* 58 (1967), 1953–66.
14. George E. Davie, *The Democratic Intellect: Scotland and her Universities in the Nineteenth Century* (1961: Edinburgh, 1964), quotations at pp. xi, 289. The best guide is Lindsay Paterson, 'George Davie and the Democratic Intellect', in Gordon Graham (ed.), *Scottish Philosophy in the Nineteenth and Twentieth Centuries* (Oxford, 2015), pp. 236–69.
15. Alexander Broadie, *A History of Scottish Philosophy* (Edinburgh, 2009), pp. 366, 368, 303. See also Alexander Broadie, 'The Rise (and Fall?) of the Scottish Enlightenment', in T. M. Devine and Jenny Wormald (eds), *The Oxford Handbook of Modern Scottish History* (Oxford, 2012), pp. 370–85.
16. Cairns Craig, 'Nineteenth-Century Scottish Thought', in Susan Manning (ed.), *The Edinburgh History of Scottish Literature. Volume 2. Enlightenment, Britain and Empire* (Edinburgh, 2007), pp. 267–76. See also Cairns Craig, *Intending Scotland: Explorations in Scottish Culture since the Enlightenment* (Edinburgh, 2009), pp. 77–144.
17. Biancamaria Fontana, *Rethinking the Politics of Commercial Society: the Edinburgh Review, 1802–1832* (Cambridge, 1985); Anand C. Chitnis, *The Scottish Enlightenment and Early Victorian English Society* (London, 1986).
18. Charles B. Bow, 'In Defence of the Scottish Enlightenment: Dugald Stewart's Role in the 1805 John Leslie Affair', *Scottish Historical Review* 92 (2013), 123–46.
19. Nicholas Phillipson, 'The Pursuit of Virtue in Scottish University Education: Dugald Stewart and Scottish Moral Philosophy in the Enlightenment', in Nicholas Phillipson (ed.), *Universities, Society, and the Future* (Edinburgh, 1983), pp. 82–101; Donald Winch, 'The System of the North: Dugald Stewart and his Pupils', in Stefan Collini et al.,

*That Noble Science of Politics: a Study in Nineteenth-Century Intellectual History* (Cambridge, 1983), pp. 23–62; Paul Wood, 'Dugald Stewart and the Invention of "the Scottish Enlightenment"', in P. Wood (ed.), *The Scottish Enlightenment: Essays in Reinterpretation* (Woodbridge, 2000), pp. 1–35; C. B. Bow, 'Dugald Stewart and the Legacy of Common Sense in the Scottish Enlightenment', in C. B. Bow (ed.), *Common Sense in the Scottish Enlightenment* (Oxford, 2018), pp. 200–23.

20. Henry Craik, *A Century of Scottish History* (1901: Edinburgh, 1911), pp. 466–7.
21. Gordon Graham, 'The Integrity of Scottish Philosophy and the Idea of a National Tradition', in Graham (ed.), *Scottish Philosophy in the Nineteenth and Twentieth Centuries*, pp. 303–22. For the early nineteenth century, see also Laurance J. Saunders, *Scottish Democracy, 1815–1840: the Social and Intellectual Background* (Edinburgh, 1950), esp. pp. 307–10.
22. Gordon Graham, 'The Nineteenth-Century Aftermath', in Alexander Broadie (ed.), *Cambridge Companion to the Scottish Enlightenment* (Cambridge, 2003), pp. 338–50. Revised text in 2nd edn (2019), pp. 334–47.
23. Robert Anderson, 'University History Teaching, National Identity and Unionism in Scotland, 1862–1914', *Scottish Historical Review* 91 (2012), 1–41.
24. Colin Kidd, *Subverting Scotland's Past: Scottish Whig Historians and the Creation of an Anglo-British Identity, 1689–c.1830* (Cambridge, 1993).
25. Robertson, *Enlightenment*, p. 644.
26. Colin Kidd, 'Teutonist Ethnology and Scottish Nationalist Inhibition, 1780–1880', *Scottish Historical Review* 74 (1995), 45–68.
27. Marinell Ash, *The Strange Death of Scottish History* (Edinburgh, 1980), pp. 10–11, 39–40. See also Colin Kidd, '*The Strange Death of Scottish History* Revisited: Constructions of the Past in Scotland, c. 1790–1914', *Scottish Historical Review* 76 (1997), 86–102.
28. Donald J. Withrington, 'Education and Society in the Eighteenth Century', in Nicholas T. Phillipson and Rosalind M. Mitchison (eds), *Scotland in the Age of Improvement: Essays in Scottish History in the Eighteenth Century* (Edinburgh, 1970), pp. 169–99; Bob Harris and Charles McKean, *The Scottish Town in the Age of the Enlightenment, 1740–1820* (Edinburgh, 2014).
29. Robert Anderson, *Education and the Scottish People, 1750–1918* (Oxford, 1995), p. 261.
30. Walter Elliot, 'The Scottish Heritage in Politics', in Duke of Atholl and others, *A Scotsman's Heritage* (London, 1932), pp. 59, 62–3.
31. James Bryce, *Studies in Contemporary Biography* (London, 1903), pp. 404–5.
32. James Lorimer, 'Scottish Nationality – Social and Intellectual', *North*

British Review 65 (August 1860), 57–82. (As usual at the time, the article was anonymous.)
33. So argues Thomas A. Markus (ed.), *Order in Space and Society: Architectural Form and its Context in the Scottish Enlightenment* (Edinburgh, 1982). This view reflects the influence of Michel Foucault.

# 3

# Dugald Stewart, William Godwin and the Formation of Political Economy

## Lina Weber

We have in this country been too much in the habit of considering Manufactures as the ultimate source of wealth, instead of making them subservient to the produce of Agriculture; & it is from this cause that we do not see the funds for Provision keep pace with those of Population; nor the conforts [sic!] of the Poor therefore increase at all in proportion to the splendour & opulence of the Rich.[1]

When Dugald Stewart (1753–1828), the renowned Professor of Moral Philosophy at the University of Edinburgh, gave this alarming analysis of Britain's current state to his students in the academic year of 1802–3, he hit the nail squarely on the head. Britain was facing an unprecedented crisis caused by the French Revolutionaries' promise of universal liberty and equality, a threat now exacerbated by the rise of Napoleon. The outlook for the heavily indebted and overextended British Empire seemed bleak. A long and hugely expensive war brought the country close to bankruptcy and revealed the increasing inequality caused by burgeoning industrialisation. Radicals like Thomas Paine and William Godwin promised Britons an end not only to monarchical despotism but also to war and poverty, while independence movements like the United Irishmen mobilised labourers and farmers to fight for representation in government and independence from London. With insurrection, misery and mob rule looming, the survival of the British Empire was at stake.[2]

Given the immense challenge that the 1790s posed to Britain's survival, strategies to fulfil the needs of the people while maintaining the state were urgently needed. The established Enlightenment science of legislation neither offered an explanation for the failure of the French Revolution nor did it proffer solutions on how to translate concern with the long-term evolution of society and morals into practical political reforms.[3] A new answer was provided by the 'science of political economy' that was beginning to take shape in Scotland. In 1799, Dugald Stewart took the radical step of separating out political economy from his course on moral philosophy. Economic subjects such as population growth and commerce had been part of political discussions and academic curricula before, but it was Stewart who brought these disparate topics together and united them within one philosophical framework. He shaped a coherent body of knowledge that was recognisable as 'political economy', a compound term seldom used before 1800.[4] Stewart's aim was highly ambitious: to provide future professional legislators with useful knowledge about policies that would make states peaceful and societies happy, while avoiding utopianism and fanaticism as well as bankruptcy and corruption.

Stewart is often presented as an epigone of the Enlightenment and his political economy is discounted as a poorly understood adaptation of Smith's principles.[5] More nuanced scholarship has by contrast shown that Stewart not only summarised and applied the principles established by his predecessors to new circumstances, but also transformed that tradition by laying his own emphasis on progress and education, topics that would become highly influential in the early nineteenth century.[6] This essay aims to further our understanding of the dissolution of the Enlightenment and the formation of political economy by focusing on those parts of Stewart's lecture course on political economy that from a modern perspective might not seem to be directly related to the subject. For Stewart framed his treatment of population growth and national wealth through discussions of marriage, property, national education and poor laws. With these subjects, he was not only contributing to contemporary discussions about social inequality but also responding to the utopianism of William Godwin's *Enquiry Concerning Political Justice* of 1793.[7]

Since Stewart never published on political economy and his own notes on his lecture course were destroyed by his son, scholars have hitherto relied on the edition that the philosopher Sir William Hamilton published in 1855–6.[8] Hamilton used autographs by Stewart from the early years of the course, now lost, and supplemented them with student notes from the later years, aiming to reconstruct what he considered a definitive version of Stewart's teaching.[9] In this essay, I go back instead to the historical beginning of the course and use a set of notes that an unidentified student took in the academic year 1802–3. It is the earliest *complete* set of notes that is extant, and it represents the course in a form very similar to that heard by a cohort of students who would leave a distinct mark on nineteenth-century British politics. Among them were Francis Horner, Francis Jeffrey, Henry Brougham and Sydney Smith, founders of the highly successful and influential *Edinburgh Review*, and a future prime minister, Henry John Temple, Viscount Palmerston.

The shape political economy assumed when first introduced as an academic subject was strongly influenced by the moral philosophy of the Scottish Enlightenment with which Dugald Stewart had grown up. He was taught by Adam Ferguson at the University of Edinburgh and by Thomas Reid at the University of Glasgow, was a close reader of Hume and the first biographer of Adam Smith.[10] When Ferguson vacated his chair in 1785, Stewart became his successor and taught moral philosophy at the University of Edinburgh until his retirement in 1810. He was a highly esteemed and successful lecturer. His moral philosophy course attracted, on average, 138 students per year, most coming from the Scottish gentry and nobility, the English aristocracy, and from abroad.[11] Stewart's classroom was, as Nicholas Phillipson tellingly summarised it, 'the nursery for British Whiggery for the next generation'.[12] Stewart's success as an outstanding teacher was supplemented by the strong influence his publications exerted. *The Elements of the Philosophy of the Human Mind* (3 vols, 1792, 1814, 1827) and *Outlines of Moral Philosophy* (1793, 2nd edn 1801) provided the philosophical basis for the introduction of political economy at the Universities of Oxford and Cambridge and were used at American and French universities until at least the middle of the nineteenth century.[13]

In teaching moral philosophy, Stewart followed the precedent set by his esteemed predecessors. The aim was practical: to prepare young students who were for destined for public careers to fulfil their moral and civic duties. Like Smith, Ferguson and Reid, Stewart therefore included political and economic issues in the moral philosophy curriculum. In 1778–9, when he replaced Ferguson (who was on a mission in America), Stewart followed the outline of his teacher, discussing population growth, riches, law, liberty, constitutional forms and national happiness under the heading of 'Politics' as the final part of the course on moral philosophy.[14] After he took over the chair in 1785, Stewart developed the curriculum further. He subdivided politics into 'political oeconomy' and the theory of government. Under the first heading, Stewart discussed population and national riches. Although he intended to supplement these subjects with questions of justice, expediency, education and the prevention of crimes in the 1790s, he did not realise this plan.[15]

Stewart's decision to separate out the lectures on political economy and to develop them into a proper academic course in 1799 was a radical step. Political economy was not, as Michael Brown has suggested, 'safer ground' than the discussion of constitutional forms.[16] In the 1790s, Smith, political economy, and philosophical speculations about politics more broadly were considered to have prepared the ground for the philosophical principles underlying the French Revolution; as such they aroused suspicion.[17] Stewart, always guarded about voicing political views, had been in France for the third time when the Revolution broke out in 1789. A cautiously approving reference to Condorcet on the issue of education that Stewart had 'written with the most innocent intention' in the first volume of his *Elements* (1792) sufficed to arouse suspicion in Edinburgh in 1793 when the least appearance of sedition was supressed vigorously.[18] Accordingly, when Stewart introduced the class, it 'made a great sensation'. Cockburn explained that the general public was unfamiliar with the writings of Hume and Smith and that the 'mere term "Political Economy" made most people start' as they expected Stewart to make 'dangerous propositions'.[19]

Given the complexity and potential danger of the topic, Stewart's course on political economy was reserved for a smaller group of the more mature students. It took place in the evening, enabling professionals such as practising lawyers to attend as well. In the lectures, Stewart provided his students with a very broad European foundation, referring to Hume, Smith, Arthur Young, Richard Price, Montesquieu, François Quesnay, Victor Riqueti, the Marquis de Mirabeau, Anne-Robert-Jacques Turgot and Cesare Beccaria. Stewart did not merely echo the opinions of his distinguished predecessors but developed this inherited knowledge in a direction of his own. He broadened the definition of political economy considerably:

> Political Œconomy has been hitherto considered as applying only to the circumstances that relate to the Wealth & Population of a State, or what have been called the resources of a Nation. I extend the term to whatever relates to Man as a Member of a political society.[20]

In thirty-eight lectures, he treated the laws fundamental to society, population, national wealth (which included questions of free trade, agricultural reform and manufacturing), poor laws and education.

For Stewart, the purpose of teaching political economy was to provide his students with knowledge that could serve as a practical guide towards creating a better future. He therefore aimed to identify general principles that were grounded in the fixed features of human nature. Since the form of government depended on the particular circumstances of a given society, it had less relevance than in earlier thinkers. History, similarly, lost the theoretical function that it once had for Hume and Smith since it only accounted for particular phenomena.[21] Stewart considered political economy as a continuation of the natural law tradition as it had been set by Hugo Grotius's *De Iure Belli ac Pacis* and the modern science of politics as it had been developed by Montesquieu, Hume and Smith.

Most important for the formation of political economy were François Quesnay and his 'sect' of Économistes (sometimes also known as the Physiocrats). For Stewart, it was not their technical language or the *tableau économique*, but their account of the social order that had advanced the new science. He conceded that the Économistes were 'too much affected by systematic notions' and technical jargon, and he criticised their arguments for an absolute executive power.[22] However, Stewart praised them for having shown that the social order was the result of 'the wisdom of Nature, & not of Human contrivance' and for redirecting the task of the politician.[23] Instead of managing the different parts of the social machine, the legislator was to protect the rights of individuals and to remove the obstacles that prevented society's progress.

Stewart also admired the methodological approach of the Économistes. Their system, he stressed, relied on a broader and more reliable basis than any other kind of political speculation. The evidence they relied on was not confined to examples from a few states or to men solely in their political capacity but was derived from 'those laws of human nature, & maxims of common sense, which every day's experience verifies'.[24] This passage is the only instance in the entire course in which Stewart used the term 'common sense'. He was in general hesitant to apply the label common sense to his philosophy, although he clearly used this Scottish method to determine the laws of nature. In the writings of the Économistes, Stewart found a methodological approach and an account of society that allowed for gradual betterment without giving way to revolution and that used a natural social order as directive guide for legislative action. He could use Quesnay and his followers as allies in his fight against the significant threat that William Godwin posed.

Between his outline of the origin and principles of the new science and the discussion of political economy proper, Stewart inserted lectures on marriage and property in his course on political economy. He explained this decision with the serious attack that the 'late rage of innovation' had made on a set of laws common to all stages of society to which marriage and property belonged.[25] Stewart singled out Godwin's *Enquiry Concerning Political Justice* (1793, revised versions in 1795 and 1798) as 'a work of very considerable genius & ability, but abounding in very erroneous & dangerous conclusions'.[26] In refuting Godwin's utopia of an egalitarian society, Stewart showed, according his student Francis Horner, 'more than usual acuteness'.[27] Since scholars commonly agree that *Political Justice* lost much of its menace when the French Revolution became less threatening to the British government in the late 1790s,[28] the question arises why Stewart, who was generally placid in temperament, felt the need to vehemently refute Godwin's system at the beginning of his course on political economy in 1802–3. The reason was that Stewart shared a dangerously large number of assumptions with Godwin.

Godwin and Stewart strongly adhered to the idea of human perfectibility. Despite their belief in a general procession towards a better future, the two philosophers were anxious about the current state of Britain, warning that the country was facing an acute social crisis brought about by an overemphasis on manufacturing. Both of them considered an increase of knowledge as the solution. Such beliefs in the progress of knowledge and concerns about social inequality were far from new in the late eighteenth century. But Godwin and Stewart went much further than any of their predecessors in the urgency they lent to the issue of poverty and in their conviction that mankind was progressing towards a better future. However, this measure of consensus between them and their shared aims made it all the more necessary for Stewart to distance himself decisively from Godwin's utopian radicalism.

In *Political Justice*, Godwin claimed that Britain's current miserable state was directly attributable to its corrupted political institutions. An overemphasis on the manufacturing of luxury goods had led to a situation where 'the inequality of property has arisen to an alarming height'.[29] An idle, insolent and rich aristocracy oppressed the lower ranks, keeping them ignorant and impoverished. According to Godwin, the human mind was shaped by its perceptions and sensations. By pressing men 'to seek the public welfare, not in innovation and improvement, but in a timid reverence for the decision of our ancestors', governments held a perfectible humanity back from progressing and realising their full potential of happiness.[30] History entailed no valuable information, no lessons for the present, no authority. It amounted to 'little else than the history of crimes' which had helped maintain unjust political institutions.[31] The new science of politics, to which *Political Justice* was meant to contribute, by contrast, 'may be reduced to this one head, calculation of the future'.[32]

Change for the better, Godwin emphasised, could be effected only by truth. Truth was all-powerful and, if studied and disseminated, would do the work by itself. Echoing the tradition of Rational Dissent, he explained that truth was to be found in moral principles that could be discovered through philosophy, introspection and individual judgement. Godwin took up Paine's distinction and argued that society was properly founded on principles of justice, defined as everything that was done for the benefit of the whole, whereas government upheld the interest of the few. The established system of property was the worst of all evils to be maintained by government. Currently, the great mass of mankind was labouring hard yet remained utterly poor while a small group of idle but rich men held all political power and made laws to preserve their own position. According to Godwin's principles of justice, however, if a man possessed more than he strictly needed to lead a moderate life, he was obliged to employ it for the increase of liberty, knowledge and virtue:

> Every man is entitled, as far as the general stock will suffice, not only to the means of being, but of well being. It is unjust, if one man labour to the destruction of his health or his life, that another man may abound in luxuries.[33]

This entitlement was a moral prescription, not a legal right founded in positive law. It was therefore not the task of the government to coerce the rich to support the poor through laws, indeed, this would itself be an exercise of governmental injustice. Rather, it was everybody's personal duty to exercise their private judgement and to grant relief if it benefited society as a whole.[34]

Despite this dire analysis of the present, Godwin promised a bright future. Since 'all government is founded in opinion', knowledge about men's true interests would bring about change for the better.[35] He stressed that the most powerful tool to discover and spread the truth was learning, particularly in the form of *conversation*. National *education*, by contrast, was counterproductive to the spread of knowledge; it only supported national governments in rendering injurious opinions permanent.[36] Study, reflection and instruction were not meant for everybody, only for 'a few favoured minds' who should aim at informing, not inflaming, the people.[37] In a typically contradictory move, however, Godwin argued for general literacy that would have revolutionary effects. 'To make men serfs and villains it is indispensably necessary to make them brutes.'[38] If the lower ranks would be enabled to read and write, the power of the aristocracy would be at an end. Although Godwin claimed that violence was ineffective in bringing about revolution and loathed the rule of the mob, he advocated anarchy as a short, violent means to free people from their prejudices and to overcome despotic governments. In Godwin's account, and despite his rejection of historical lessons, anarchy seemed to be a regular transition mechanism that had occurred 'in the history of almost every country' and had great potential, if done at the right moment of society's development, to bring about the best form of human association.[39]

The English utopian predicted a post-political and post-economic future society. There would be no private property, social rank or government, and consequently neither poverty nor war. Individuals would be freed from all forms of coercion and cooperation, including marriage, 'the worst of all properties'.[40] The pernicious division of labour of civilised nations would be replaced by an 'extensive composition of labour'; everyone would perform the tasks they were most skilled for or work in agriculture for half an hour per day and spend the rest of the day benevolently contributing to the public good.[41] Eventually, mind would overcome matter, making sleep and procreation unnecessary and eradicating illness and death. Godwin dared predict that this future state of humanity would be realised 'at no great distance'. Some people currently alive would be able to experience it.[42]

Stewart was faced with a difficult task. He needed to show that change for the better was possible but that the realisation of progress neither depended on Physiocratic legal despotism nor led to Godwinian egalitarianism and anarchy. Stewart's philosophy was, like Godwin's, oriented towards the future and aimed to 'illustrate that theoretical perfection to which human Society must gradually tend, if not arrested in its progress by the imperfections of positive Institutions'.[43] Stewart stressed that the experience of human history and global expansion showed that society was constantly changing. Improvements in knowledge, discoveries and technical innovation were the forces driving progress. The advances in the art of navigation, for example, made the discovery of the new worlds possible, ushering in 'a new Æra in the history of the Species'.[44] As a result of the invention of the printing press, the introduction of bills of exchange and the evolution of public credit, modern societies differed fundamentally from their ancient predecessors. The break between the past and the present was decisive. Consequently, historical policies became inapplicable to modern circumstances and history lost the theoretical function it had for the Enlightenment science of legislation.[45]

For Hume and Smith, the past had been intimately connected with the present and they seldom ventured to predict the future. Political prophesying was, in the words of Hume, 'a violent prejudice against almost every science'.[46] On the few occasions that Hume and Smith dared make statements about the possible future, they did so to warn Britain about the dire consequences that the current politics of warmongering and public borrowing would have. The most that could be expected from the advocated changes was the avoidance of ruin.[47] Stewart, by contrast, firmly adhered to the belief that human actions could shape the future and that mankind was progressing towards perfection. Although not so obviously utopian, this piecemeal perfectibilism placed Stewart much closer to Godwin than to the Scottish Enlightenment.[48]

Unlike Godwin, Stewart did not provide a detailed account of what the future he envisioned might look like, but it is clear that there was a limiting factor for human progress according to his account, namely, the natural order. The change needed to realise this natural order, Stewart emphasised over and over again, needed to be gradual and free. Legislation could not force society to change or, for example, population to grow. The main task of the politician was to adapt political institutions and to remove obstacles, allowing the natural order to manifest itself. 'The progress of Human Reason', Stewart was convinced, 'will gradually rectify the imperfections of legal regulations, & in this, as in other instances, restore by degrees the more simple & beautiful arrangements of nature'.[49] Commerce, including the trade in corn, would be free, monopolies would be abolished, and agriculture liberated from the remnants of feudalism. As a consequence, the human character would be enabled to develop to its full potential and happiness obtained.

Where Stewart sharply disagreed with Godwin was over the question whether the fundamental laws of human nature could be changed. The prime examples were marriage and property, two themes prominent in traditional natural jurisprudence. In contrast to Godwin, Stewart claimed that marriage resulted from the unchangeable physical condition of the human species. Since mothers were not capable of nursing their dependent babies at the same time as providing for all other needs, they had to have the aid of men. Relationships had to be monogamous because of the natural balance between the sexes, a physico-theological argument that was given new strength by demographical statistics.[50] Property, defined as the right of exclusive possession and transfer, similarly, was a condition of nature. For humans to subsist, they needed to labour. Stewart grounded the right to property acquired by labour not in a contract or a convention but in a 'natural sentiment' that was 'engraven on the heart of every Man'.[51] Stewart ended his lecture on the issue with a strong warning:

> To the freedom from Restraint in the employment of property, Great Britain owes all her Wealth & Prosperity. All restraint in this respect is a deduction from the general mass of Wealth. The opinions held lately by some great Law Characters, that it is the first duty of government to provide food for the People by compelling the Farmer to bring his produce to Market would if fully acted on shake all rights of Property to their foundations, & lead, in their result, to all the consequences of Mr. Godwin's System.[52]

Providing for the poor was a question of justice that was of the utmost importance for political economy and for contemporary Britons. Stewart argued that neither the government nor the individual was best able to administer justice; it was properly a matter for the community. The model was provided by Scotland. Aware that several of his students were English, Stewart gave a historical outline of both the English and the Scottish systems of poor relief.

Referring to Smith, Stewart identified the effect that the established system of compulsory provision for the poor through parishes had on the prices of labour as 'the greatest defect in English Jurisprudence'.[53] The complicated regulations of the English poor laws were not only directly opposed to the simple arrangement of nature, but they were also highly expensive and ineffective. Stewart explained that the English poor laws established 'a sort of community of goods, by taking from the deserving to bestow on the worthless'. They made the idle and profligate imprudent and multiplied 'Inhabitants who are a pest and a burthen to the State' while checking the increase of the industrious middle classes 'whose morals and whose habits are the surest foundations of its strength'.[54]

Poor relief in Scotland provided a wise contrast since it relied on the active humanity of individuals as members of society. Stewart gave a fairly accurate description of the system in place in Lowland Scotland that was based on kirk parishes rather than on local government. Although laws imposing a uniform rate were set up under James VI and Charles II as a copy of the English poor legislation, they were never carried into effect. Instead, local communities collected charitable contributions at church doors, imposed fines on immoral behaviour and levied contributions from the heritors (landowners), who assessed themselves. To ensure the prevention of fraud, the poor were inscribed on a roll and conferred all their property to assessors. The salaries of the treasurer of the Kirk session and the parish schoolmaster, who acted as secretary, amounted to £2 per year and were the only expenses for the community. This was 'an instance of frugality & integrity in the management of a public concern absolutely without example in the history of Europe'[55] and made the Scottish peasants into an exemplar of industry and morality.

In addition to the physical well-being of the lower orders, Stewart made political economy responsible for their happiness. He argued that the division of labour was necessitated by human nature and that it consolidated the social union by making the various members useful to each other. An extreme subdivision of labour, however, narrowed man's attention and depressed his faculties. Referring to Ferguson, Stewart exclaimed, 'To obviate this effect is, in the present state of things, one of the most important Problems of Political Economy. A well regulated System of National Education seems to be the only effectual remedy.'[56] The aim was not, as for Ferguson, to inculcate civic virtue but reason and prudence. Here, again, Scotland provided the model. Stewart explained that a cooperation of local heritors and the kirk made a basic education more accessible in Scotland than in any other European country. Even members of the lower classes were provided with a basic knowledge of writing, Latin, arithmetic and mechanics.

For Stewart, education was the key to effecting change for the better and to unlocking mankind's true potential. He was convinced that knowledge and instruction would prevent the poor from adopting pernicious habits, such as spending money on tea in an imitation of their superiors instead of on food, and from committing crime. Although Smith too had considered education as the most appropriate remedy for the numbing effects that the division of labour had on the human mind, Stewart's confidence in the power of knowledge to facilitate progress went much further:

> For my own part I am convinced that it is from the mistaken prejudices & speculative errors of Mankind that all their miseries take their rise; and that every increase of knowledge, by less diminishing the effects of these, will add both to their virtue & happiness.[57]

Although Stewart claimed that an increase in knowledge would force political institutions to adapt to the new social forces, he did not share Godwin's belief that educating the lower orders would lead to revolution. To the contrary, a more comprehensive education would consolidate the social union and enable society to move closer towards harmonious perfection.

By introducing a course dedicated to political economy Dugald Stewart made a significant contribution to the formation of a new science. Its scope, method of enquiry and practical significance set the body of knowledge that Stewart identified as political economy clearly apart from the Enlightenment science of legislation. Given the prevailing suspicion in 1790s Britain that political economy had contributed to the French Revolution, this was a courageous and radical step. However, the inclusion of the issues of marriage and property, which had been taught as part of natural law, serves as a stark reminder that political economy was just starting to achieve coherence as a distinct science. The border with moral philosophy, in particular, was still permeable.

That a major philosopher of international standing chose to start the first lecture course on political economy by engaging with Godwin shows that the threat radical utopianism posed to British debate was not over by 1800. Godwin's ideas continued to be taken seriously and their influence needed to be restricted. This was particularly the case for Stewart, who shared Godwin's assessment of the current state of Britain and his belief in perfectibility. Although his criticism was serious, it remained philosophical. Personally, Stewart and Godwin seemed to have been on good terms.[58]

The new emphasis that Stewart put on poor relief, education and gradual reform proved highly influential in the early nineteenth century. His conception of political economy as a science that provided the tools to increase the human capability of understanding and shaping social and political mechanisms was appealing to men, as well as women, who had become increasingly polarised over politics.[59] Scotland's community-based administration of justice in the form of poor relief and the basic education that Stewart upheld as exemplary became widely praised. Malthus, in the second edition of his *Essay on the Principles of Population*, lauded the 'quiet and peaceable habits of the instructed Scotch peasant' and the beneficial effect that the Scottish system of poor relief and education had on the national character.[60] It was the seemingly realistic promise of a happier world without poverty, fanaticism or revolution that made Stewart's political economy so attractive for Britons in the early nineteenth century.

# Notes

1. 'Notes of Lectures on Political Œconomy by Professor Dugald Stewart 1802–3', Columbia University, Seligman Library, 1802E St 4, I, f. 205f.
2. Gregory Claeys, *The French Revolution Debate in Britain: The Origins of*

Modern Politics (New York, 2007); Gareth Stedman Jones, An End to Poverty? A Historical Debate (New York, 2012); Mark Philp, Reforming Ideas in Britain: Politics and Language in the Shadow of the French Revolution, 1789–1815 (Cambridge, 2013).

3. See Anna Plassart, The Scottish Enlightenment and the French Revolution (Cambridge, 2015); Richard Whatmore, The End of Enlightenment (London, forthcoming).
4. On the evolution of the concepts of economy and political economy, see Keith Tribe, The Economy of the Word: Language, History, and Economics (Oxford, 2015), pp. 21–88.
5. See, for example, Murray Milgate and Shannon Stimson, After Adam Smith: A Century of Transformation in Politics and Political Economy (Princeton, 2011), pp. 97–120.
6. István Hont, 'Dugald Stewart's Evening Class in Political Economy at the University of Edinburgh, 1800–1809' (unpublished paper, [1986]), University of St Andrews Special Collections; Stefan Collini, Donald Winch and John Burrow, That Noble Science of Politics: A Study in Nineteenth-Century Intellectual History (Cambridge, 1983), pp. 23–61; Knud Haakonssen, Natural Law and Moral Philosophy: From Grotius to the Scottish Enlightenment (Cambridge, 1996), pp. 226–60; Plassart, The Scottish Enlightenment, pp. 157–86.
7. For the English discussion of poverty, see Niall O'Flaherty, 'Malthus and the "End of Poverty"', in Robert Mayhew (ed.), New Perspectives on Malthus (Cambridge, 2016), pp. 74–105; for the Scottish discussion on the poor laws, see Rosalind Mitchison, The Old Poor Law in Scotland: The Experience of Poverty, 1574–1845 (Edinburgh, 2000), pp. 118–25.
8. The lectures on political economy are published as volumes VIII and IX of Hamilton's The Collected Works of Dugald Stewart, Dugald Stewart, Lectures on Political Economy. Now First Published. To Which Is Prefixed, Part Third of the Outlines of Moral Philosophy, I (Edinburgh, 1855); Lectures on Political Economy, II (Edinburgh, 1856).
9. Stewart, Lectures on Political Economy, I, pp. xx–xxiii.
10. The importance of moral philosophy for the Scottish Enlightenment is well known, see Richard B. Sher, Church and University in the Scottish Enlightenment: The Moderate Literati of Edinburgh (Edinburgh, 1985); Haakonssen, Natural Law.
11. Dugald Stewart, William Hamilton and John Veitch, Biographical Memoirs of Adam Smith, William Robertson, Thomas Reid. To Which Is Prefixed a Memoir of Dugald Stewart, with Selections from His Correspondence (Edinburgh, 1858), p. xxxiv.
12. Nicholas Phillipson, 'The Pursuit of Virtue in Scottish University Education: Dugald Stewart and Scottish Moral Philosophy in the Enlightenment', in Nicholas Phillipson (ed.), Universities, Society, and the Future (Edinburgh, 1983), p. 88.
13. Shin Kubo, 'George Pryme, Dugald Stewart, and Political Economy at

Cambridge', *History of Political Economy* 45 (2013), 61–97; Pietro Corsi, 'The Heritage of Dugald Stewart: Oxford Philosophy and the Method of Political Economy', *Nuncius* 2 (1987), 89–144; Phillipson, 'Pursuit of Virtue', pp. 82–5.

14. Josiah Walker, 'Abbreviations from Lectures on Moral Philosophy Delivered by Dugald Stewart Professor of Mathematics in the University of Edinburgh 1778–9', Edinburgh University Library, MS Gen. 2023.80; Adam Ferguson, *Institutes of Moral Philosophy: For the Use of Students in the College of Edinburgh* (Edinburgh, 1769).
15. 'Lectures on Moral Philosophy Delivered by Professor Dugald Stewart 1789–90', Edinburgh University Library, Coll-1881 Gen. 1989, [n.p.]; Archibald Bell, 'Lectures on Moral Philosophy by Dugald Stewart Esq., Delivered in the University of Edinburgh 1793–4', Edinburgh University Library, Dc.4.97, ff. 291–331; Dugald Stewart, *Outlines of Moral Philosophy: For the Use of Students in the University of Edinburgh* (Edinburgh, 1793), pp. 299f.
16. Michael Brown, 'Dugald Stewart and the Problem of Teaching Politics in the 1790s', *Journal of Irish and Scottish Studies* 1 (2007), 114.
17. Ryan Walter, 'Defending Political Theory after Burke: Stewart's Intellectual Disciplines and the Demotion of Practice', *Journal of the History of Ideas* 80 (2019), 387–408; Emma Rothschild, *Economic Sentiments: Adam Smith, Condorcet, and the Enlightenment* (Cambridge, MA, 2001), pp. 52–7.
18. Stewart to William Lord Craig, 15 February 1794, printed in Stewart et al., *Biographical Memoirs*, lxxi. For the incident, see Gordon Macintyre, *Dugald Stewart: The Pride and Ornament of Scotland* (Portland, 2003), pp. 73f., 84–91.
19. Henry Cockburn, *Memorials of his Time* (Edinburgh, 1856), p. 170.
20. 'Notes of Lectures', I, f. 65.
21. See Haakonssen, *Natural Law*, pp. 226–60.
22. 'Notes of Lectures', I, ff. 61, 83.
23. 'Notes of Lectures', I, f. 61.
24. 'Notes of Lectures', I, f. 63.
25. 'Notes of Lectures', I, f. 85.
26. 'Notes of Lectures', I, f. 87.
27. '39. To William Erskine, 23 Jan. 1800' in Francis Horner, Kenneth Bourne and William Banks Taylor, *The Horner Papers: Selections from the Letters and Miscellaneous Writings of Francis Horner, M.P., 1795–1817* (Edinburgh, 1994), p. 108.
28. See Mark Philp, 'Introduction', in *William Godwin: An Enquiry Concerning Political Justice* (ed. Mark Philp, Oxford, 2013), pp. xxii–xxxii; Pamela Clemit, 'Godwin, Political Justice', in Pamela Clemit (ed.), *The Cambridge Companion to British Literature of the French Revolution in the 1790s* (Cambridge, 2011), p. 99.
29. William Godwin, *An Enquiry Concerning Political Justice, and Its Influence*

on *General Virtue and Happiness* (2 vols, London, 1793), I, p. 34. The first edition is used here since Stewart's library, now held by the University of Edinburgh, contains a copy of it with his bookplate.
30. Godwin, *Political Justice*, I, pp. 31f.
31. Godwin, *Political Justice*, I, p. 5.
32. Godwin, *Political Justice*, II, p. 468.
33. Godwin, *Political Justice*, II, pp. 791.
34. Godwin, *Political Justice*, I, pp. 87–9.
35. Godwin, *Political Justice*, I, p. 105.
36. Godwin, *Political Justice*, II, p. 670.
37. Godwin, *Political Justice*, I, p. 207.
38. Godwin, *Political Justice*, II, p. 479.
39. Godwin, *Political Justice*, II, p. 738.
40. Godwin, *Political Justice*, II, p. 850.
41. Godwin, *Political Justice*, II, pp. 823, 859.
42. Godwin, *Political Justice*, II, pp. 871f.
43. 'Notes of Lectures', I, f. 55. Stewart made this statement in a lecture on jurisprudence that was part of his moral philosophy course but that the unidentified student included in his notes on the political economy class.
44. 'Notes of Lectures', I, f. 71.
45. Haakonssen, *Natural Law*, pp. 232f.
46. In the essay 'Whether the British government inclines more to absolute monarchy, or to a republic', David Hume, *Political Essays* (Cambridge, 1994), p. 28.
47. Collini et al., *That Noble Science*, pp. 39f. For Hume's and Smith's predicted futures, see Lina Weber, 'Doom and Gloom: The Future of the World at the End of the Eighteenth Century', *History* 106 (2021), 409–28.
48. For the suggestion that Stewart's perfectibilism had Christian and Reidian origins, see Haakonssen, *Natural Law*, pp. 237–40, 258–60.
49. 'Notes of Lectures', II, f. 147.
50. 'Notes of Lectures', I, ff. 87–100.
51. 'Notes of Lectures', I, ff. 103f.
52. 'Notes of Lectures', I, f. 107.
53. 'Notes of Lectures', II, f. 159.
54. 'Notes of Lectures', I, f. 172.
55. 'Notes of Lectures', II, f. 178. For an account of Scotland's poor laws, see Mitchison, *The Old Poor Law*.
56. 'Notes of Lectures', II, f. 15.
57. 'Notes of Lectures', II, f. 212.
58. Godwin visited Stewart at Kinneil in 1816; Macintyre, *Dugald Stewart*, p. 189.
59. Corsi, 'The Heritage'; Jane Rendall, 'Adaptations: History, Gender, and

Political Economy in the Work of Dugald Stewart', *History of European Ideas* 38 (2012), 143–61.
60. Thomas Robert Malthus, *An Essay on the Principle of Population, or, a View of Its Past and Present Effects on Human Happiness*, 2nd edn (London, 1803), pp. 329, 497, 555.

# 4

## The French Revolution and the Transformation of Moderatism: The Silence of the Scribes

### John S. Warren

Silences confound the historian. Bob Harris, in his reassessment of Scotland during the French Revolution, surveys the curious absence that enveloped Scotland's mid-1790s political repression like an invisibility cloak: Scottish artisan radicalism existed, but was 'rarely accessible to the historian's scrutiny'.[1] Not only was the noise of protest stilled; the liberalism of the Moderate Enlightenment also fell mute. The coming of the French Revolution marked a major fissure in the history of the dominant Moderate Party in the Kirk.

At the zenith of the Scottish Enlightenment in the early 1760s the 3rd Earl of Bute – a man of science and learning – controlled political patronage in Scotland's institutions. At the apex of his system were the University Principals of Edinburgh and Glasgow.[2] His choice to replace John Gowdie as Principal of Edinburgh University in 1762 was William Robertson (1721–93): in Bute's words to his political fixer Baron Mure, 'From the minute I first fixed on him for our great undertaking, I determined to assist him in obtaining the Principal's chair in Edinburgh or Glasgow.'[3] Robertson went on to lead both the University of Edinburgh and an enlightened Moderate establishment in the Church of Scotland that favoured free enquiry and the cultural leadership of a learned clergy.

Robertson circumvented traditionalist resistance to Moderatism by guiding recalcitrants toward acceptance, submission or secession, not least by intruding new, Moderate ministers into hitherto traditionalist congregations. In the Inverkeithing patronage case

(1752), which established his reputation as a kirkman, Robertson made the revealing statement that 'there can be no society where there is no subordination'.[4] By the time of the Schism Overture 1765–6, Robertson was tacitly encouraging secession, which removed dissident voices from the Kirk.[5] Moreover, the growing influence of Moderatism drove out powerful and articulate opponents, such as the talented anti-Moderate satirist, the Reverend John Witherspoon (1723–94) who left Scotland in 1768 for the presidency of the Presbyterian college at Princeton in New Jersey.

There is a tendency for historians to see the differences between traditionalists and Moderates as representing stark divisions: traditionalists devout yet politically liberal, the Moderates tolerant of both patronage and intellectual deviation.[6] Ian Clark, however, notices the inner contradictions in Moderatism, while Laurence Whitley, like David Allan, sees that 'the Evangelical wing of the Kirk and the Moderates was less polarised than has sometimes been thought'.[7] Secession prospered and contradictions flourished, which would in the long run enable post-Disruption Evangelicals in the later nineteenth century to rewrite the history of Moderatism as one of failure.[8]

The major source of division was the law of patronage, and the tensions which flared up between congregations and patrons (typically landowners or the Crown) in the appointment of ministers, but were complicated by the operation of a hierarchy of Kirk courts and the mechanics of Kirk finance.[9] Congregations did not pay the teinds, which fell rather on heritors or landowners.[10] The teinds financed the stipends and manses on which the church ministry and mission depended.[11] Yet while the non-heritor members of the congregation did not pay for minister, church, or manse, they demanded the right to choose the presentee.[12] Tensions in the Kirk were complex, involving matters of funding, as well as of doctrine and judicature.

Robertson maintained a delicate balancing act driven by the needs of a Kirk establishment co-extensive with the state, yet autonomous from it. He was happy enough to see the diehards of the original reactionary Secession kept outside from the Kirk.[13] But his stance shifted when dealing with the second Secession. Thomas Gillespie (1708–74), deposed in the 1752 Inverkeithing case, set up the Secessionist Presbytery for Relief in 1761.[14] The Relief Church however was not intended to be schismatic, and Gillespie avoided association with the churches of the first Secession.[15] In this instance, it was Robertson who took the side of Presbyterian orthodoxy. Kenneth Roxburgh identifies Robertson's criticism of Gillespie's deposition and indiscipline as expressive of 'a very real concern over the danger of Independency within the Church of Scotland'.[16]

Notwithstanding his position of leadership in enlightened Scotland, Robertson remained a remarkably staunch, orthodox representative of Presbyterian establishment and its hierarchy of judicatures. Yet Robertson's beliefs, and indeed Moderate theology more generally, as I. D. L. Clark notes, remained elusive.[17] As a result, historians have found it a slippery task to discover the inner Moderate faith. Thus Clark, Richard Sher and Colin Kidd have interrogated Moderate theology largely by way of Moderatism's wider intellectual contexts than from anything clinching or decisive in Moderate theology itself. For Kidd the Moderates' 'stadialist detachment from the Reformation sat comfortably with an acute sense of Protestant superiority'.[18] Moderates considered themselves no more footloose regarding the Confession of Faith than traditionalists, but more respectful, Christian Stoics indeed, in their conformity to established doctrine and church polity.[19]

More recently, Thomas Ahnert has overturned the received assumption that the Moderates – as the party of Enlightenment in the Church of Scotland – flirted with natural theology, while their orthodox opponents in the Popular or Evangelical Party of the Kirk were so thirled to Calvinist views regarding the imperfections of human reason, that they, conversely, had little truck with anything that smacked of natural religion. Scholars have, it transpires, got this entirely the wrong way round. Rather it was the Moderates who tended to emphasise the limitations of natural knowledge and to stress that philosophy on its own was an inadequate substitute for divine revelation, whereas the orthodox members of the Popular Party were committed to upholding a form of natural theology. These differences surfaced in the 1750s when the newly formed Moderate grouping attempted to thwart the attempts of the orthodox to prosecute the leading Enlightenment philosophers David Hume and Lord Kames for heresy. According to Ahnert, Hume and Kames were denounced by the orthodox in the 1750s not for their adherence to natural religion but for their sceptical interrogation of the natural theology which was such an important adjunct to the orthodox Calvinist theology of the Kirk.[20]

Doctrine as such was never a central preoccupation of moderate clerics. Subscription to the Confession of Faith, indeed, became a matter of disguised equivocation; often discreetly circumvented, but never wholly or openly repudiated (though it is worth pointing out that qualified subscription had deeper pre-Moderate roots, nor was it confined exclusively to that party in the Kirk).[21] Notwithstanding the ritual fencing between Evangelical and Moderate over patronage and the Confession, we should be aware that such divisions between church parties disguised the ways that lay politicians exploited church appointments and ecclesiastical differences for their own temporal ends.

Robertson's Moderate policy thus had its limits, and a problematic shelf life. By 1780 circumstances had changed, sufficient for Robertson to see serious difficulties ahead for his well-established, smooth, self-regulating church administration. In 1778 William Robertson and the 'coming man' in British politics, Henry Dundas (1742–1811), the MP for Midlothian, ensured the appointment of Robertson's son William over the Foxite Whig Henry Erskine, for the legal post of procurator.[22] But otherwise Dundas was not quite to Robertson's fastidiously genteel taste. Moreover, Dundas was the harbinger of new Erastian pressures which threatened the operational autonomy of Robertson's delicate Moderate machine.[23] Whereas Robertsonian Moderatism envisaged a strengthened Kirk liberated from temporal politics, Dundas aimed to absorb the Kirk within his own political network.[24]

Unpropitious circumstances happened to coincide with a furious personality clash. The radical Whig historian Gilbert Stuart (1743–86), who believed Robertson's influence over university patronage had denied him the chairs of public law and universal civil history at Edinburgh, conducted personal attacks on Robertson in print, casting aspersions against his character, and exploiting Robertson's controversial support for Catholic relief.[25]

Robertson's son William became embroiled in his father's predicament, eventually fighting a duel – albeit ritualised – with Stuart.[26] Robertson also found himself in conflict with the pro-American Revolution radical Whig, David Erskine, Earl of Buchan (1742–1829), elder brother of Henry Erskine and Thomas Erskine (1750–1823), over the Society of Antiquaries. These events were compounded by Robertson's difficulties over Catholic relief (1779–80) amid anti-Catholic riots, including threats to his own home.[27] In the sudden eruption of popular violence and the hostility of influential interests, Robertson's impeccable political insight deserted him. Catholic relief was not simply a sign of enlightened tolerance in Scotland, but exposed a furtive political-military bargain; a specific consequence of the American Revolution and the military disaster at Saratoga in 1777.[28]

Roman Catholic relief became enmeshed with a discreet agenda to promote Catholic recruitment in Scotland to fight Britain's colonial war in America; but it pitched Scottish political interests into dangerous conflict.[29] Unfortunately, this military factor opened the door on a world Robertson did not understand well; the British armed forces, in which Scotland's elite were significantly over-represented, to which they were personally committed and possessed serious interests.[30] Robertson opposed American independence, but this was treacherous political quicksand. Supporters of the war were committed to army recruitment in Scotland; indeed were actively pursuing recruitment for rank, rewarding the quasi-feudal influence Scots landowners possessed over their tenants and communities: but the implication that Roman Catholics were clandestinely being recruited to fight Protestants in America proved disastrous when discovered, exposing volatile political and religious tensions.[31] For Donovan, Catholic military recruitment delivered the death blow to Roman Catholic relief in Scotland: the law was passed in England, but only with the provision that it did not apply in Scotland, through powerful political pressure from elite Scottish interests.[32] Rarely had Robertson found himself so unexpectedly exposed. Dundas deftly avoided the fallout, but the alarming and unexpected turn in politics led the fading Robertson to resign, with suddenness, to a future in Scotland of rancour, and worse, that he no longer quite understood or could master.[33] His Moderate administration of the Kirk devolved to Professor George Hill (1750–1819) of St Andrews University, an academic theologian and ardent practitioner of nepotism.[34] Hill was closely linked to Henry Dundas, who became Chancellor of the University of St Andrews in 1788, the same year that Hill became the Professor of Divinity at St Andrews. In 1791 Hill became Principal of St Mary's College in a university dominated by the Hill-Dundas nexus. The two men worked in tandem, both locally and nationally. The post-Robertson Moderate Party was an engine of nepotism, connections and conservatism. This second generation Moderatism was to be very different in character from its forebear.

Such differences were further compounded by the trauma of the French Revolution. This was because the response of the British government to the French Revolution, was to crush all signs of radicalism, as harbingers of revolution, anarchy and barbarism. Even Foxite Whiggism – though at some remove from radical politics – was tarred by association. As Jim Smyth and Alan McKinlay note, the Foxites 'were not republicans, but, nonetheless, they were included in this all-out assault'.[35] The reactionary trend would culminate in the parliamentary suspension of Habeas Corpus and the Scottish Act anent Wrongous Imprisonment in May 1794.[36]

Henry Dundas not only 'managed' Scottish politics, ensuring a reliable phalanx of Scottish MPs at Westminster in support of William Pitt the Younger, the long-standing and limpet-like prime minister since Christmas 1783, but was also a pivotal figure in the campaign of repression by way of his role as home secretary. Dundas displayed a deftness in managing his countrymen. Possessed of a cold, shrewd, directing mind, Dundas discreetly steered the mood of society, encouraging a turn towards loyalism and military volunteering, and astutely gauged the strengths of the landed interest in their communities. For Cockburn, Dundas 'knew the circumstances, and the wants, and the proper bait of every countryman worth being attended to', indeed he was 'the Pharos of Scotland'. Like the warning beacon of a lighthouse Dundas's leadership of Scottish society during the 1790s presaged danger as well as potential safety: 'Who steered upon him was safe; who disregarded the light was wrecked.'[37] Dundas turned out to be a dangerous, ruthless and highly skilled operator, ultimately indifferent to the fragility of the Enlightenment, which he otherwise courted when it suited him.

Already exposed to the political wiles of the Dundas-Hill machine, the Kirk – and the Moderate Party in particular – fell into line. In spite of some Moderate sympathy at first with the early stages of the French Revolution, which bore some resemblance to a cross-Channel version of the 1688 Revolution, the Moderates proved staunchly loyal in their support of government and its policies of anti-radical repression.[38] However, the radicalism of Paine's *Rights of Man*, the activities of the Friends of the People and the British Convention alarmed the douce literati, and the ongoing eruptions of violence in the course of the Revolution in France induced a fear of the mob. From the early 1790s the Kirk followed the lead of government.[39] The turn to conservatism was evident not only among second-generation Moderates, but also among veterans of enlightened Robertson-era Moderatism. Alexander Carlyle (1722–1805) articulated the lurid Moderate view of a revolutionary mob in his sermon on the death of Lord Hailes in 1792:

> following the example so lately set before them by that very foreign enemy on whose aid they can only rely, to raise an ignorant, an unruly and desperate mob ... to perpetrate their wicked purposes, and through rapine, havoc and blood: to overturn religion, law, and the ancient constitution, that, under pretence of a free democracy, they may acquire dominion and wealth to themselves.[40]

Loyalist conservatism was not the monopoly preserve of the Moderates, but also inflected their Popular/Evangelical Party within the Kirk. During the 1770s and 1780s, the Popular/Evangelical Party had been moving in the direction of a Foxite Whig connection. But the French Revolution 'stifled' this trend.[41] The Popular Party, like the Moderates, embraced an ideology of political conservatism during the 1790s. A broad consensus emerged in the Kirk that materialism and atheism were culprits for the mayhem in Paris.[42]

Crucially, France's chaotic Revolution disturbed the tranquillity on which a liberal Enlightenment depended.[43] During the second half of the eighteenth century Moderatism had established a place of respected influence for the leaders of the 'republic of letters'. Polite Moderate clerics enjoyed an informal accord with Scotland's landed elite, many of whose members enjoyed rights of patronage in the Kirk. Scotland's clerical literati cultivated an easy, mutually beneficial accommodation with landowners: a relationship that gave the Moderates a sense of rank and privilege, and bestowed on the landed interest a borrowed air of intellectual cultivation and literary taste. But this socially conservative tendency had its counterpoint, at least until the 1780s, in the Moderates' liberal promotion of free enquiry and intellectual liberty. The literati had theorised on the matter of society with brilliant insight, novel ideas and liberal good taste, testing the limits of difficult subjects and controversial boundaries.[44] In particular, the Moderates had refined the methods of conjectural history and the new social science into the earliest form of evolutionary theory, applied to society before its application to biology; a socio-historical theory developed by the literati into evolutionary gradualism. The ferocity of British political reaction to the French Revolution changed everything. The liberal Whig Sir James Mackintosh, initially an apologist for the French Revolution and close to the Friends of the People, passed through an Edinburgh medical education without any suggestion of evolution or transformism disturbing his conventional views.[45]

The Moderates' abrupt abandonment of notions of political evolution was articulated by another veteran Moderate minister, Thomas Somerville (1740–1830):

At the commencement of the French Revolution I had too precipitately expressed my wishes for its success, and hailed it as the dawn of a glorious day of universal liberty and happiness; nor were my sentiments changed by Mr. Burke's eloquent publication, which, when I first read it, appeared to me to contain the ranting declamations of aristocratic pride and exuberant genius.

However, Somerville went on, 'The atrocities committed in Paris in August and September 1792 opened my eyes ... The very existence of civil society was in danger.'[46] The Moderates' initial indulgence of the French Revolution, an event embraced at first even by William Robertson, vanished overnight.[47] Pocock has seen Dugald Stewart's career thereafter as a series of retreats from Hume; and Stewart's philosophical disciple Sir James Mackintosh, who trenchantly rebutted Burke on the French Revolution in *Vindiciae Gallicae* (1791), compromised with Burke after observing the disorders of the French Revolution at first hand in 1792.[48]

Dundas calculatedly conducted a coordinated policy with London to overwhelm radicalism wherever it might arise, through arrest and trial for alleged revolutionary conspiracies, with draconian punishments. Lord Cockburn, no impartial spectator of course, understood what was being unleashed by the government and courts:

> these trials, however, sunk deep not merely into the popular mind, but into the minds of all men who thought. It was by these proceedings, more than by any other wrong, that the spirit of discontent justified itself throughout the rest of that age. It was to them that peaceful reformers appealed for the practical answer to those, who pretended to uphold our whole Scotch system as needing no change.[49]

Cockburn went on to describe the oppressive, claustrophobic nature of a society so constructed: 'There was then in this country no popular representation, no emancipated burghs, no effective rival of the Established Church, no independent press, no free public meetings.'[50]

Nevertheless, the Lord Justice-Clerk, Lord Braxfield, who played a central role in the trials of Scots radicals for sedition in 1793, utterly lacked Dundas's sleight of hand, and proved a provocative and distracting presence in the courtroom. In his final jury summation at the trial of Thomas Muir, Braxfield unwisely spelled out the nature of unreformed, undemocratic British liberalism: 'A government in every country should be just like a corporation; and, in this country, it is made up of the landed interest, which alone has a right to be represented; as for the rabble, who have nothing but personal property what hold has the nation of them?'[51] By the way, this was also to unmask the far-from-democratic credentials of Scotland's otherwise liberal Enlightenment. The Moderate literati of eighteenth-century Scotland had never subscribed to democratic ideals.[52] Moderate liberalism arrived via political economy, judged more suited to advancing liberty and distributive justice than the intoxicating claims of democracy: civil liberty was guided by the invisible hand of economic freedom and trade.[53] But Braxfield's outspokenness also presented a more immediate problem for Dundas.

There were alternatives. Henry Dundas and his nephew Robert Dundas, the Lord Advocate, were in no doubt that the imported Treason Act of 1709 was problematic; it was foreign to Scots law, ill-regarded, and ill-understood by Scots lawyers. So in May 1794 Dundas commissioned John Bruce (1744–1826), a former Professor of Logic at Edinburgh, to conduct an investigation and report on the practices and procedures of historic treason trials.[54] In the wake of the Pike Plot Dundas resorted to the Special Commission of Oyer and Terminer, last used in the 1715 and 1745 risings, for the cases of Robert Watt and David Downie, who were charged under the 1709 Treason Act.[55] Dundas wanted assured success; which led to the adoption of English judicial process and a jury of twelve, as well as diminishing the role of the notorious Braxfield who sat on the Commission as merely one judge on a panel of nine.[56] In the Watt trial the Lord President, Ilay Campbell, declared that Scotland had not just adopted the English treason statute, but ‹the whole body of writing' – in effect, English law lock, stock and barrel.[57]

The striking feature of the Pike Plot in 1794 was the ready-made convenience of the guilty, more than the quaintly old-fashioned pikes supposedly ushering in violent revolution. In the ensuing case, the government sought to deliver a calculated public message of cold terror in a disturbingly elaborate public production, of traitors dramatically brought to book: an excuse for shock therapy which might underscore policy through retributive state theatre. In the trial of Robert Watt, Barrell discovers the rewriting of the feudal law of treason as a 'modern' treason; a 'treason of the hour' in the prosecutor Anstruther's case; redefining 'what it was to "depose" a king' and made almost any hotheaded disturbance a planned assault on the king's person, and the king, still on the throne, and with all his resources intact, as effectively or 'figuratively' deposed.[58] Watt's 'plot', though nobody ever quite established that it really existed, was sufficient to warrant conviction for his possession, in Barrell's words 'for imagining something that had never entered his imagination': exploiting the possibilities of the antiquated Anglo-Norman word 'imaginer' in Edward III's 1351 Treason Act.[59] Anstruther had stretched the limits of the treason law beyond the precedents understood by the leading English commentators.

Watt and Downie's trials for treason proved to be the only ones of the period that sentenced the accused to death, though Downie was eventually reprieved. In spite of Dundas's quasi-reformist legal sophistry, the outcome of the trial was scarcely unexpected. The changes retained the inescapable authority of sovereign, lethal retribution; with death now hygienically delivered before disembowelling, in a refined demonstration of mature, late eighteenth-century civility.[60] The Edinburgh execution of Watt was planned as a state spectacle – cold in its ominous ceremony, implacable in its outcome:

> Two Chief Constables of the shire of Edinburgh, in black, with batons, two county constables with batons. The Sheriff-Depute and Sheriff-Substitute, dressed in black, with white gloves and white rods. Six county constables, two and two, with batons, the hurdle painted black (drawn by a white horse), in which were seated the executioner dressed in black, with the axe in his hand

and a supporting cast of a few dozen under-constables and two hundred members of the Argyllshire Fencibles.[61] The macabre execution of Watt reached its powerful climax when the traitor's severed head was held up to the crowd by the executioner, declaring, 'This is the head of a traitor.'[62] The authorities meant business, and the crowd attending the spectacle was duly shaken:

> When the platform dropped, little agitation was perceptible amongst the spectators ... But the appearance of the axe, a sight to which they were totally unaccustomed, produced a shock instantaneous as electricity; and when it was uplifted, such a general shriek or shout of horror burst forth, as made the executioner delay his blow, while numbers rushed off in all directions to avoid the sight.[63]

The *coup de théâtre* had its intended effect: radicals were cowed, Moderates of a liberal persuasion fell silent.[64]

The anti-Revolutionary reaction of the 1790s silenced the Moderate Enlightenment. Moreover, a combination of external political pressures and internal changes in the character of Moderatism effected a major transformation in its attitude to Scotland's Enlightenment legacy. Post-Robertson Moderatism was an empty shell. No longer did it represent Enlightenment values and tastes, rather it survived in a hollowed-out form as the Dundas-Hill network. But when this connection was confronted by the threat of the French Revolution it retained no principled resolve to defend Enlightenment tenets, and degenerated into an arm of counter-revolutionary repression.

A vivid encapsulation of the new order of things was the Leslie affair of 1805, when the Moderates mounted an energetic and concerted campaign to prevent the appointment of John Leslie to the Chair of Mathematics at Edinburgh. The Leslie controversy revealed the strange and ironic metamorphosis of Moderatism into a force of illiberal conservatism. For now, in a stunning 'reversal'[65] of their previous positions, it was the Moderates who opposed free inquiry and the values of the Enlightenment, and the Evangelicals who, at the very least, acquiesced in Leslie's appointment to the professoriate. Moderate opposition hinged on the notorious footnote xvi of Leslie's *Experimental Enquiry into the Nature and Propagation of Heat*, which endorsed Hume's arguments about causation. Scandalised that Leslie should align himself so publicly with one of the most theologically destructive of Hume's arguments, the Moderates protested, reviving a lapsed claim of avisandum, a corporate right of Edinburgh's clergy to warn the university against the appointment of a candidate whose views were heterodox. The Leslie controversy was a reliable index of political and cultural change. The Moderates, according to J. B. Morrell, had abandoned the cause of 'intellectual liberty'.[66] Indeed, the Moderates, transformed by Hill's leadership and buffeted by the pressures of Britain's anti-Revolutionary reaction to events in France, now rejected the very idea of 'moderation'. Tellingly, Charles Bradford Bow describes the second-generation Moderates of the Hill-Dundas era as a 'Counter-Enlightenment movement'.[67]

## Notes

1. Bob Harris, *The Scottish People and the French Revolution* (London, 2008), p. 6.
2. Roger L. Emerson, 'Lord Bute and the Scottish Universities 1760–1792', in Karl Schweizer (ed.), *Lord Bute: Essays in Re-interpretation* (Leicester, 1988), pp.147–80.
3. Richard B. Sher, *Church and University in the Scottish Enlightenment* (1985: Edinburgh, 2015), p. 114.
4. Sher, *Church and University*, pp. 52–7; Jeffrey Smitten, *William Robertson: Minister, Historian and Principal* (Edinburgh, 2017), pp. 98–100; *Annals of the General Assembly of the Church of Scotland* (Edinburgh, 1838), pp. 231–3.
5. Sher, *Church and University*, pp. 133–4.
6. Sher, *Church and University*, p. 36; Laurence Whitley, 'The Operation of Lay Patronage in the Church of Scotland from the Act of 1712 to 1746' (University of St Andrews PhD thesis, 1994); I. D. L. Clark, 'From Protest to Reaction: The Moderate Regime of the Church of Scotland, 1752–1805', in N. T. Phillipson and Rosalind Mitchison (eds), *Scotland in the Age of Improvement* (1970: Edinburgh, 1996), pp. 200–24.
7. Clark, 'From Protest', pp. 201ff.; Laurence Whitley, *A Great Grievance: Ecclesiastical Lay Patronage in Scotland until 1750* (Eugene, OR, 2013), p. 267; David Allan, *Scotland in the Eighteenth Century: Union and Enlightenment* (London, 2002), p. 70.
8. Robert Rainy, *Three Lectures on the Church of Scotland* (Edinburgh, 1872); Thomas M'Crie the younger, *The Story of the Scottish Church from the Reformation to the Disruption* (London, 1875), p. 489; A. T. N. Muirhead, *Reformation, Dissent and Diversity: the story of Scotland's Churches, 1560–1960* (London, 2015), pp. 74–7.
9. John Connell, *A Treatise on the Law of Scotland respecting Tithes, and the stipends of the parochial clergy* (3 vols, Edinburgh, 1815); A. J. H. Gibson, *Stipend in the Church of Scotland* (Edinburgh, 1961); 'Reasons for Dissent', *Scots Magazine* 14 (1752), 224–7.

10. J. M. Duncan, *Treatise on the Parochial Ecclesiastical Law of Scotland* (Edinburgh, 1869), p. 291.
11. Duncan, *Treatise*, p. 76; William Buchanan, *Treatise on the Law of Scotland on the subject of Teinds or Tithes* (Edinburgh, 1868), p. 7.
12. R. M. Sunter, *Patronage and Politics in Scotland, 1707–1832* (Edinburgh, 1986), pp. 68–74.
13. Whitley, *Great Grievance*, pp. 197–8.
14. Kenneth Roxburgh, *Thomas Gillespie and the origins of the Relief Church in 18th century Scotland* (Bern, 1999), pp. 86–94; *Annals of the General Assembly*, pp. 275–80.
15. Roxburgh, *Gillespie*, pp. xiii, 95–9, 160, 170–1.
16. Roxburgh, *Gillespie*, p. 82; Muirhead, *Reformation*, pp. 105–24.
17. Clark, 'From Protest', p. 209.
18. Colin Kidd, 'Subscription, the Scottish Enlightenment and the Moderate Interpretation of History', *Journal of Ecclesiastical History* 55 (2004), 502–19.
19. Sher, *Church and University*, p. 35.
20. Thomas Ahnert, *The Moral Culture of the Scottish Enlightenment 1690–1805* (New Haven, CT, 2015).
21. C. S. Sealy, 'Church authority and non-subscription controversies in early 18th century Presbyterianism' (University of Glasgow PhD, 2010), pp. 70, 99, 101–3; Roxburgh, *Gillespie*, pp. 22, 31–2; Gavin Struthers, *The history of the rise, progress, and principles of the Relief Church* (Glasgow, 1843), pp. 9–10.
22. Sher, *Church and University*, p. 129.
23. Clark, 'From Protest', pp. 210–13.
24. R. L. Emerson, *Academic Patronage in the Scottish Enlightenment* (Edinburgh, 2008), pp. 180–1.
25. Smitten, *Robertson*, pp. 189–95.
26. Henry Brougham, *Works* (2 vols, London, 1856), II, p. 276.
27. Sher, *Church and University*, p. 287.
28. Richard M. Ketchum, *Saratoga* (New York, 1997).
29. R. K. Donovan, 'The Military Origins of the Roman Catholic Relief Programme of 1778', *Historical Journal* 28 (1985), 79–102.
30. Neil Davidson, *Discovering the Scottish Revolution 1692–1746* (London, 2003), pp. 162–5; Stephen Conway, 'The British Army, "Military Europe," and the American War of Independence', *William and Mary Quarterly* 67 (2010), 69–100; James Hayes, 'Scottish Officers in the British Army, 1714–63', *Scottish Historical Review* 37 (1958), 23–33.
31. Donovan, 'Military Origins', pp. 90–101.
32. J. G. Kyd (ed.), *Scottish Population Statistics* (Edinburgh, 1952), p. xvii; National Records of Scotland, Introduction, Catholic Parish Registers; accessed 17 December 2020.
33. Smitten, *Robertson*, pp. 194–5; Sher, *Church and University*, pp. 282–96;

Alexander Du Toit, 'A species of false religion': William Robertson, Catholic relief and the myth of Moderate tolerance', *Innes Review* 52 (2001), 167–88; Clark, 'From Protest', p. 211.
34. Emerson, *Academic Patronage*, pp. 477, 497, 508–9; Michael Fry, *The Dundas Despotism* (1992: Edinburgh, 2004), p. 179.
35. Jim Smyth and Alan McKinlay, 'Whigs, Tories and Scottish Legal Reform, c. 1785–1832', *Crime, Histoire et Sociétés/Crime, History and Societies* 15 (2011), 111–32, at p. 113.
36. Henry Meikle, *Scotland and the French Revolution* (Glasgow, 1912), pp. 102–3; Atle L. Wold, 'The Scottish Government and the French Threat, 1792–1802' (University of Edinburgh PhD, 2003), pp. 59–72, 85–6.
37. Henry Cockburn, *Life of Francis Jeffrey* (Edinburgh, 1872), p. 74.
38. Ahnert, *Moral Culture*, p. 124; Harris, *Scottish People*, pp. 138–9.
39. Sher, *Church and University*, p. 305; Emma V. MacLeod, *A War of Ideas: British Attitudes to the Wars against Revolutionary France 1792–1802* (Abingdon, 2018), pp. 141, 150.
40. Alexander Carlyle, *Sermon on the death of Sir David Dalyrmple, Bart., Lord Hailes* (Edinburgh, 1792), p. 32; William Brydon, 'Politics, Government and Society in Edinburgh, 1780–1833' (University of Wales PhD, 1988), pp. 129–77.
41. John R. McIntosh, *Church and Theology in Enlightenment Scotland: The Popular Party, 1740–1800* (East Linton, 1998), pp. 231–2.
42. John R. Mcintosh, 'The Popular Party in the Church of Scotland 1740–1800' (University of Glasgow PhD, 1989), pp. 235, 245, 248–9, 271, 279–82, 295–6, 465; Harris, *Scottish People*, p. 56.
43. Wold, 'Scottish Government', pp. 16–37, 56–9; Gordon Pentland, 'The freethinkers Zetetic society: an Edinburgh radical underworld in the eighteen-twenties', *Historical Research* 91 (2018), 314–32; John M. Robertson, *A History of Freethought in the nineteenth century* (2 vols, London, 1929), I, p. 8.
44. Anna Plassart, *The Scottish Enlightenment and the French Revolution* (Cambridge, 2015), pp. 35–46, 71–2.
45. Jane Rendall, 'The Political Ideas and Activities of Sir James Mackintosh (1765–1832): A Study in Whiggism between 1789 and 1832' (University College London PhD, 1972).
46. Thomas Somerville, *My Own Life and Times* (Edinburgh, 1861), pp. 251, 264, 266–7.
47. Richard B. Sher, '1688 and 1788: William Robertson on Revolution in Britain and France', in P. Dukes and J. Dunkley (eds) *Culture and Revolution* (London, 1990); Smitten, *Robertson*, p. 221.
48. Rendall, 'Mackintosh', p. 87; J. G. A. Pocock, *Virtue, Commerce and History* (Cambridge, 1985), p. 298.
49. Henry Cockburn, *Memorials of his Time* (Edinburgh, 1856), p. 102.

50. Cockburn, *Life of Jeffrey*, pp. 70–1, 260–1.
51. *An Account of the Trial of Thomas Muir the Younger, of Huntershill before the High Court of Justiciary at Edinburgh on the 30th/31st of August 1793 for sedition* (New York); accessed 2 December 2018, p. 122.
52. C. B. Macpherson, *The Real World of Democracy* (Toronto, 2006) pp. 7–14.
53. Plassart, *Scottish Enlightenment*, p. 46.
54. Emma MacLeod, 'The English and Scottish State Trials of the 1790s Compared', in M. T. Davis, E. MacLeod and G. Pentland (eds), *Political Trials in an Age of Revolutions: Britain and the North Atlantic, 1793–1848* (Cham, 2019), pp. 79–107.
55. Smyth and McKinlay, 'Whigs, Tories and Scottish Legal Reform'.
56. MacLeod, 'The English and Scottish State Trials'.
57. John Barrell, *Imagining the King's Death: Figurative Treason, Fantasies of Regicide, 1793–1796* (Oxford, 2000), p. 269.
58. Barrell, *Imagining the King's Death*, pp. 269, 275, 277; Wold, 'Scottish Government', p. 136.
59. Barrell, *Imagining*, pp. 29–36.
60. *Caledonian Mercury* (13 October 1794).
61. *Scots Magazine* 56 (1794), 578–83, 625–34.
62. *Scots Magazine* 56 (1794), 651–2.
63. *Gentleman's Magazine* 66 (1794), 953; Harris, *Scottish People*, pp. 122–3.
64. Harris, *Scottish People*, pp. 58, 117; Meikle, *Scotland and the French Revolution*, p. 89.
65. C. B. Bow, 'In Defence of the Scottish Enlightenment: Dugald Stewart's Role in the 1805 John Leslie Affair', *Scottish Historical Review* 92 (2013), 123–46, at p. 137.
66. J. B. Morrell, 'The Leslie Affair: Careers, Kirk and Politics in Edinburgh in 1805', *Scottish Historical Review* 54 (1975), 63–82, at p. 65
67. Bow, 'In Defence of the Scottish Enlightenment', p. 145.

# 5

# James Mackintosh: The Science of Politics after the French Revolution

## Richard Whatmore

According to Whig accounts of historical change the French Revolution passed a democratic baton from a radical Enlightenment to a new era of greater liberty, rights and progress.[1] James Mackintosh (1765–1832) has been a reliable exemplar in this strain of historiography, as a liberal archetype and perpetual friend of reform, from his defence of the French Revolution, *Vindiciæ Gallicæ*, to his final speeches supportive of the Reform Bill.[2] In this chapter Mackintosh's sense of his own times is reconstructed to emphasise the sharp disjunction between the Enlightenment era and the period that followed; a disjunction which had little to do with positive evaluations of democracy and everything to do with adjusting to a world in which expanding commerce became the dominant reason of state. This meant that large states, in order to compete with their rivals, prioritised the economic domination of weaker states. The example of Scotland became significant because this small state appeared to have bucked the trend. Mackintosh was a unionist who believed in the fundamental importance of Scotland's former independence.[3] While he supported the Anglo-Scottish model of union for Ireland and ultimately for India and Canada, he continued to argue that Europeans were failing to address the Enlightenment legacy, which, following Burke, he termed the collapse of 'the European commonwealth'. This process had endangered small states, and the problem was so acute that Mackintosh held it to be impossible thereafter to articulate a convincing liberal philosophy.

In the crisis period of the British constitution in the 1770s and 1780s, when the empire appeared to be collapsing and Adam Smith labelled the whole a corrupt mercantile system because self-interested businessmen and legislators made money at the expense of the public good, there was a worry across Scotland about the impact upon the Union of 1707.[4] For numerous commentators, the Enlightenment era of strategies to prevent wars of religion from breaking out anew was replaced by one in which international peace was buffeted by the need of states to expand their markets; civil peace too was under threat from populations seduced by luxury goods, which were held to be corrosive of the national mores necessary for the maintenance of states. At the Union a bankrupt Scotland gave up its parliament and national sovereignty in return for union with a rapidly commercialising England. Seventy years later, Scotland was enjoying the benefits of urbanisation and expansive trade while successfully retaining its distinctive culture, religious establishment and laws. Scots worried before and after 1707 that their larger neighbour would take their wealth, ruin their culture and subvert their religion.[5] But by the 1770s and 1780s the greater worry was that Scotland would be ruined by the collapse of the British constitution through bankruptcy, civil war or military defeat.

Few philosophers of the Scottish Enlightenment, including Hume, Smith, Ferguson and Reid, believed that the constitution was likely to last, as Britain's rulers were addicted to wars for empire. Large markets were the key to commercial success and generated revenues for expensive military technology.[6] Few commentators expected Britain's version of commercial society to be sustainable; the fanatic lust for luxury and power it involved seemed like a translation of religious enthusiasms into everyday politics. In the maelstrom of concern about renewals and translations of Reformation-style superstitions, crucial symptoms of the scale and extent of the crisis surfaced on the imperial peripheries – North America, India, Ireland.[7] Treatment of areas deemed to be abused by English power showed the character of the whole and explained why the rotten structure would crumble.

Opponents of mercantile states waging war for empire had long argued that Scotland provided a counter argument to the inevitability of the decline or disappearance of states that could not compete militarily or economically with larger rivals. Union of the kind achieved in 1707 offered a lifeline to weak states facing modern political and economic realities. Equally, the case of Scotland could refute assertions that Britain was a typical mercantile polity guided by reason of state. Scotland could favourably be compared to Ireland in particular, but also to India and North America.[8] Different forms of union ultimately modelled on that of 1707 were recommended for small states across Europe,[9] sparking marked interest in Scotland and its history.[10] The Scottish model of union was naturally followed in the case of Ireland in 1800–1, and was paraded as an attractive option for small states at the Congress of Vienna.

What happened to the figures who followed their Enlightenment teachers in accepting that Britain was unlikely to last as a polity? Their trajectory underlines the topsy-turvy nature of political thought after Enlightenment and the consequential difficulties of establishing the new philosophy of liberalism. A key figure was Mackintosh. After an education at King's College Aberdeen, Mackintosh moved to Edinburgh to train in medicine. In the mid-1780s, alongside Benjamin Constant and others who later became notable liberals, he attended Dugald Stewart's lectures on moral philosophy. Stewart had succeeded Ferguson in the chair of moral philosophy in 1785, and thereafter conceived a teaching programme designed to revise the science of the legislator for altered circumstances. Reid's Common Sense philosophy challenged the luminaries of the science, Hume and Smith, and Stewart agreed with Reid that an excess of scepticism was poisoning national culture.[11] But irrespective of the philosophical foundation of the science, Scottish philosophers tended to view one of the main goals of the science as the evaluation of Scotland's place in a modern world of increasingly commercial societies. Mackintosh shared this objective and saw 'the science of politics' as 'a grand experiment in the improvement of the social order, and the portion of freedom and happiness that can be created by political institutions'.[12]

Having abandoned medicine, Mackintosh left Scotland for London in 1787 with the intention of becoming a lawyer. During the Regency Crisis of the late 1780s, Mackintosh sensed that Britain was on the edge of revolution.[13] When, at the commencement of the French Revolution, Louis XVI and his people appeared to come together to create a new nation, Mackintosh saw the ills of Britain confirmed. Another prominent critic of contemporary Britain, Burke, famously saw things differently. Burke had been in the vanguard of those who defended the American Revolution for its similarities to England's Revolution of 1688.[14] Burke thought the treatment of Ireland and India indicted imperial policy so profoundly that existing political relationships could not be maintained.[15] Yet Burke also argued in *Reflections on the Revolution in France* of November 1790 that events in France were a world away from 1688 or 1776.[16] Rather, a further species of fanaticism had been unleashed, an excessive lust for liberty that was destroying the institutions that sustained France as a polity – the church, the king and the nobility.[17]

In the following controversy Mackintosh was lauded as the most able Whig voice, and *Vindiciæ Gallicæ* appeared quickly in three editions from April 1791. According to the Glaswegian poet Thomas Campbell, significant opponents of Burke such as Thomas Paine were 'deficient in the strategetics of philosophy' while 'Mackintosh met Burke, perfectly his equal in the tactics of moral science'.[18] The popularity led to Mackintosh's acquaintance with Whig magnates sympathetic towards the Revolution.[19] Burke was now an enemy to his long-time mentee Charles James Fox. Mackintosh named a son after the radical orator and might well have been expected to take Burke's place. As the Revolution became bloodier, the kind of patronage Mackintosh required to dedicate himself to the radical Whig cause was not forthcoming. Rather, he was called to the English bar in 1795.[20]

Mackintosh was reconciled with Burke before the latter's death in 1797. Some have seen this as a key moment in Mackintosh's life as he gave up revolutionism for Burke's patriotism and moderate reform. William Godwin and Samuel Taylor Coleridge, both then friends of liberty, were critical, the latter calling Mackintosh a 'great Dung fly'.[21] Godwin asked his former friend why he was being described as a 'savage desolator' and 'superficial and most mischievous sciolist'.[22] In fact, Mackintosh's conversion was hardly monumental, as Burke immediately perceived. Mackintosh, ever obsessed with the fate of weaker nations, came to a different conclusion about the crisis tactics most suited to saving such states. In this he accepted one of Burke's major conclusions about modern conditions but continued to reject others. Mackintosh then set about working out means of defending such states in a world marked by fanaticism and unintended consequences, especially the surprising rise to prominence of Britain as a political model for Europe.

The *Vindiciæ* held that the French Revolution had been caused by a variant of Smithian mercantile systems: corrupt cabals to self-interested ends, in the church, at court and among the aristocracy. Feudal barbarism characterised French manners under the Old Regime.[23] There was a parallel with the state of Scotland and its feudal landowning class, but that was healthily being eroded by the progress of commerce. Yet France, unlike Scotland and England, experienced revolution because all other means of reform had failed. Events in France were altogether understandable: 'Men will not long dwell in hovels, with the model of a palace before their eyes.'[24] It was a rebellion against 'the fate of beggared artisans, and famished peasants, the victims of suspended industry, and languishing commerce'.[25]

Furthermore, revolution was a normal means to liberty, and the French had learned the tactics of popular revolution from the North Americans, who had in their turn followed the English.[26] In each case rebellion and revolution responded to fanaticism and enthusiasm in religion, politics and economy. The misery of the French people explained the bloodletting. At the time of writing, in late 1790 and early 1791, Mackintosh could claim that the excesses of the Revolution were minimal compared with violence in English, Scottish and French history. Perhaps 20,000 lives had been lost in France, nothing compared to 'the slaughter that established American freedom or the fruits of the English Revolution'.[27] Transient evil in conditions of emerging liberty was necessary and anarchy likely to be short-lived; despotic governments, by contrast, might be permanent. To establish liberty, the Dutch had experienced almost a century of war, England a civil war and the Scots and Irish ceaseless conflict. More recently still the English had faced two rebellions in Scotland, the experience of a standing army and a gargantuan public debt because of foreign wars.[28]

Mackintosh's greatest challenge was to justify the French Revolution as an uprising of a virtuous populace reclaiming its rights and uniting to govern itself. Above all, there was no evidence for Burke's assertion that the Revolution was an organised 'conspiracy for the abolition of Christianity', 'one of the most extravagant chimeras that ever entered the human imagination'.[29] The fact was that 'whatever excellence, whatever freedom is discoverable in Governments, has been infused into them by the shock of a revolution'.[30] The French Revolution was in accordance with the principles of politics and the tactics of acquiring liberty: '[T]he most enlightened politicians have recognized the necessity of *frequently recalling Governments to their first principles.*' This 'truth' had been 'suggested to the penetrating intellect of Machiavel, by his experience of the Florentine democracy, and by his research into the history of ancient Commonwealths'.[31] The circumstances of France explained the introduction of a single legislative chamber rather than a division of powers between legislative authorities. The latter were presumed to exist in Britain but did not in reality because of collusion among the landed interest. In fact, 'Governments of balance and control have never existed but in the vision of theorists' – for example, the deluded Jean-Louis De Lolme.[32] Mackintosh saw much to praise in the French Revolution. Primary assemblies, the 'subordination of elections', were a 'masterpiece of legislative wisdom', being 'as great an improvement on representative Government, as representation itself was on pure Democracy'.[33] Burke's conclusions and language were 'contemptuous, illiberal, and scurrilous'.[34]

The most controversial element of Mackintosh's book concerned Britain. England, he argued, had become free in 1688, being 'the first example in civilized Europe of a Government which reconciled a semblance of *political*, and a large portion of *civil* liberty with stability and peace'.[35] In 1688 'an asylum for freedom of thought which made England the preceptress of the world in philosophy and freedom' was created. This ensured the rise of 'the school of sages, who unshackled and emancipated the human mind; from among whom issued the Lockes, the Rousseaus, the Turgots, and the Franklins, the immortal band of preceptors and benefactors of mankind'. Such figures in turn directed a silent but grand '*moral* Revolution, which was in due time to ameliorate the social order'.[36] Superstition, prejudice and despotism had been challenged; 'progress of opinion' which led in turn to the events in America and France. Ironically, while this was happening, liberty declined in Britain. Britons had not purified 'the polluted fountain' of constitution and society, in which the landed interest played far too great a role and the powers of the monarch were excessive.[37] Accordingly, Britain's constitution was not an apt model for France. Indeed, 'no party in the assembly considered the English model', including such purported Anglomanes as Jean-Jacques Mounier and Trophime-Gérard, Marquis de Lally-Tollendal.[38] Britain was in a situation similar to pre-revolutionary France in that liberty had been lost and needed to be restored.

At this stage Mackintosh was optimistic about the future of Europe in general and the small states like Scotland in particular, because the French Revolution was part of the diffusion of enlightened manners through society in accordance with the growth of commerce. Mackintosh, unlike Smith, had faith in men of property and trade as natural reformers, cosmopolitans and lovers of liberty. In a key paragraph of *Vindiciæ* he praised merchants rather than landed proprietors, an exact reversal of the popular Physiocratic, neo-Harringtonian or Country-party arguments that being tied to the soil guaranteed moderation and stability.[39]

Britain needed a revolution against the Gothic manners and notions of chivalry defended in Burke's paean to aristocracy. Such change was due, for 'society is inevitably progressive' and 'commerce has overthrown that "feudal and chivalrous system" under whose shade [aristocracy] first grew'.[40] The dominion of the landed aristocracy meant that little could be done to ameliorate the division between the rich and poor.[41] That Britain stood by at the dismemberment of liberty in Poland and promoted slavery in Jamaica were consequences of a lingering feudal culture, itself overly influenced by antiquity which could not 'boast one philosopher who questioned the justice of servitude, nor with all her pretended Public virtue, one philanthropist who deplored the misery of slaves'.[42] Mackintosh traced a lineage of right reasoners about modern liberty – defenders of the 'science which teaches the rights of man, the eloquence that kindles the spirit of freedom' – from George Buchanan, John Milton, James Harrington, Algernon Sidney, Locke, Andrew Fletcher and James Molyneux to Richard Price.[43]

The fulcrum of Mackintosh's argument was that the French Revolution was leading to a pacific Europe in which commerce and enlightened manners would ameliorate the evils of the past. The French had renounced conquest, so the only source of hostility between Britain and France lay in the colonies. The latter were 'commercially useless and politically ruinous' and would not last.[44] Wars should therefore cease. Mackintosh rejected Montesquieu's prediction that the growth of armies would turn Europe into an armed camp, making civil conflict more likely.[45] True, the French Revolution had created an enormous army, 150,000 strong, but Mackintosh was not worried for this was a citizen army and entirely popular.[46] Mackintosh had identified the forces capable of putting the genie of fanaticism back in its bottle. An era of peace and liberty was to be anticipated and unions like 1707, for commerce and security, might become commonplace in such conditions.

When Burke called for a crusade against revolutionary France in his successive letters on a regicide peace in 1796, warning William Pitt never to relent in the battle against Jacobinism, he confessed that he had been wrong in his *Reflections*.[47] Against all odds, France had become militarily stronger despite destroying the pillars of state. What Burke now identified as republican patriotism masquerading as a religion of universal liberty and rights had led the French Republic to defeat its enemies and commence the acquisition of territories.[48] Although invasion was termed liberation, clearly France was putting an end to Europe's patchwork of principalities and republics and redrawing the map of the continent in a fashion only dreamt of by Louis XIV. Britain alone had the means to challenge the revolutionary Leviathan.[49] Whatever the cost, including the ruin of Britain, the defeat of France would be worthwhile, so dangerous was the threat to the cultures and states of the old Europe that Burke, like his friend Edward Gibbon, so venerated.[50]

In reviewing Burke's letters in the *Monthly Review* Mackintosh admitted that the Revolution had changed his politics too. The rosy anticipation of a peaceful world was gone. Mackintosh no longer downplayed the violence or the victims. The French Revolution had disturbed the peace of nations, although the invasion of France by Austria and Prussia in 1791 had made things worse.[51] More war would not lead to peace. Burke was mistaken in this. One example was the actions of Catherine the Great 'and her accomplices' in Poland who 'perpetrated the greatest crime which any modern government has ever committed against another nation' while using the 'extirpation of Jacobinism' as a justificatory ruse.[52] Although Burke downplayed the danger of despots, Mackintosh called Burke brilliant and a friend of liberty, a seer and a sage. This led to correspondence and a visit by Mackintosh to Beaconsfield after Christmas 1796.

Two things had changed for Mackintosh. Firstly, he no longer had faith in revolutionary strategies for improving the world; 'a melancholy experience has undeceived me on many subjects in which I was then the dupe of my own enthusiasm'.[53] Mackintosh later recalled his 'emotion on the murder of General Dillon, on the 10th of August, on the massacre of the prisons, on the death of the king'.[54] Secondly, Mackintosh admitted to Burke that 'I can with truth affirm that I subscribe to your general principles, and am prepared to shed my blood in defence of the laws and constitution of my country.'[55]

This was an important move for Mackintosh. In the circles where he moved the question was how England after 1688 had gradually succumbed to arbitrary power and economic corruption. The weaker elements of the empire, whether Bengal, Ireland or Scotland, were threatened by Britain's decline. Burke had agreed with the diagnosis of the ills of Britain in the 1770s and 1780s, but unlike Mackintosh in 1791 he refused to see France as a state turned successfully from tyranny to liberty and thus as the potential model. Burke had faith that the British form of union was better prepared to cope with the bleaker and more brutal aspects of modern commercial and political conditions, especially the destruction of weaker states. In his final years, he intensively studied Emer de Vattel's notion of Europe as a pacific commonwealth of nations.⁵⁶ Burke recognised that the French Revolution failed not just because revolutionary governments were closer to states of tyranny than liberty, but also because a republican empire was being created. States across Europe were being eaten up and smaller ones made an endangered species. Burke was fascinated by the parallel between the events of the 1790s and the partitions of Poland from 1772 which signalled the failure and ultimately collapse of any sense of a commonwealth of Europe.⁵⁷ Mackintosh, equally obsessed with the Polish question, came to an identical verdict.⁵⁸ The First French Republic's foreign policy was a further illustration of a deeper Continental malaise.

The events of the Revolution forced Mackintosh towards Burke's conclusion that Europe's only free state capable of maintaining itself militarily was Britain. However, Mackintosh had less faith than Burke in relying upon Britain to restore old Europe. Britain was not a natural defender of other free states, as the recent experience of Poland, Corsica, Geneva and the Dutch Republic revealed. In fact, Britain itself still had to undergo reform as a free polity. Hence Mackintosh could not even now tell Burke 'that I can ... assent to all your opinions on the present politics of Europe'. For Burke this meant that Mackintosh's agreement 'does not extend beyond the interior politics of this island; but that with regard to France and many other countries he remains as frank a Jacobin as ever. This conversion is none at all.'⁵⁹ Burke was right. Mackintosh remained a friend of liberty and the people, far closer in his politics to Fox. However, his concern for small states far exceeded that of Foxite Whigs. Burke had raised the right issue in his regicide peace letters, namely, that the great failure of the modern world was the threat towards and the instability of weak states. But he continued to have too much faith in unreformed, illiberal, Britain. Britain had to defend such polities, though Burke was mistaken in recommending ceaseless war as a legitimate means to such an end.

It was incumbent upon Mackintosh to propose an international system whereby smaller states and weaker peoples were protected from the lust for empire and military power of the great. This was a central theme of the thirty-nine lectures he gave at Lincoln's Inn between February and June 1799 and repeated January to March

1800, the preface to which appeared as *A Discourse on the Law of Nature and Nations*. Praising Burke as a genius, Mackintosh's text was a commentary upon and rejoinder to Burke's regicide-peace letters.[60] It was undoubtedly Burke that led Mackintosh to study Vattel, whom he called an 'abridger' of Pufendorf. The modern study of the law of nations had been systematised by Grotius and corrected by Pufendorf. Tragically the latter's work was now 'oftener found on the shelf than the desk of the general student'.[61] Mackintosh's grand goal was to restore the law of nations as a branch of legislative science. To be effective it had to encompass 'the principles of national independence, the intercourse of nations in peace', privileges of ambassadors, the commerce of private subjects, just war, neutral powers and 'limits of lawful hostility'.[62] Mackintosh hoped that 'the system of the law of nations as it has for the last two centuries existed in Europe' could become a set of laws acceptable to all the major powers, giving legal authority to the claims of small states to remain independent.[63] He placed his faith in what he termed the unanimity of the human race with regard to the rules of duty and the fundamental principles of morals.[64] Europe itself could be purged of war because it had become a 'closer society' due to similar manners, institutions, religion, languages and the links established by commerce.[65] The lectures moved from the philosophy of human nature and morality via the conjectural and actual history of rude and civilised societies to the nature of liberty and the means of preserving it.

Mackintosh was, however, silent on the transition from the current war of Europe's empires to a rule-governed, legally established pacific harmony of states. He acknowledged that the French Revolution was doomed to failure. Attempts to change by violence ancient habits would always be ineffectual and lead to a 'ferocious tyranny'.[66] He now called the French Revolution 'a conspiracy against God and man, the chief scourge of the world, and the chief stain upon human annals'.[67] Mackintosh remained unconvinced, however, by Burke's treatment of Britain's constitution. In the lectures he asserted that 'there is scarcely any subject which has been less treated as it deserved than the government of England'.[68] Mackintosh later admitted that he was unhappy with the lectures because he had been 'agitated by so many feelings, in the year of the conquest of Switzerland'.[69] In fact only Burke had 'recognised both the malignity and the strength of the revolution'.

In short, Burke had moved towards Mackintosh's appreciation of the power of events in France just as Mackintosh accepted Burke's view that they were becoming a force for evil, by destroying the existing system of states. Burke had ultimately failed because while he had 'wisdom to discover the truth, there was not power, and perhaps there was not practical skill, to make that wisdom available for the salvation of Europe'.[70] Yet Mackintosh had no solution either to the problem of collective laws protective of liberty. This became clear in his defence of the French royalist Jean Peltier for libelling Bonaparte. Here too Britain was praised as free but imperfectly free, while imperialist France was accused of destroying Europe in violation of the law of nations.[71] Mackintosh was victorious in this case partly because he successfully argued that Britain was the state where the true rights of man characterised domestic law and where the rights of nations defined international policy.[72] The Glorious Revolution had created a polity capable of combatting enthusiasm and superstition. In the new century, in a 'long series of conflicts between the greatest power in the world and the only free press now remaining in Europe', Britain could be portrayed as a defender of 'smaller states . . . devoted . . . to the arts of peace, to the cultivation of literature and the improvement of reason'.[73] Such arguments, more Burkean in tone than the lectures on the law of nations, convinced a British jury but had little purchase against the counterargument of Bonaparte's defenders, that Peltier's call for the assassination of a head of state had to be contrary to the law of nations, or such a law was not recognised by Britain. Mackintosh's greatest legal success underlined how little progress he had made in his philosophic mission.

Mackintosh focused more upon the predicament of small states in the new century. Instead of Burke's war policy, he looked for juridical means whereby Britain could defend fragile polities. Yet Mackintosh underlined an ever-more Burkean view of the Revolution in the pages of *The Edinburgh Review*. It had unleashed new forms of superstition, especially 'among the vulgar', and amounted to a 'system of infidelity' turned 'furious and frantic as the atheistical fanaticism of the Reign of Terror'.[74] Mackintosh hoped that such an era could not last, despite 'the ignorance of the multitude' and the 'immature state, even in the highest minds', of appreciation of truth.[75] Mackintosh admitted that 'the extraordinary and unfortunate events of our times have indeed damped the sanguine hopes of good men and filled them with doubt and fear'.[76] The solution was the gradual development of institutions backed by people of moderation and wealth. Accordingly, when creating the Bombay Literary Society, he recommended the study of political economy as having 'the greatest tendency to promote quiet and safe improvement in the general condition of mankind; because it shows that improvement is the interest of the Government, and that stability is the interest of the people'.[77] He acknowledged that national insecurity had extinguished 'hopes of improvement' in the present but progress was to be anticipated in the longer term.

Mackintosh's near-Godwinian forecast of better times did not prevent him from criticising the schemes of fellow liberals. His friend Constant attacked Europe's era of revolution-inspired war as ancient barbarism 'so much at variance with the habits and pursuits of civilized, commercial and luxurious nations, that it cannot be long-lived in such an age as ours'. This was, said Mackintosh, as utopian in 1815 as his own hopes for peace in 1791.[78] In fact, 'liberty is one of the luxuries which only a few nations seem destined to enjoy – and they for only a short period'.[79] Mackintosh was sceptical about France's prospects because the populace had become addicted to conquest and war. Constant's plan for the French to adopt a version of Britain's constitution lacked a foundation in popular manners, and Mackintosh predicted that the Bourbon monarchy of Louis XVIII would never return after fleeing Paris at the beginning of the Hundred Days.

As Bonaparte's empire collapsed, a recurring theme for Mackintosh was to play down the overall influence of the French Revolution in the decline of 'the commonwealth of Europe'.[80] This had relied upon a balance of power established in earlier centuries and had been so successful that 'no great violation of national independence had occurred from the first civilisation of the European states till the partition of Poland'.[81] Disregarding the questionable accuracy concerning Europe, the notion that it was a peaceable union of interlinked powers respecting each other's sovereignty made no sense beyond the Continent, as Mackintosh admitted.[82] Mackintosh's controversial opinion reiterated Burke's view[83] and deployed it to lambast Viscount Castlereagh, the foreign secretary, for decisions at the Congress of Vienna. Mackintosh's condemnation was 'the most painful public duty which I have ever felt myself called upon to perform'.[84] Castlereagh was found wanting for refusing to restore many of Europe's formerly sovereign powers. For Mackintosh, Fox and Burke had allied 'to dissuade England from tyranny' in Ireland, North America and Poland.[85] Mackintosh described post-1815 international relations as a 'repartition of power' or concert of large European states in corrupt cabal against smaller and weaker states: 'Europe can no longer be called a commonwealth, when her members have no safety but in their strength.'[86] The Congress of Vienna was following Bonaparte in having 'adopted every part of the French system, except that they have transferred the dictatorship of Europe from an individual to a triumvirate'.[87]

Writing about Poland seven years later, Mackintosh repeated that 'conquest and extensive empire are among the greatest evils', while 'the division of mankind into independent communities is among the greatest advantages which fall to the lot of men'.[88] Again he claimed that the division of Poland marked the end point for the European commonwealth: 'Till the first Partition, the right of every people to its own soil had been universally regarded as the guardian principle of European independence.'[89] Britain had failed in Poland and was failing now by refusing to acknowledge the independence of the former Spanish colonies in South America.[90] Burke had foreseen the tragic development before others. In an account of the loss of liberty in Denmark Mackintosh called Burke 'a fond, and therefore fearful, lover of European liberty' and praised his brilliance in recognising that liberty might well 'be driven from her ancient seats and leave the inhabitants of Europe to be numbered with the Asiatic slaves'. Burke was equally correct that 'every evil is to be hazarded for her preservation'.[91]

Ultimately Mackintosh saw himself as restoring Burke to the camp of the friends of liberty. Mackintosh shared with Burke,

Richard Price and the philosophers of the Scottish Enlightenment a vision of a Britain reformed so that the republican patriotism of its public culture was channelled towards trade rather than towards war (although a more military patriotism was always retained for times when necessity dictated, and when commerce could be relied upon to underpin national security). Britain had to be committed to permanent involvement in mainland Europe to prevent modern versions of universal monarchy from arising once again. Such themes he explored in an unfinished history of England. The question was how to create a world in which Britain could play such a role. Mackintosh found no strategies sufficient to move Britain or Europe back to the position after 1688 and found his own generation to be wanting. He was sceptical of every liberal philosophy promising an altered world of liberty. The example of Scotland as a counterpoint remained and towards the end of his life he identified the kinds of union that ought to characterise the place of Canada with the 'British Confederacy'.[92] The fear remained that Britain itself was lacking in liberty and this translated into refusal to defend liberty and peace abroad. Mackintosh's final work, in defence of reform, echoed many of the assaults upon the British polity first enunciated in *Vindiciæ Gallicæ*.[93]

## Notes

Thanks to Colin Kidd, Knud Haakonssen and Lina Weber for comment on earlier versions.

1. Lynn Hunt, *Inventing Human Rights. A History* (New York, 2007); Dan Edelstein, *The Enlightenment. A Genealogy* (Chicago, 2010); Jonathan Israel, *The Enlightenment That Failed* (Oxford, 2019); Annelien de Dijn, *Freedom. An Unruly History* (Cambridge, MA, 2020).
2. Jonathan Israel, *Revolutionary Ideas: An Intellectual History of the French* (Princeton, 2015), p. 265; Patrick O'Leary, *Sir James Mackintosh: The Whig Cicero* (Aberdeen, 1989).
3. Mackintosh, 'An Account of the Partition of Poland' (1822), in *The Miscellaneous Works of the Right Honourable Sir James Mackintosh* (3 vols, London, 1854), II, p. 363 [henceforth MW].
4. Adam Smith, *An Inquiry into the Nature and Causes of the Wealth of Nations*, ed. R. H. Campbell, A. S. Skinner and R. B. Todd (2 vols, Oxford, 1976), Book III, ch. 1, at I, p. 380.

5. Colin Kidd, *Union and Unionisms: Political Thought in Scotland, 1500–2000* (Cambridge, 2008).
6. Istvan Hont, *Jealousy of trade: International Trade and the Nation-state in Historical Perspective* (Cambridge, MA, 2005); Michael Sonenscher, *Before the Deluge: public debt, inequality, and the intellectual origins of the French Revolution* (Princeton, 2007); Lina Weber, 'Doom and gloom. The future of the world at the end of the eighteenth century', *History* 106 (2021), 409–28.
7. J. G. A. Pocock (ed.), *Three British Revolutions: 1641, 1688, 1776* (Princeton, 1980); Christopher A. Bayly, 'Ireland, India and the Empire: 1780–1914', *Transactions of the Royal Historical Society* 10 (2000), 377–97.
8. Edmund Burke, 'To Samuel Span, Esq., Master of the Society of Merchants Adventurers of Bristol' in *Two Letters from Mr. Burke to Gentlemen in the City of Bristol* (London, 1778), pp. 11–13.
9. Jean-Louis De Lolme, *An Essay, Containing a Few Strictures on the Union of Scotland with England* (London, 1787).
10. Richard Whatmore, 'Rights after the revolutions', in *Philosophy, Rights and Natural Law: Essays in Honour of Knud Haakonssen*, ed. Ian Hunter and Richard Whatmore (Edinburgh, 2019), pp. 484–524.
11. Knud Haakonssen, 'Dugald Stewart and the science of a legislator' and 'The Science of a Legislator in James Mackintosh's Moral Philosophy', in *Natural Law and Moral Philosophy from Grotius to the Scottish Enlightenment* (Cambridge, 1996), pp. 226–93.
12. Mackintosh, *Vindiciæ Gallicæ. Defence of the French Revolution and its English Admirers* (3rd edn, London, 1791), p. 110.
13. [Mackintosh], *Arguments Concerning the Constitutional Right of Parliament to Appoint a Regency* (London, 1788), pp. 7–10.
14. Burke, *Speech of Edmund Burke, Esq., on American Taxation: April 19, 1774* (London, 1775).
15. Burke, *Thoughts on the Cause of the Present Discontents* (London, 1770).
16. Edmund Burke, *Reflections upon the Revolution in France* (London, 1790), 7th edn, p. 21.
17. J. G. A. Pocock, 'Edmund Burke and the Redefinition of Enthusiasm', in Keith Michael Baker (ed.), *The French Revolution and the Creation of Modern Political Culture* (Oxford, 1987–94), 4 vols, 3:19–43.
18. James Mackintosh, *Memoirs*, I, pp. 59–60.
19. Anon., 'Sir James Mackintosh', *The National Magazine* 1 (1830), 11.
20. Christopher J. Finlay, 'Mackintosh, Sir James, of Kyllachy (1765–1832)', ODNB: <https://www.oxforddnb.com/view/10.1093/ref:odnb/9780198614128.001.0001/odnb-9780198614128-e-17620>.
21. William Christian, 'James Mackintosh, Burke, and the Cause of Reform', *Eighteenth-Century Studies* 7 (1973), 193–206.
22. Godwin to Mackintosh, 27 January 1799, published in Godwin, *Thoughts*

*Occasioned by the Perusal of Dr. Parr's Spital Sermon* (London, 1801), p. 13.
23. Mackintosh, *Vindiciæ*, pp. 66–74, 94–106.
24. Mackintosh, *Vindiciæ*, p. 122.
25. Mackintosh, *Vindiciæ*, p. v.
26. Mackintosh, *Vindiciæ*, p. 106.
27. Mackintosh, *Vindiciæ*, pp. 173–4.
28. Mackintosh, *Vindiciæ*, pp. 167–8.
29. Mackintosh, *Vindiciæ*, p. 140.
30. Mackintosh, *Vindiciæ*, p. 107.
31. Mackintosh, *Vindiciæ*, pp. 108.
32. Mackintosh, *Vindiciæ*, pp. 264–5.
33. Mackintosh, *Vindiciæ*, pp. 240–1.
34. Mackintosh, *Vindiciæ*, p. vi.
35. Mackintosh, *Vindiciæ*, p. 328.
36. Mackintosh, *Vindiciæ*, p. 329.
37. Mackintosh, *Vindiciæ*, pp. 330–4.
38. Mackintosh, *Vindiciæ*, p. 260.
39. Mackintosh, *Vindiciæ*, pp. 136–7.
40. Mackintosh, *Vindiciæ*, p. 197.
41. Mackintosh, *Vindiciæ*, p. 268.
42. Mackintosh, *Vindiciæ*, p. 269.
43. Mackintosh, *Vindiciæ*, pp. 308–11.
44. Mackintosh, *Vindiciæ*, p. 280.
45. Mackintosh, *Vindiciæ*, p. 55.
46. Mackintosh, *Vindiciæ*, pp. 282–90.
47. Edmund Burke, *Two letters addressed to a Member of the present Parliament, on the proposals for peace with the regicide Directory of France* (London, 1796), p. 6.
48. Burke, *Two letters*, p. 7.
49. Burke, *Two letters*, p. 9.
50. J. G. A. Pocock, *Barbarism and Religion: Volume 1* (Cambridge, 1999).
51. Mackintosh, 'The French War of 1793', MW, III, pp. 174–6.
52. Mackintosh, 'The French War', MW, III, p. 177.
53. Mackintosh to Burke [November 1796] in *Memoirs of the Life of Sir James Mackintosh*, I, pp. 87–8.
54. Mackintosh to Richard Sharp, 9 December 1804, *Memoirs*, I, p. 133.
55. Mackintosh to Burke [November 1796] in *Memoirs of the Life of Sir James Mackintosh*, I, p. 88.
56. Emer de Vattel, *Droit des gens* (1758). Cf. Iain Hampsher-Monk, 'Edmund Burke's changing justification for intervention', *Historical Journal* 48 (2005), 65–100; Richard Bourke, 'Edmund Burke and the Politics of Conquest', *Modern Intellectual History* 4 (2007), 403–32.

57. Anna Plassart, 'Edmund Burke, Poland, and the Commonwealth of Europe', *Historical Journal* 63 (2020), 885–910.
58. Hampsher-Monk, 'Edmund Burke's changing justification', 99.
59. Burke to French Laurence, 25 December 1796, *The correspondence of Edmund Burke*, ed. Thomas W Copeland (Cambridge, 1958–78), 10 vols, IX, 204–5.
60. Mackintosh, MW, I, pp. 381, 387.
61. Mackintosh, MW, I, pp. 351, 355.
62. Mackintosh, MW, I, p. 383.
63. Mackintosh, MW, I, p. 384.
64. Mackintosh, MW, I, p. 353.
65. Mackintosh, MW, I, p. 348.
66. Mackintosh, MW, I, p. 375.
67. Mackintosh to George Moore, 6 January 1800, *Memoirs*, I, p. 125.
68. Mackintosh, MW, I, p. 377.
69. Mackintosh to Richard Sharp, 9 December 1804, *Memoirs*, I, p. 133.
70. Mackintosh to Sharp, 9 December 1804, *Memoirs*, I, pp. 128–9.
71. James Mackintosh, *The Trial of John Peltier, esq for a Libel Against Napoleon Buonoparte* (London, 1803), p. 127.
72. Mackintosh, *The Trial*, pp. 154–80.
73. Mackintosh, *The Trial*, pp. 83–5.
74. Mackintosh, 'Review of Madame de Staël's *De l'Allemagne*', *Edinburgh Review* (1813), in MW, I, p. 554.
75. Mackintosh, 'Review of Madame de Staël', MW, I, p. 559.
76. Mackintosh, 'Discourse read at the opening of The Literary Society of Bombay, 26 November 1804', MW, I, pp. 577–8.
77. Mackintosh, 'Discourse', MW, I, p. 577.
78. Mackintosh, 'The State of France', MW, III, p. 199.
79. Mackintosh, 'The State of France', MW, III, p. 202.
80. Mackintosh first used the phrase in his defence of Peltier, MW, III, p. 251.
81. Mackintosh, 'Speech on the Annexation of Genoa to the Kingdom of Sardinia, delivered in the House of Commons on the 27th of April, 1815', MW, III, p. 351.
82. Mackintosh, 'Memoir on the Affairs of Holland', MW, I, pp. 567–70.
83. Plassart, 'Edmund Burke, Poland, and the Commonwealth'.
84. Mackintosh, 'Speech on the Annexation of Genoa to the Kingdom of Sardinia', MW, III, p. 310.
85. Mackintosh, 'Speech on the Annexation', MW, III, pp. 316–17.
86. Mackintosh, 'Speech on the Annexation', MW, III, pp. 349–50.
87. Mackintosh, 'Speech on the Annexation', MW, III, p. 351.
88. Mackintosh, 'An Account of the Partition of Poland', MW, II, p. 362.
89. Mackintosh, 'An Account', MW, II, p. 381.
90. Mackintosh, *Substance of the speech of Sir James Mackintosh in the House*

of Commons, June 15, 1824 on presenting a petition from the merchants of London for the recognition of the independent state established in the countries of America formerly subject to Spain (London, [1824]).
91. Mackintosh, 'Sketch of the Administration and Fall of Struensee', *Edinburgh Review* (1827), in MW, II, pp. 406–7.
92. Mackintosh, 'Speech on the Civil Government of Canada, delivered in the House of Commons, on the 2nd of May, 1828', MW, III, pp. 481–5.
93. Mackintosh, 'Speech on the Second Reading of the Bill to amend the Representation of the People of England and Wales, delivered in the House of Commons, 4th July 1831', MW, III, pp. 526–58.

# 6

# Scotland's Freethinking Societies: Debating Natural Theology, 1820–c.1843

*Felicity Loughlin*

Of course, Edinburgh, it was said, was built on hypocrisy. It was the city of Hume, the home of the Scottish Enlightenment, but then what had happened? Petty Calvinism had flourished in the nineteenth century and the light had gone elsewhere; back to Paris, to Berlin, or off to America, to Harvard and the like, where everything was now possible.

Alexander McCall Smith, *The Sunday Philosophy Club* (2004)

These musings of the fictional Edinburgh resident, moral philosopher and eponymous protagonist of Alexander McCall Smith's *Isabel Dalhousie* novels neatly encapsulate the conventional portrait of the intellectual transformation of post-Enlightenment Scotland. Scholars commonly identify a turning point in the early nineteenth century with the steady decline of the Moderate Party of the Kirk, whose members had actively participated in the Scottish Enlightenment, held prominent roles in the universities, emphasised morality over dogma and forged friendships with as notorious a sceptic as David Hume. A new chapter in Scottish intellectual life is traditionally associated with the rise of the Evangelical Party, which discouraged the combination of ministerial and professorial roles and championed the importance of doctrinal orthodoxy. Yet by painting the landscape of post-Enlightenment Scotland in such broad brushstrokes, several interesting features of its religious and intellectual transformation are omitted from the frame.

Strikingly, it is seldom recognised that insurgent Calvinist Evangelicalism was mirrored by the concomitant appearance of freethinking circles and communities, most notably the 'Zetetic' societies in Edinburgh (1820) and Glasgow (1824).[1] Taking their name from the Greek *zētein*, 'to seek' or 'enquire', these radical groups met weekly on Sunday evenings to debate controversial philosophical and theological topics, attracting audiences of three to four hundred at their peak. Dominated by male members of the middling and working classes – including retailers, shop owners, artisans, skilled labourers, apprentices and factory workers – they provided a hub for unbelievers of various stripes, including atheists, deists and sceptics. Despite periodic waves of persecution, in which several individuals affiliated with these groups were prosecuted for selling or circulating blasphemous books, descendants of the 1820s freethinking societies remained active into at least the early 1840s. Although the surviving reports of their debates and activities are patchy, extant lectures and newspaper articles preserved in the freethinking press provide a remarkable window onto forgotten dimensions of intellectual change in the post-Enlightenment period.

This chapter explores a question that was tackled repeatedly by many of Scotland's freethinkers over the twenty-year period between the establishment of the Zetetic societies and the last blasphemy prosecution of 1843: what is the scope and legitimacy of natural theology? That is, how far can rational arguments demonstrate or corroborate divine truths? This was a question that had divided Scottish Christians in the previous century. As M. A. Stewart has shown, responding to trends south of the border and on the Continent, numerous eighteenth-century Scots experimented with natural theology, sparking 'bitter conflicts between conservative and progressive parties in the Kirk'.[2] Until recently, it was generally agreed that while all Scottish Christians stressed the supremacy of revelation over reason, the Moderates were more optimistic about the potential of natural theology to discern or demonstrate divine truths than the Evangelicals, who placed greater emphasis on the utter depravity of fallen humanity.[3] Thomas Ahnert, however, has dramatically reversed this picture, showing convincingly that 'paradoxical though this may seem, the enlightened Moderate clergymen in the Presbyterian Church of Scotland were actually more sceptical about a natural, philosophical religion of reason than their more orthodox, traditional counterparts'.[4] In this the Moderates were closer to Hume, whose writings on religion included a dramatic critique of the epistemological and philosophical foundations of rational arguments for fundamental religious teachings. By the early nineteenth century, then, the precise status and utility of natural theology remained unresolved. How did the members of Scotland's freethinking societies engage with this unsettled theological problem? And how far did they respond to the legacy of Hume in doing so?

Scottish freethinkers reckoned with two broad types of natural theological arguments, based respectively on *a priori* and *a posteriori* reasoning. The former, often described as first-cause arguments, were deduced from logical propositions. The latter, commonly known as design arguments, were by far the more popular form of natural theology and were based on our experiences and observations of the external world and the living organisms within it. Hume had famously undermined *a posteriori* claims for God's existence and attributes, arguing that they rested on an unproven assumption that the order of things in the material world had not existed since eternity, and that they erroneously sought to deduce an infinite being from the evidence of finite phenomena. Nineteenth-century Scottish theologians took such criticisms on board. Few displayed the unbridled confidence in *a posteriori* demonstrations of God's existence and attributes displayed by the politician Henry Brougham in his *Discourse of Natural Theology* (1835).[5] Nevertheless, many Scottish Evangelicals displayed a lively interest in the potential of *a posteriori* arguments to discern or corroborate a variety of scriptural truths.

In 1816, for instance, William Laurence Brown, Professor of Divinity at Marischal College in Aberdeen, published his *Essay on the Existence of the Supreme Creator*, which deduced the existence of an infinitely powerful, wise and good God from observations of external nature and the constitution of the human mind. Brown referred in several places to the *Natural Theology* (1802) of the English theologian William Paley, who had done much to reinvigorate the design argument south of the border. As Paul Baxter has shown, Scottish Evangelicals tended to disagree with Paley's optimistic vision of external nature, preferring to focus on human nature in their own experimentations with the design argument, and drawing attention to change and decay as much as harmonious adaptation to corroborate divine truths.[6] Perhaps the most notable contributor to Scottish natural theology was Thomas Chalmers, whose popular *Astronomical Discourses* (1817) appealed to the magnitude of the heavens and the probability of extraterrestrial life to enhance Christian piety and bolster evangelical soteriology.[7] Chalmers expanded his natural theological arguments in his *Bridgewater Treatise* (1833), which appealed to the human mind's adaptation to external nature to defend the existence of an infinite, omnipresent and benevolent deity.[8] Other leading Evangelicals also dabbled in *a posteriori* natural theology, including the scientist David Brewster, who argued that geology helped to confirm revealed teachings about the regeneration of corrupt humanity, and the minister John Fleming, who believed natural theology should be given greater priority in Presbyterian seminaries.[9]

Numerous members of Scotland's freethinking societies rejected attempts to align rational arguments or scientific discoveries to the demonstration of Christian theological principles. In 1823, a Dundonian materialist named William Henry Steuart, a frequent correspondent to the British freethinking newspaper, *The Republican*, characterised Chalmers's *Astronomical Discourses* as a 'vain attempt ... to reconcile the glorious discoveries of modern science with the foolish, self-conceited, and gross absurdities of the meek, the well known, and renowned Moses'.[10] Responding to the burgeoning Evangelical interest in geology, Steuart expressed the view of many fellow unbelievers when he lamented that 'the beautiful principles, not only of Astronomy, but of Geology are interwoven with all the jargon which priestcraft ever invented'.[11] James Affleck, a grocer and founding member of the Edinburgh Zetetic Society, echoed these sentiments. For Affleck, recent astronomical and geological developments had only proved that our understanding of nature remained limited. On this basis, human beings were ill-equipped to use such discoveries to demonstrate the being and attributes of a supposed creator, for 'what reason have we, while unacquainted with all the secondary causes in nature to pretend to expound the first? As well might a child, unacquainted with the alphabet, attempt to decipher the hieroglyphics of the ancients.'[12]

Nevertheless, while unbelievers unanimously rejected the 'scripturian's god', opinion was divided over the extent to which *a posteriori* reasoning could prove the existence and attributes of a deity. Some favoured deism, including an anonymous thinker from Aberdeen, who argued in 1828 that the harmonious 'properties, powers, and nature of the universe' signalled its design by a divine being.[13] By contrast, many of the most vocal members of Scotland's freethinking communities rejected the validity of such claims. Some followed Hume's lead by pointing out that it was just as plausible that the world was eternal than that it was created *ex nihilo* by an intelligent deity. According to Affleck, Christians had 'written and harangued much about the mechanical arrangement of animal bodies' in their attempts to prove a 'designing workman', but such arguments depended on the unproven assumption that such animals had not always existed.[14] Affleck, like many other freethinkers, instead favoured the materialism of the eighteenth-century *philosophe* Baron d'Holbach, whose *Système de la Nature* had posited the eternity of the world in place of its creation by an imaginary immaterial deity. For Affleck, recent geological evidence that whole species had periodically suffered extinction added weight to the materialist view that the 'prolific principle in nature' was capable of producing 'organized beings' without the need for a divine creator.[15]

Others also cited geological arguments to counter traditional *a posteriori* arguments for intelligent design. An anonymous Edinburgh Zetetic argued that on the basis of the 'internal structure' of the earth, 'and the anfractuousness of its surface, we may as reasonably believe it to be a lump of cooled dross, as a well-planned and a well-executed world'.[16] Steuart was equally confident that geology tended to disprove the design argument. He praised a manuscript written by a friend on 'The Age of the World' (1821), which had calculated that the time needed to produce the largest salt mountains on earth was 48,032 years, proving that the planet was at the very least 'thousands of thousands of ages old'.[17] For Steuart these findings tended to favour the materialist view that the earth, 'in place of being created out of *nothing*, about six thousand years ago, has continued to roll in the immensity of space, during the endless ages of eternity'.[18]

Several freethinkers took aim at works such as Brown's *Essay*, which had presented *a posteriori* arguments to demonstrate the existence of an almighty, benevolent god. In retaliation, several freethinkers delved into the thorny problem of evil. Affleck adopted a particularly strident approach in a lecture delivered to the Edinburgh Zetetics in the early 1820s. Echoing Philo in Parts X and XI of Hume's *Dialogues Concerning Natural Religion* (1779), he drew attention to the undeniable existence of moral and physical evil in the world, which testified that the Deity, 'either from want of power, or from want of will, or perhaps from want of both, has only given a certain portion of happiness to this world, and has, as it were, carelessly thrown it down, and left his creatures to struggle with one another about its possession and division'.[19] Affleck stressed that the fleeting experience of happiness in life was insufficient to demonstrate the existence of a benevolent creator deity, as such joys were substantially mitigated by suffering. 'Partial evils' could not be proven to be generally productive of 'universal good', nor could the experience of misery be excused on the grounds that it inspired our own charitable instincts.[20] Surveying the existence of moral and physical evil in the world, he concluded by quoting Lucifer in Lord Byron's play *Cain* (1821), who had urged suffering souls to 'look the Omnipotent tyrant in His everlasting face, and tell him that His evil is not good!'[21] James H. Simson of the Glasgow Zetetic Society agreed with Affleck and asserted that theologians could never appeal to *a posteriori* arguments to prove the existence of a benevolent, omnipotent deity. Epicurus' old questions, he pointed out, had never been answered: 'God either wills that evil should exist, or he does not. If he wills the existence of evil, where is his goodness? If evil exists against his will, how can he be all powerful? If God is both good and omnipotent, whence is evil?'[22]

Affleck's impassioned discussion of the problem of evil also moved the argument beyond the Enlightenment debate by responding to the new vogue for phrenology, a pseudo-science that argued that the size and shape of parts of the brain determined human character traits and behaviour.[23] Originating in Germany with Johann Gaspar Spurzheim and Franz Josef Gall, it attracted widespread interest across Britain, where its chief champion was the Edinburgh lawyer and deist George Combe, who established the Edinburgh Phrenological Society in 1820. Phrenologists such as Combe had emphasised that moral actions were largely dependent on the relative development of particular organs within the brain. Those with the most advanced intellectual faculties were more liable to act morally by exerting control over their feeling faculties. Drawing on phrenological language, Affleck argued that if God had given certain individuals 'strong natural propensities and passions' without an equal share 'of reason calculated to keep them in control', they would naturally form bad habits. On this basis, the Deity must be assumed to have set in motion the evil actions committed by such individuals, 'whilst he himself lurks in the back ground, secure and unseen, like the incendiary, who rejoices because he is at a great distance from the calamity which he has raised'.[24]

Although freethinkers' critiques of natural theology tended to concentrate predominantly on *a posteriori* modes of reasoning, a fracas in an Edinburgh bookshop in 1837 sparked controversy over the less popular *a priori* defence of God's existence and attributes, which aimed to proceed from logical propositions. The antagonist in the affair was William Honyman Gillespie (1808–75), a lawyer, ardent Evangelical and enthusiastic anti-infidel controversialist.[25] An intelligent but fractious personality, his biographer described him rather revealingly as a man who was 'best liked by those who understood him best', and whose 'mental faculties were more highly developed than his affections'.[26] Strolling on a 'conspicuous street' in Edinburgh in 1837, he was shocked at the sight of a new edition of the notorious deist Thomas Paine's *Age of Reason* (1794–1807) in the window of a small bookshop. As he demanded an explanation from the proprietor, a fellow customer interrupted to inform him of the existence of a freethinking society in Edinburgh, which met weekly on Sunday evenings.[27] Incensed by this discovery, Gillespie arranged a meeting with a member of the Edinburgh group and issued a challenge to the society, requesting them to respond in writing to his own work of natural theology, *The Argument, A Priori, For the Being and Attributes of God* (1833).

Published three years earlier, Gillespie's *Argument* stemmed from a chance reading of Hume's *Dialogues* at the tender age of twenty-one, which had reportedly left him in a 'perturbed condition' and 'aroused a spirt of inquiry'.[28] Convinced by Hume's critique of the *a posteriori* argument, he remained confident that a modified version of the *a priori* argument would demonstrate once and for all the being and attributes of God.[29] Gillespie conceded that Hume had rightly identified the fallacies inherent in the *a priori* argument as it had been articulated in Samuel Clarke's well-known *Demonstration of the Being and Attributes of God* (1704), which rested on the unproven assumption that everything that exists must have a cause.[30] To overcome this difficulty, Gillespie drew inspiration from common-sense philosophy and based his demonstration of God's existence on the mind's intuitive conviction of the necessary existence of infinite extension and infinite duration. For Gillespie, such existences were necessary because it was impossible for anyone to conceive of their non-existence, as 'every one, by a review, or reflex examination of his own thoughts, will find, it is utterly beyond his power to do so'.[31] On the same principles, he aimed to prove the necessary indivisibility of infinite extension and duration, which in turn proved that they formed a single substance or being, distinct from the divisible material universe. Gillespie concluded by attempting to combine this demonstration with *a posteriori* arguments to prove that this being was also intelligent, all-powerful and free.

Despite an initial promise to meet Gillespie's challenge, the Edinburgh freethinkers passed the buck to the larger Glasgow Zetetic Society. A willing champion was found in the materialist George Simpson, Secretary of Glasgow's Working Men's Association, whose closely argued *Refutation of the Argument A Priori* led Gillespie to acknowledge that the 'western atheists' of Glasgow commanded 'talent and acquirements very superior' to the 'easterns' of Edinburgh.[32] Not content with merely refuting Gillespie, Simpson set out to demolish the entire *a priori* theological tradition, beginning with Samuel Clarke, 'the first and greatest authority' in such arguments.[33] At the heart of Simpson's critique was his objection to applying 'metaphysical abstractions' and 'mathematical reasonings' to ontological questions regarding real existences. As Simpson argued, 'if their god be a real being – an agent; he cannot be a heap of abstractions: if made up of abstractions, he cannot be an agent'.[34] At best, *a priori* reasoning could demonstrate the idea that 'something' has existed from all eternity, and the necessary existence of abstract qualities such as infinite space and duration, none of which were ever disputed. For Simpson, the 'garden of Hesperides, with its golden fruit, may as soon be expected to spring up from the vapour of the Atlantic, as that the mere abstraction brought out by the argument *a priori*, should be proved a deity'.[35] Simpson noted that Christian thinkers had themselves recognised the 'irrelevancy' of such claims. He cited an unfavourable review of such arguments in the *Edinburgh Review* as a case in point, and might have added Sir William Hamilton, Professor of Logic and Metaphysics at Edinburgh, who reportedly claimed that Gillespie's demonstration could not 'rise above Spinozism' to prove an infinite and intelligent deity distinct from nature.[36]

Finally, he critiqued the misleading use of language in *a priori* demonstrations by thinkers such as Clarke and Gillespie. He objected above all to their use of the term 'necessity', which departed from the usual definition of the term as 'that which must be' and adopted the 'much attenuated' definition of 'that which is the contrary of an express contradiction'.[37] For Simpson, such a construction allowed *a priori* reasoners to 'work miracles'. 'Necessity', he argued, was 'their magic rod by whose power they banish the material universe from the class of self existences, and foist a nonentity into its place'.[38] He concluded that natural theological arguments such as Gillespie's represented an 'extraordinary attempt to prop up, on rational principles, what has nothing to do with such principles, but which must ever remain a matter of faith'.[39] Gillespie detected distinct Humean echoes here, particularly the Great Infidel's claim in the *Essay on Miracles* that 'our most holy religion, is founded on *Faith*, not on *reason*'.[40]

Yet Simpson's *Refutation* also targeted 'heresies' in Hume's philosophy. He was unconvinced by the sceptic's view of causation and necessity, which argued that we can only identify probable rather than certain causal relationships on the grounds that we cannot prove that nature will always act uniformly. For Simpson, this sceptical approach could only apply to 'matters of chance'. By contrast, in the operations of nature 'all is fixed and immutable as the truths of geometry themselves'. As acknowledged by all departments of physical science, an 'experiment once fairly and fully verified, nothing remains but to adopt the result as a determinate principle'. On this basis, Simpson disagreed with Hume's view that it was impossible to demonstrate the necessary existence of matter. For Simpson, its existence was a 'matter of knowledge, a matter of absolute certainty'. As such, given that it was necessary for *something* to exist from eternity, it was far more likely to be matter, 'of whose existence everything testifies in the strongest, the most irresistible manner', than 'an aggregate of imaginary perfections, physical as well as moral, without a body for their habitation or a medium for their existence'.[41]

Gillespie issued a lengthy response to Simpson, much of which rested on the claim that his adversary had confused the relative demands of mathematical and metaphysical reasoning. Simpson chose not to retaliate, which his adversary happily interpreted as an admission of defeat.[42] Gillespie continued to develop his demonstration of God's existence and attributes, culminating in a final sixth edition in 1872. Along the way he issued further challenges to Britain's infidels to confront his *a priori* reasoning, prompting a duel with the English freethinker Charles Bradlaugh in 1867.[43] Despite Gillespie's view that he had gained the upper hand over Simpson, the controversy was fondly remembered by Scottish freethinkers. At an 'atheistic supper' held at a tavern in Glasgow's George Square in 1844, glasses were raised in memory of 'the late and respected "Antitheos"'.[44]

Scotland's freethinkers not only tackled natural theological claims for God's existence and attributes, they also confronted rational arguments for the soul's immortality and the existence of an afterlife. As Ahnert has shown, the Scottish Enlightenment had seen Moderates and Evangelicals diverge over the ability of unassisted human reason to discern these fundamental Christian doctrines.[45] For the Moderates, philosophical arguments could at best offer hints of the soul's immortality. They failed to provide a definitive, compelling demonstration of a future state; certainty could only derive from the gospel. In Hume's 'Essay on the Immortality of the Soul' he similarly rejected the utility of philosophical arguments for this belief, asserting that "tis the Gospel and the gospel alone that has brought *life and immortality to light*'.[46] By contrast, eighteenth-century Evangelicals had tended to emphasise that, while revelation offered the paramount testimony of a future state, the light of reason also enabled humankind to discern compelling evidence of the soul's immortality.

In picking up this debate, some freethinkers repeated arguments that had been made by the Moderates in the previous century. This included the fact that many ancient philosophers, despite their remarkable reasoning abilities, had remained ignorant of the soul's supposed immortality.[47] Other freethinkers concentrated on the popular argument that the existence of injustice in this world, which frequently saw the wicked go unpunished and the virtuous suffer, increased the likelihood of the existence of an afterlife in which the balance would be rectified.[48] As one anonymous member of the Edinburgh Zetetic Society argued, if 'God cannot make all his creatures happy in this life; how is it possible for him to do it in the next?'[49] Another member of the group offered a different retort, arguing that it was in fact debatable whether the virtuous and wicked did not always receive the just deserts for their actions in this life, as we are not always fully aware of the consequences of our actions.[50]

Many members of Scotland's freethinking communities engaged with the philosophical argument most frequently brought forward in defence of the soul's immortality, which asserted that unlike the body, the soul was an immaterial and indivisible substance, free from the change and decay that affected matter. In response to such claims, Hume had emphasised our inability to determine the nature of any substance.[51] By contrast, numerous members of Scotland's freethinking communities confidently asserted materialist philosophies of the human mind. Some were swayed by their observations of anatomy classes. This included an anonymous physician, who had studied anatomy and physiology at the University of Edinburgh. This individual argued in 1824 that the dissecting room proved the universal principle of decomposition 'in vivid colours' and made it impossible to believe the 'unphilosophical distinction' that was commonly drawn between body and soul.⁵² This physician acknowledged that their materialist position left them in a minority among their fellow students and teachers. Strikingly, however, this anonymous thinker did attribute materialist views to the late public lecturer John Murray, 'the most celebrated chemist of the age', and to John Leslie, the incumbent Professor of Natural Philosophy, whose appointment had sparked controversy in 1805.

Although we cannot be certain that Murray and Leslie shared the materialist views of human life, other freethinkers certainly did. One anonymous speaker at the Edinburgh Zetetic Society, who also referred to observing 'a pale and lifeless corpse' on the dissecting table, rejected the doctrine of the soul's immortality on similar grounds.⁵³ The available evidence, they argued, suggested that the 'principle which lately animated the body' was simply the result of the arrangement of the 'material particles, of which it was composed'. This speaker appealed to phrenology to defend their assertion that human mind was material and therefore mortal. Although George Combe had repeatedly rejected the accusation that phrenological theories were materialistic, many Christian thinkers were unconvinced. So too, it appears, were members of Scotland's freethinking communities. As this anonymous Edinburgh Zetetic argued, phrenology had proved that the mental and moral qualities long thought to be the province of an immaterial soul were in fact the result of an individual's physical organisation, rooted in 'the composition and structure of his brain and nervous system'.⁵⁴

Similar themes were on display in a lecture delivered to the Glasgow Zetetic Society in 1842 by an anonymous factory worker. The speaker argued that phrenology had dramatically transformed the state of the debate, for 'if brain is admitted to be the real existence of mind, and thought and feeling only its qualities, the theory of the immortal spirit is gone for ever'.⁵⁵ The speaker added that attempts to reconcile phrenology with Christianity by claiming that the brain was simply the organ of an immaterial soul were doomed to fail. Ultimately, all phrenologists would reject the chimerical belief in an immortal, immaterial soul. For once it is accepted that the thought and feeling are the function of the material brain, any remaining immaterial substance would be a complete nonentity: 'What then is the soul? The external senses are gone – it cannot receive new ideas – it cannot perceive existence – it cannot reflect on the past – it cannot anticipate the future – it cannot feel – it cannot engage in adoration – what then is it?'[56] Acknowledging that leading phrenologists such as Combe had been eager to rebut the charge of materialism, the speaker explained that this was a prudent policy, which had been adopted to flatter the prejudices of 'spiritualists' and to encourage them to engage in phrenological enquiries.[57]

In probing the rational arguments for fundamental divine truths, members of Scotland's nineteenth-century freethinking circles picked up the unsettled dispute over natural theology that had divided Scottish thinkers of the Enlightenment. Their debates took place in an altered theological landscape. The Moderates, who had been more sceptical about reason's ability to discern certain fundamental divine truths and had been central participants in the intellectual culture of the previous century, were on the decline. By contrast, numerous Evangelicals were experimenting with natural theology of various kinds and drawing attention to the harmonious relationship between science and religion. Unlike Christian thinkers of either camp, Scotland's freethinking communities entirely rejected the validity of revelation and took the debate on natural theology in different directions, responding as they did so to new developments in astronomy, geology and phrenology. The most vocal members of these groups were materialists, who were firmly persuaded of the non-existence of an immaterial, creator deity and an immortal soul. In this, they also departed from Hume, who had acknowledged that such beliefs could not be definitively verified or falsified by philosophical reasoning. The bold materialism of thinkers such as d'Holbach was consequently more popular with many members of the freethinking communities than the philosophical scepticism of Scotland's 'Great Infidel'.

Humean influences can, however, be detected in the manner in which Scottish freethinkers strove to conduct their debates over natural theology. Strikingly, several individuals consciously aimed to remain free from a spirit of dogmatism and echoed Hume's well-known commitment to open, tolerant and courteous philosophical dialogue.[58] Simpson of Glasgow, for instance, had contrasted his own approach to Gillespie's controversialist style, which he described as 'fierce – not gallant; haughty and cavalier, not courteous'.[59] A similar commitment to the Humean ideal of open philosophical exchange was displayed by the anonymous Edinburgh Zetetic who debated the soul's immortality, who declared that they wished 'it to be understood, that I am not dogmatical, but open to conviction by fair reasoning'.[60] Affleck's discussion of the eternity of the world similarly asserted that 'by a calm consideration of this subject, we shall find it involved in much obscurity' and added that there were good reasons 'for being sceptical and forebearing with one another'.[61] Responding to English freethinkers who objected to the Edinburgh Zetetics' willingness to use the term 'god' to refer to the principle that vivifies matter, the anonymous president of the group argued that

> you cannot more effectually aid the cause of truth, than by cheerfully trying how far you can yield to opposing parties. Go always as far *with them* as truth and reason allow you to go – when you come to this point, state that you must stop – *not* because you are *unwilling*, but because you are *unable* to proceed.[62]

Significantly, the freethinkers' debates over natural theology encourage us to rethink the classic portrait of Scotland's post-Enlightenment intellectual culture as sketched by Isabel Dalhousie at the beginning of this chapter. Firstly, they prompt us to question the great chasm that is often drawn between the intellectual concerns of the Scottish Enlightenment and those of the nineteenth century. As the dispute over natural theology reveals, there were elements of continuity as well as transformation and some eighteenth-century debates continued to reverberate in the post-Enlightenment period. Although the question of natural theology acquired new modulations in the hands of Scottish freethinkers, its dominant strains would have been familiar to the eighteenth-century literati. Secondly, this exploration of Scotland's freethinkers reveals that the intellectual and religious landscape of post-Enlightenment Calvinist Scotland was more diverse than is often recognised. In particular, by extending our gaze beyond the elite of church and university, we discover new controversies and recognise that the early nineteenth century was an age in which unbelievers acquired unprecedented organisation and visibility. Natural theology was just one of many subjects that engaged Scotland's freethinking communities. Members of these groups also displayed a keen interest in subjects including the relationship between religion and morality, biblical criticism, the science of human nature, the relationship between church and state, and questions of social reform. As in the case of natural theology, many of these themes overlapped with questions that were actively debated within the intellectual and religious mainstream. By paying greater attention to unbelievers, and the responses they elicited, we therefore stand to gain a richer, more textured picture of the evolution of Scotland's intellectual culture in the post-Enlightenment age.

## Notes

1. The notable exception is Gordon Pentland, 'The Freethinkers' Zetetic Society: An Edinburgh Radical Underworld in the 1820s', *Historical Research* 91 (2018), 314–32. See also Felicity Loughlin, 'Scotland's Last Blasphemy Trials: Popular Unbelief and its Opponents, 1819–1844', *English Historical Review* 137 (2022), 794–822.
2. M. A. Stewart, 'Religion and Rational Theology', in A. Broadie and C. Smith (eds), *The Cambridge Companion to the Scottish Enlightenment* (Cambridge, 2019), pp. 33–59, quotation at p. 33.
3. As illustrated in I. D. L. Clark, 'The Leslie Controversy, 1805', *Records of the Scottish Church History Society* 14 (1963), 189–97.
4. Thomas Ahnert, 'Philosophy and Theology in the Mid-Eighteenth Century', in D. Fergusson and M. Elliott (eds), *The History of Scottish Theology, Volume II: From the Early Enlightenment to the Late Victorian Era* (Oxford, 2019), pp. 56–68, quotation at p. 66.
5. Henry Brougham, *Discourse of Natural Theology, Showing the Nature of the Evidence and the Advantages of the Study* (London, 1835).
6. Paul Baxter, 'Science and Belief in Scotland, 1805–68: The Scottish Evangelicals' (University of Edinburgh PhD, 1985), pp. 108–55.
7. On the broader Evangelical interest in the theological implications of astronomy, see Bill Jenkins, 'Evangelicals and the plurality of worlds debate in Scotland, 1810–55', *Journal of Scottish Historical Studies* 35 (2015), 189–210, and Colin Kidd, 'Extra-Terrestrials and the Heavens in Nineteenth-Century Theology', in Fergusson and Elliott, *Scottish Theology, Volume II*, pp. 390–403.

8. Thomas Chalmers, *On the Power, Wisdom and Goodness of God, As Manifested in the Adaptation of External Nature to the Moral and Intellectual Constitution of Man* (London, 1833).
9. David Brewster, 'The sciences connected with Natural Theology', *Monthly Chronicle* 3 (1839), 115; John Fleming to Thomas Chalmers, 2 January 1836, New College Library, Edinburgh, MS CHA.4.179.43. Cited in Baxter, 'Science and Belief', pp. 118–21.
10. W. H. Steuart, 'To Mr. R. Carlile, Dorchester Gaol', *The Republican* (2 May 1823), 558.
11. W. H. Steuart, 'To Mr. Richard Carlile, Dorchester Gaol', *The Republican* (30 January 1824), 137.
12. James Affleck, 'A Discourse, Delivered before the Edinburgh Zetetic Society, on the Absurdity of Public Worship', *The Republican* (31 January 1823), 144.
13. W. G., 'To Mr. Carlile', *The Lion* (7 November 1828), 591–2.
14. James Affleck, 'On the Personality of the Deity, A Discourse Delivered before the Edinburgh Freethinkers' Zetetic Society', *The Republican* (28 February 1823), 268–9.
15. Affleck, 'Personality of the Deity', 269.
16. Anon., 'On Providence. A Discourse delivered before the Edinburgh Zetetic Society', *The Republican* (7 February 1823), 171.
17. Anon., 'The Age of the World', *The Republican* (30 January 1824), 135.
18. Steuart, 'To Mr. Carlile', *The Republican* (30 January 1824), 137.
19. James Affleck, 'On the Power and Goodness of the Christian Deity. A Discourse delivered before the Edinburgh Zetetic Society', *The Republican* (21 February 1823), 234.
20. Affleck, 'On the Power', 237–9.
21. Affleck, 'On the Power', 235; Lord Byron, *Cain: A Mystery* (London, 1821), p. 14.
22. J. H. Simson, 'A Letter to William McGavin, Esq. in Vindication of Mr. Owen', *The Republican* (13 May 1825), 585.
23. See especially Roger Cooter, *The Cultural Meaning of Popular Science: Phrenology and the Organization of Consent in Nineteenth-Century Britain* (Cambridge, 1984), pp. 201–23.
24. Affleck, 'On the Power', 236.
25. On whom, see James Urquhart, *The Life and Teaching of William Honyman Gillespie of Torbanehill* (Edinburgh, 1915), pp. 17–42.
26. Urquhart, *Gillespie*, pp. 28, 31.
27. The story is recounted in 'An Examination of Antitheos's "Refutation of the Argument *a priori* for the Being and Attributes of God"', in William Gillespie, *The Necessary Existence of God* (Edinburgh, 1843), pp. 10–12.
28. Urquhart, *Gillespie*, p. 18.
29. William Gillespie, *An Argument, A priori, for the Being and Attributes of God* (Edinburgh, 1833), pp. 3–11.

30. Gillespie, *Argument*, pp. 22–5.
31. Gillespie, *Argument*, p. 38. See also p. 49.
32. Gillespie, 'Examination', footnote, pp. 11–12.
33. G. Simpson [Antitheos], *Refutation of the Argument A Priori for the Being and Attributes of God* (Glasgow, 1838), p. iv.
34. Simpson, *Refutation*, pp. 10–11.
35. Simpson, *Refutation*, p. 86.
36. Simpson cited 'Art. VI. Review of Dr Robert Morehead's *Dialogues on Natural and Revealed Religion*', *Edinburgh Review* 52 (October 1830), 113. On Hamilton, see the letter addressed to him from Gillespie, 30 March 1844, enclosed in Gillespie, *Necessary Existence of God* (Edinburgh, 1843), Glasgow University Library, BC32-c.22.
37. Simpson, *Refutation*, p. 22.
38. Simpson, *Refutation*, p. 83.
39. Simpson, *Refutation*, p. 82.
40. Gillespie, 'Examination', p. 222.
41. Simpson, *Refutation*, pp. 23–4.
42. Simpson, *Refutation*, p. 8.
43. Charles Bradlaugh and W. H. Gillespie, *Atheism or Theism? Debate between Iconoclast, the Accredited Champion of British Atheists and W. Gillespie* (London, 1869).
44. 'Atheistic Demonstration in Glasgow', *The Movement, Anti-Persecution Gazette, and Register of Progress* (2 October 1844), 375.
45. Thomas Ahnert, *The Moral Culture of the Scottish Enlightenment, 1690–1805* (New Haven, CT, 2015), pp. 45–51, 96–105.
46. David Hume, *Essays on Suicide, and the Immortality of the Soul, ascribed to the late David Hume, Esq.* (London, 1783), p. 23.
47. Anon., 'On the Immortality of the Soul: A Discourse delivered before the Edinburgh Freethinkers' Zetetic Society', *The Republican* (14 February 1823), 204. On the Moderates' use of this argument, see Ahnert, *Moral Culture*, pp. 99–103.
48. Examples include the Moderate Hugh Blair and the Evangelical John Witherspoon, as shown in Ahnert, *Moral Culture*, pp. 83, 105.
49. Anon., 'On Providence', 168.
50. Anon., 'On the Immortality of the Soul', 201.
51. Hume, *Essays on Suicide and the Immortality of the Soul*, pp. 23–6.
52. Anon., 'Doctor in London, to the Priest in Dundee', *The Republican* (29 October 1824), 540.
53. Anon., 'On the Immortality of the Soul', 198–99.
54. Anon., 'On the Immortality of the Soul', 199.
55. Anon., *Essay on the Question does our Experience in the Present World warrant us to expect a future state of conscious existence: delivered in the Zetetic Hall, Nelson Street* (Glasgow, 1842), p. 8.
56. Anon., *Essay on the Question*, p. 10.

57. Anon., *Essay on the Question*, p. 9.
58. On Hume's commitment to philosophical conversation of this kind, see James A. Harris, *Hume: An Intellectual Biography* (Cambridge, 2015), pp. 297–9.
59. Simpson, *Refutation*, p. iii.
60. Anon., 'On the Immortality of the Soul', 198.
61. Affleck, 'Personality of the Deity', 264.
62. Anon., 'The President of the Edinburgh Zetetic Society to Mr. Abel Bywater, of Sheffield Park', *The Republican* (12 November 1824), 602. There was no permanent president of the society; a member of the group was temporarily appointed to the role at the start of each meeting. See 'Precognition: Declarations of John Kesson & others, November 1822', *National Records of Scotland*, Edinburgh, AD/14/22/253, f. 3.

# 7

# Christian Isobel Johnstone: Radical Journalism and the Ambiguous Legacy of the Scottish Enlightenment

## Jane Rendall

Christian Isobel Johnstone (1781–1857) was the only woman to edit a major British periodical in the first half of the nineteenth century, though she has rarely attracted the attention of scholars. She was also a novelist, educationalist, and prolific journalist, with a distinctively Scottish voice, which admirably illustrates the ambiguous legacy of the Scottish Enlightenment.[1] Her view of that Enlightenment was partly expressed in a reference to the 'mazy and intricate, or hedged and primrose paths' of the world of Henry Mackenzie and Dugald Stewart.[2] But she also wrote in the spirit of the Enlightenment of future social improvement and the continuing progress of civilisation, to be achieved partly through the extension of its educational hopes and practices to the working classes. She went beyond the eighteenth-century Enlightenment, in that she was deeply committed to egalitarian values, drawn both from the political ideals of the French Revolution and from a rational, benevolent Presbyterianism indebted to the New Light wing of the Secession.[3] She supported manhood suffrage, rejected racial prejudice and tentatively supported the rights of women. While she respected the language of Adam Smith and political economy where it promised greater prosperity, she also believed in interventionist poor law reform. Notwithstanding her strong opposition to complacent assumptions of Western superiority, Johnstone was also deeply versed in the stadial history of the Scottish Enlightenment, and her writing did not escape the hierarchical assumptions inherent in that developmental approach.

Christian Johnstone was born Christian Todd, the daughter of James Todd and Jean Campbell, in the parish of St Cuthbert's, Edinburgh. At her birth in June 1781, three weeks after her parents' marriage, her father was listed as a medical student. In December 1796 she married Thomas McCliesh, a printer; on her second marriage, in June 1815, to John Johnstone, a schoolteacher from Dunfermline, James Todd's occupation was also recorded as that of a printer. Though we have no further details of her upbringing or education, Christian Todd seems to have been rooted in the world of the Edinburgh printing trades.

More, however, can be surmised about her background. In November 1814 she divorced her first husband under Scottish law for adultery: the divorce papers reveal that she was married to Thomas McCliesh 'in his father's house Nicolson Street by the Rev. Frederick McFarlane some time Antiburgher Minister Edinburgh' in December 1796, at the age of fifteen, in what is likely to have been an irregular marriage.[4] The Secession originated in a split from the Kirk over the law of patronage, with the Antiburgher Seceders breaking away from the Secession in 1747 over the Burgess Oath. A further division between Old and New Light Antiburghers followed at the end of the century. The Nicolson Street Antiburgher congregation was led by the dominant figure in that church, Rev. Adam Gib, until his death in 1788. After a contentious period, Rev. Frederick Macfarlane replaced him as minister, but after internal battles in May 1792 he led his followers to found the second Antiburgher church in Edinburgh, on Potterrow.[5] These conflicts took place at a time of steady growth in the Seceding churches, especially in urban districts; in Edinburgh by 1835–6 they made up 30 per cent of churchgoers.[6] It may also be relevant that in the battles within the Nicolson Street congregation, female members could and did vote for and against their chosen minister on a number of occasions, though the principle of female voting was and remained a contentious issue within the Seceding churches.[7] It is relevant to her future career that Johnstone had associations with a Seceding church strongly committed to a congregation's right to call its own minister, in which female voting was practised and debated. Her second marriage, shortly after her divorce, was probably also an irregular one.[8]

Little is known of Johnstone before the publication of her best-known novel, *Clan-Albin*, published anonymously in 1815 a few months after Walter Scott's *Waverley*.⁹ It is possible, though not certain, that she also published an earlier novel, *The Saxon and the Gael* (1814).¹⁰ *Clan-Albin* is set in the Highlands during the Napoleonic wars, when clearances by Anglo-Scottish lairds left little option but emigration, and later in occupied Ireland and then Spain. It criticises British rule in Ireland, the conduct of the Peninsular War and the brutal hierarchies of the British army. The novel is sympathetic to Scottish and Irish Gaelic-speaking cultures, the Scottish hero finally marrying an Irish bride and creating in an abandoned glen a prosperous, improved, religiously tolerant quasi-utopian community.

In 1817, probably on the advice of William Blackwood, John Johnstone was nominally appointed editor of a newly established newspaper, the *Inverness Courier*, and the couple went to Inverness. But the historian of the newspaper suggests 'Mrs Johnstone was evidently the leading writer and ... generally spoken of as editor.'¹¹ A pattern was established for the future of a joint enterprise in which Christian Johnstone took the leading role in editorial work and writing, while her husband focused on the business side. In these years she undoubtedly developed her editorial and reviewing skills. The newspaper paid much attention to ethnographic and antiquarian work on the Highlands, as well as to the literary works of Scott, Galt, Hogg and Susan Ferrier, outshining its rival, the *Inverness Journal*. But the politics of the editors did not always meet the approval of the local elites who were their readers, for instance over the reporting of Peterloo.¹²

The couple returned to Edinburgh in late 1824, and John Johnstone established his printing business there. In 1826, Christian Johnstone published, pseudonymously, her bestselling work, the *Cook and Housewife's Manual*, ostensibly written by Meg Dods, a character from Scott's novel *St Ronan's Well*, as were the other characters who figure in the introductory dialogues about cookery set in the Cleikum Inn, together with Dr Redgill from Ferrier's *Marriage*. These dialogues mimic the masculine, tavern-based conviviality of the 'Noctes Ambrosianae' in *Blackwood's Edinburgh Review*. This extremely successful work demonstrates the ease with which Johnstone could both parody and adopt the masculine voice in her writing, while effacing her own name and personality.[13] Her last novel, *Elizabeth de Bruce* (1827) had a disappointing reception, and she abandoned the novel for journalism and shorter tales.[14]

In Edinburgh she came into contact with the radical bookseller and publisher, William Tait, who in March 1832 set up the monthly *Tait's Edinburgh Magazine*, printed by John Johnstone, and costing 2s 6d. Both Tait and Johnstone were committed to the campaign against taxes on unstamped newspapers, and for cheaper news and instruction. In August 1832 the Johnstones established the first of two periodicals, the weekly *Schoolmaster, and Edinburgh Weekly Magazine*, which carried on its masthead an epigraph from Lord Brougham, 'The Schoolmaster is abroad' and cost 1½d.[15] Early issues of the magazine indicate the Johnstones' political and educational mission. The initial address criticised simple instruction in factual 'useful knowledge': 'it is evidently thought better that they should read of the growth of the tea-plant, than watch the progress of legislation, or inquire into *rights of industry*'.[16] Adam Smith's endorsement of universal education was quoted.[17] In a series 'On the Moral Training of Children', the 'enlightened writer' Elizabeth Hamilton was repeatedly cited for her advocacy of a rational education that encouraged critical questioning instead of rote learning.[18] The aim of *The Schoolmaster* was 'to be political, in so far as the science of politics is connected with social wellbeing'.[19] Fiction often carried a political or educational message. Christian Johnstone reprinted from *Clan-Albin* 'The Flogged Soldier', describing the brutalities of the British Army, and from her *Nights of the Round Table* 'The Two Scotch Williams', an exemplary story of the education of William Cullen and William Hunter.[20] The Johnstones knew their readership. In October 1832 they noted that 'a very considerable proportion of our readers are connected with the Secession Church'.[21] In June 1833 *The Schoolmaster* was transformed into a monthly periodical, *Johnstone's Edinburgh Magazine*, sold for 8d, and published by Tait. With the same masthead, it conveyed the same mixture of fiction, political news and reviews. Its first issue reported the discontent at the payment of a 6 per cent church rate tax among Edinburgh tradesmen, William Tait's imprisonment for the cause and his triumphal release and escort from prison by a crowd of 8,000 drawn from the Trades of Edinburgh.[22] As Scottish Voluntaryism grew in strength, *The Schoolmaster, Johnstone's Edinburgh Magazine* and *Tait's* all contributed to the onslaught on church establishments.[23]

In June 1834 *Johnstone's Edinburgh Magazine* merged with *Tait's Edinburgh Magazine*, Christian Johnstone taking half-ownership and becoming co-editor with William Tait.[24] The price for *Tait's* readers had already been reduced from 2s 6d to 1s in February 1834, to appeal to a wider public. The merger recognised the appeal of *Johnstone's*, which had enjoyed considerable success in Scotland. With a circulation claimed at 5,000 just before it merged, it was outselling *Tait's*, *Blackwood's* and other expensive rivals.[25] By the mid-1830s, of *Tait's* existing circulation of just over 4,000, 2,800 went to England and just over 1,000 to Scotland.[26] The Scottish identity of *Tait's* was important to it, though Tait still sought to increase sales and advertising in England.

Johnstone and Tait worked together as co-editors to appeal to a middle-class readership attracted by the magazine's cheapness, radicalism, literary strengths and attention to Scottish affairs.[27] Tait corresponded with contributors and managed the business of the periodical, while Christian Johnstone made the editorial decisions and chose the contents of each issue; they collaborated on difficult issues, as they did over problems with Thomas De Quincey in 1840.[28] Johnstone was in charge of the Literary Register of short reviews for each issue. The Political Register was written by James Johnston Darling until his death in June 1842, when Johnstone probably took over responsibility.[29] Her output was enormous: according to the *Wellesley Index*, she was responsible for 443 articles from 1832 to 1847, Tait for 97.[30] Her editorship has been called 'the high point of the magazine's history', and she was undoubtedly one of the leading shapers of Scottish public opinion in this period.[31] Yet, constrained by gender, she continued to avoid publicity, rejecting the identity of a public intellectual; although she was clearly known within Edinburgh literary circles, Tait rightly wrote in 1833 that she was 'scarcely known to fame'.[32] The editorial invisibility she cultivated allowed her to exercise an assertive and forceful political voice. The *Wellesley*

*Index*, following contemporary comments, has suggested that 'under [Johnstone's] leadership the fine explosions of radicalism disappeared, and the journal became primarily a literary magazine'.[33] But this greatly underestimates Johnstone's radical agenda.

Underlying that agenda was her continuing commitment, in the spirit of the Enlightenment, to the advancement of knowledge among all classes of the population. Though in this respect she might be seen as following in the tradition of Elizabeth Hamilton and Dugald Stewart, as a firm believer in equality Johnstone extended her political message further. All her writing on education encouraged self-education for the working classes, in Mechanics' Institutes and Halls of Science, and she poured mocking scorn on the 'Society for the Effusion of Useful Knowledge'.[34] In 1836 Johnstone supported the message of the English radical Perronet Thompson 'Let no man be frightened by the word "democracy"', and by 1842 she was sympathising with the Chartists and endorsing Joseph Sturge's attempts to bring together working- and middle-class reformers of the suffrage.[35]

*Tait's Edinburgh Magazine* ensured its appeal to 'our Scottish readers' with its extensive coverage of domestic politics and religion alongside fiction and poetry. Johnstone gave significant attention to the progress of radicalism in Scotland. Her article of May 1833 on 'The Spy System' recalled the Radical War of 1820; which led to a libel action against *Tait's*.[36] In January 1837 in a lengthy and impassioned leading article she hailed the memory of 'the illustrious brand of patriots, now familiarly termed THE SCOTTISH POLITICAL MARTYRS', the transported radicals of the 1790s.[37] Tait and the Johnstones were all active supporters of the campaign led by the radical Joseph Hume for an appropriate memorial.[38] Among parliamentary politicians, *Tait's* supported the philosophic radicals, especially the Scots Lord Brougham and Joseph Hume. In July 1834 Johnstone began a series of political dialogues among characters supposedly from Edinburgh life; in the first dialogue they gossip about the Edinburgh by-election of June 1834 and the chances of the radical candidate James Aytoun against the Whigs, implying the strong connection between radical politics and Secessionist dissent.[39] In March 1835 she introduces 'a respectable Edinburgh wool-stapler', Tam

Glen, speaking a broad Scots, into these conversations, and later prints Glen's fictional letter to the Edinburgh MP, the Whig Sir John Campbell, in which Glen asks 'What in the world's become o' Hairy Brougham?', referring to Brougham's embittered absence from the Whig ministry formed in April 1835.[40]

From her earliest contributions to *Tait's*, Johnstone advocated the doctrines of Smithian political economy, whether in relation to the freeing of trade from all restrictions or in significantly reducing government expenditure. Later, she actively supported repeal of the Corn Laws.[41] However, she was also deeply concerned by the appalling conditions of the labouring poor of Scotland. In two lengthy articles she surveyed the evidence provided by the Church of Scotland's Report to the General Assembly, the *New Statistical Account of Scotland*, and Dr W. P. Alison's *Observations on the Management of the Poor in Scotland* (1840). She wrote of the opposition of many Scottish landowners to a new and compulsorily assessed poor rate, and of the speculations of 'benevolent visionaries', led by the Evangelical Thomas Chalmers, who imagined that Christian philanthropy could meet the needs of the poor without the intervention of government. She called for a new inquiry, independent of the Church of Scotland, to meet the needs of 'extensive and extreme destitution, of the innocent as well as the improvident and profligate'.[42] But she found the report of the new body of Poor Law Commissioners for Scotland – dominated by the interests of landowners and the Church of Scotland – deeply disappointing.[43] In October 1842 she reviewed Edwin Chadwick's *Report on the Sanitary Condition of the Labouring Population*, focusing on the Scottish evidence and argued that its importance could not be overrated.[44]

Throughout her editorship Johnstone both celebrated and encouraged Scottish literature. In her five-part review of Lockhart's *Life of Sir Walter Scott* (1837–8) she had no reservations in praising the works of 'a man of great genius', notwithstanding his flaws and unattractive politics.[45] She encouraged and mentored young and lesser known writers, especially those writing in Scots, praising and publishing the work of the young poet Robert Nicoll and reviewing favourably the unknown Scottish novelist Grace Webster.[46] *Tait's Edinburgh Magazine* occasionally carried a selection of poetry, sometimes called 'A Feast of the Poets', which usually included unknown Scottish poets.[47]

Yet in spite of a continuing commitment to Scottish politics and literature, Johnstone expressed scant sympathy for Romantic nationalism or notions of greater Scottish autonomy within the United Kingdom. However, her religious positions bore the hallmark of Scotland's New Light Secession. Indeed in her tale 'The Sabbath Night's Supper' she defended the Scottish Sabbath as arising from a Presbyterianism 'which has ever allied itself with the spirit of independence, and the sternest assertion of the principles of civil liberty'.[48] In April 1841 she comments on the debate around women's right to vote in the election of ministers and elders and its practice in the United Secession Church, satirically contrasting this with the reluctance of leading Evangelical ministers to accept this right in principle, in spite of their appeal for women's support.[49] But her position was based less on doctrine than on issues of church governance. In October 1841, reviewing a biography of the missionary John Campbell, she admired the Independent congregations of Scotland for their many achievements, including Sabbath schools, cheap tracts, missions and Magdalen asylums.[50] The principle of the independence of the church from the state outweighed doctrinal and national differences. The preachers and writers she admired included the Baptist Robert Hall, the Methodist Adam Clarke, the Unitarian Rammohun Roy and the Quakers William and Mary Howitt.[51] Throughout her journalism she lamented the corrupt episcopal establishments of the Churches of England and Ireland, and their unjust imposition of tithes.[52]

Johnstone was committed to equality for women, and employed writers such as Harriet Martineau, Catherine Gore, Mary Russell Mitford, Amelia Opie and Eliza Meteyard. She also reviewed personally most works written by women, and defended their right to contribute to debates on all major national issues. So in favourably reviewing Martineau's *Illustrations of Political Economy* in 1832 she fully supported the abilities of women like Martineau and Jane Marcet to expound 'the intricacies of political economy'. She welcomed Martineau's *Life in Demerara*, for its commitment to freeing an enslaved population.[53] In January 1834 she commented critically on Julia Pardoe's travel book on Portugal by suggesting 'a small dash of politics . . . in regard to the great struggle now depending [the civil war in Portugal] . . . might have been introduced, without subjecting Miss Pardoe to the charge of being either impertinent, or unfeminine'.[54] She gave encouraging reviews even to authors to whom she was not politically sympathetic, like the conservative historians of English queens, Hannah Lawrance and Agnes Strickland, and the author of advice-books to women, Sarah Ellis, whose *Daughters of England* (1842) and *Wives of England* (1842) were seemingly less restrictive than others in that genre.[55] However, while she praised Maria Edgeworth, she also found her work flawed by a sense of caste and lacking 'religion, poetry, passion'.[56]

In her fiction and reviews, Christian Johnstone consistently supported women's rights to employment and showed sympathy for the claim to vote. In *The Schoolmaster* she ran a regular 'Column for the Ladies', and in reporting the discovery that a plasterer in Glasgow was found to be a woman asked: 'Why does no-one open mechanical arts to women?'[57] In her tale 'Violet Hamilton' the heroine's mother-in-law lamented, 'I know that the woman who turns her talents to any profitable purpose, is, in some occult sense – I own I do not comprehend how it is – but she is in our society, degraded.'[58] While Johnstone condemned the exploitation of urban needlewomen, she was ready to defend women's outdoor employment, especially in societies of small peasant proprietors.[59] She was also prepared to defend the idea of women's participation in political life. In her first contribution to *Tait's* in the tale 'The Ventilators', on the only spaces then provided for women to watch proceedings in the House of Commons, the heroine Margaret Clifford intervenes to ensure the reforming side wins the vote.[60] In another tale, 'Blanche Delamere', the wealthy heroine takes active steps to improve the conditions of those who worked her Irish and West Indian estates, sets up an orphanage to train girls in artisan trades and invests in a factory on her lands in England.[61] In a review of *Woman and Her Master* (1840), Johnstone praises Lady Morgan as 'the champion and philosophical historian of her sex' and praised her history of women as 'a brave and gallant beginning of that grand agitation' on behalf of 'the natural rights of their sex'.[62]

In Johnstone's review of the Scotswoman Marion Reid's *A Plea for Woman* (1843), published by Tait, she made her full, if cautious, support for the feminist case very clear. She appealed to the memory of Catherine Macaulay and Mary Wollstonecraft, at a time when most women writers feared to use the latter's name. She did suggest that though many improvements had been made since Wollstonecraft's time, the challenge was still to lift women to social and civil equality. They needed not only education but employment to be self-supporting. She agreed with Reid on the necessity of legal reform to protect married women, even if the time was not yet ready for mixed juries or legislative assemblies. But, in principle, she wrote 'we can see very little objection to women participating, as Mrs Reid contends they should, in the same political franchises that men enjoy'.[63]

Johnstone believed that all peoples were potentially equal, and she condemned contemporary racism. Reviewing Edmund Abdy's book of travels in the United States in November 1835, she comments on his very critical analysis of American racism that he greatly underestimated the extent of colour prejudice in Britain and its commitment to 'white ascendancy'.[64] In this area she drew on the language of Enlightenment. Although she had parodied the idea of the stadial history of civilisation, wittily, in the discourse on the four stages in the history of cookery in her cookbook, she employed it in her many reviews of works by travellers and missionaries. She criticised Henry Lytton Bulwer's writing on France in November 1838 because he lacked the profundity and judgement needed for the 'philosophical historian of a great nation'.[65] She explored the interplay of material, cultural and political structures, approving the comparative analysis of Norway, Sweden and Prussia by the Orcadian Samuel Laing, whose admiration of the small proprietors and liberal politics of Norway she heartily endorsed.[66] In other reviews of travel literature she frequently draws comparisons with the state of the Scottish Highlands in the past, whether she was writing of the murderous inclinations of a Nawab of Hindostan, the feudal structures of the 'Caffre' or Xhosa peoples, or the customs of fosterage in Circassia.[67]

She did not however accept that a comparative approach should automatically lead to assumptions of cultural superiority often linked to imperial expansion and militaristic initiatives. In August 1837, reviewing *The Wrongs of the Caffre Nation*, she condemned the conduct of the war of 1834–6 between the Cape Colony and the Xhosa people: 'There is no darker page in the history of civilized nations than their first dealings with those whom, terming barbarians, they treat like brutes.' Finally, she said, there was 'a voice in England' to make the extreme oppression of the Xhosas heard.[68] In reviews touching on all the Australian colonies she joined the humanitarian chorus of the mid- to late 1830s in condemning the treatment of their indigenous peoples, 'this ill-treated, despised and degraded race'.[69] She supported the Quaker James Backhouse's account of his time there and 'the humane and enlightened opinions held by all reflecting men' in defending the natural capacity of the indigenous peoples,[70] and agreed with William Howitt in *Colonization and Christianity* (1838) that the cruel and unjust treatment by Englishmen of the indigenous peoples of Tasmania and the Cape Colony threw into question the very claim of her countrymen to be Christians.[71]

In particular, she questioned the common trope of the degradation of women in the earliest stages of society.[72] Reviewing Marianne Postans's *Cutch; or Random Sketches of Western India* (1839), she suggests in relation to Postans's description of the 'degraded social condition and daily drudgery' of the women of Cutch, now part of Gujarat, that the daily labours of working women in Britain were no better or even greater than those Postans described.[73] She commended Anna Jameson's similar argument on indigenous Canadian women in her *Winter Studies and Summer Rambles* (1839).[74] When reviewing George Catlin's *Adventures among the North American Indians*, however, she accepted his portrayal of indigenous American women as 'drudges and slaves', though she also described the evidence he provides of delicacy, tenderness and maternal affection among such women.[75]

At the same time as questioning crude assumptions of savagery and barbarism, Johnstone continued to believe in the desirability of rightly directed improvement, shaped by commerce and Christianity, towards a higher level of civilisation. In 1833, reviewing a work on Sierra Leone, she expressed the general disappointment that the king's speech from the new Whig administration did not mention 'the monstrous iniquity, the national sin, of colonial slavery', and called for further efforts by the friends of emancipation.[76] Five years later, in 1838, in reviewing Joseph Sturge and Thomas Harvey's *The West Indies in 1837*, she condemned the compensation to slave-owners paid in 1833, and the violation of the agreement then made to train apprentices to free labour.[77] A month later she approved Lord Brougham's denunciation of the Orders in Council enabling planters in British Guiana to bring indentured labour from India, this latter 'the foundations of a new scheme of slavery as flagitious as that which ... is hardly yet extirpated'.[78] Yet she also quoted Sturge when writing of Antigua, where abolition was in effect, that black slaves though in better domestic circumstances there were 'not yet elevated above the stage of moral and intellectual childhood'. That is, though part of the human family, they did not yet meet expectations of the free black subject, although in a rapid state of improvement.[79] Johnstone, like Sturge, hoped for a Christian, domesticated and industrious society to develop there in the future.

Johnstone was highly critical of the continuing expansion of the British Empire. She distrusted governments in the colonies of settlement, Canada, Australia and southern Africa. Reviewing a history of New South Wales by the radical Presbyterian John Dunmore Lang, she echoed his view of the government there in 1833 as 'despotic', and welcomed his zeal for representative government and civil rights for former convicts, as well as his campaigns against the episcopal establishment.[80] In two critical reviews of 1838 she questioned the self-interested, flattering representations of the new colony of South Australia by its commissioners and by the South Australian Land Company, and urged caution on potential Scottish emigrants, who were directly targeted with the promise of a 'New Utopia'.[81] She was also hostile to military interventions. In four reviews of 1843 she emphasised the injustice and folly of the British invasion of Afghanistan in 1839–42, and commented on Lady Sale's journal of events which illustrated that 'whatever is noblest, and also whatever is hard, selfish, cruel and insolent in the military principle'.[82]

What is increasingly noticeable is her admiration for evangelical missionary endeavours and their association with the message of civilisation. In November 1838, reviewing Sir James Alexander's *Discoveries in the Interior of Africa*, she wrote of the missionary stations he encountered as 'moral *oases*' and 'the most beautiful feature in the African wilderness'.[83] In the 1840s she helped in the lionising of key missionary figures. In 1842, reviewing *Missionary Labours* by Robert Moffat, the Scottish Congregationalist missionary to the northern Cape, she wrote that 'the missionary to barbarous or half-civilized countries is the true hero of modern times'; Moffat is hailed as the civiliser of 'the barbarous tribes of South Africa', shaping a civilising process which brought houses, a chapel, a school, improved irrigation and new tools to indigenous settlers.[84] In June 1843, reviewing the memoirs of John Williams, the well-known London Missionary Society missionary to the South Pacific, she celebrated his similar efforts 'to make civilization proceed hand-in-hand with evangelization'. In both reviews she noted the advantages of the presence of missionary wives, giving 'the influence, instruction and example, of Christian matrons'.[85]

Johnstone was a woman of influence: a humanitarian, a religious dissenter and a political radical who challenged imperial power and many instances of racial oppression. But in spite of these impressive challenges, she was deeply imbued with the developmental assumptions of the Enlightenment and the imperative to progress towards a form of civilisation rooted in the commerce and Christianity of middle-class Britain, a Britain which despite its failings she still thought offered the best prospects of liberty. Though not always optimistic for the future of an empire she believed deeply flawed by militarism and corruption, she constantly encouraged her Scottish and English readers to share her hopes for a rightly deployed civilising mission. The legacy of Enlightenment merged with the force of evangelicalism to create a powerful version of middle-class radicalism.

# Notes

1. However, I am greatly indebted to: Dorothy McMillan, 'Figuring the Nation: Christian Isobel Johnstone as Novelist and Editor', *Etudes Ecossaises* 9 (2003), 27–41; Alexis Easley, *First Person Anonymous: Women Writers and Victorian Print Media, 1830–70* (Aldershot, 2004),

ch. 3; Ian Duncan, *Scott's Shadow: The Novel in Romantic Edinburgh* (Princeton, 2007), pp. 99–100, 287–305; Pam Perkins, *Women Writers and the Edinburgh Enlightenment* (Amsterdam, 2010), Ch. 3.

2. 'Gallery of Living Authors and Periodical Writers. No II. – Lord Brougham', *Johnstone's Edinburgh Magazine* [JEM] 1 (February 1834), 340–8, at p. 343.
3. Callum Brown, *The Social History of Religion in Scotland since 1730* (London and New York, 1987), pp. 35–6.
4. National Records of Scotland, CC8/6/1526, Process of Divorce: Christian Isabella Todd v. Thomas McCleish, 7 October 1814, Condescendence for pursuer. Nonconformity was the major reason for irregular marriage; the kirk session would retrospectively record such marriages on payment of a small fine. See T. C. Smout, 'Scottish Marriage, Regular and Irregular 1500–1940', in R. B. Outhwaite (ed.), *Marriage and Society: Studies in the Social History of Marriage* (London, 1981), pp. 204–36.
5. Brown, *Social History of Religion*, pp. 34–8; Rev. Robert Small, *History of the Congregations of the United Presbyterian Church from 1733 to 1900*, 2 vols (Edinburgh, 1904), vol. 1, pp. 68–9, 427–8, 444. After further conflict within the Potterrow congregation, in May 1796 Macfarlane left it, and, in marrying McCliesh and Todd, was carrying out services unofficially.
6. Brown, *Social History of Religion*, p. 61.
7. Small, *History . . . of the United Presbyterian Church*, vol. 1, pp. 428, 714; for a discussion of women's voting within the Secession churches, see pp. 711–16.
8. The marriage was conducted in Edinburgh by the Rev. Robertson on 24 June 1815, and registered in Dunfermline on 29 July 1815. The Rev. Joseph Robertson of Leith Wynd Chapel was notoriously willing to conduct such marriages. See Leah Leneman, *Promises, Promises: Marriage Litigation in Scotland 1698–1830* (Edinburgh, 2003), p. 4.
9. On this novel, see, besides works cited in note 1: Juliet Shields, 'From Family Roots to the Routes of Empire: National Tales and the Domestication of the Scottish Highlands', *English Literary History* 72, no. 4 (2005), 919–40; Andrew Monnickendam, 'Introduction' to Christian Johnstone [CJ], *Clan-Albin: A National Tale* (Glasgow, 2003).
10. The evidence is discussed in Perkins, *Women Writers*, pp. 211–12.
11. [James Barron] *A Highland Newspaper. The Inverness Courier, 1815–1967* (Inverness, 1909), p. 9.
12. *Inverness Courier*, 26 August and 23 September 1819; generally, for her editorship I have relied on Perkins, *Women Writers*, pp. 213–15, and my own reading of the *Inverness Courier* and *Inverness Journal*.
13. See Pam Perkins, 'A Taste for Scottish Fiction: Christian Johnstone's *Cook and Housewife's Manual*', *European Romantic Review* 11, no. 2

(2000), 248–58; Perkins, *Women Writers*, pp. 243–7; Duncan, *Scott's Shadow*, pp. 287–9.
14. Duncan, *Scott's Shadow*, p. 290.
15. John S. North (ed.), *Waterloo Directory of Scottish Newspapers and Periodicals, 1800–1900* (Waterloo, ON, 1989), p. 512.
16. 'Address', *The Schoolmaster, and Edinburgh Weekly Magazine* 1 (4 August 1832), 1.
17. 'Education of the People', *Schoolmaster* 15 (10 November 1832), 225–6.
18. 'A Friend to Early Education', 'On the Moral Training of Children, Letter VI', *Schoolmaster* 41 (11 May 1833), 289–91.
19. 'Address', *Schoolmaster*, 1.
20. CJ, 'The Flogged Soldier' and 'The Story-Teller. Mrs Johnstone. The Two Scotch Williams', *Schoolmaster* 1 (4 August 1832), 9–13 and 20 (15 December 1832), 313–7; CJ, *Clan-Albin*, ed. Monnickendam, pp. 245–52; CJ, 'The Two Scotch Williams', in *Nights of the Round Table: or, Stories of Aunt Jane and Her Friends*, 2nd series (Edinburgh, 1832) pp. 261–91.
21. 'Rise, Progress, and Present State of the Secession Church', *Schoolmaster* 12 (20 October 1832), 180–1.
22. 'Clerical Disturbances in Edinburgh', *JEM* 1 (September 1833), 72–3.
23. For instance, see: 'Church Establishments versus Voluntary Churches', *Schoolmaster* 34 (23 March 1833), 177–9; 'Fruit of Church of England Establishments', *Schoolmaster* 37 (13 April 1832), 231–2; for the growth of the Scottish Voluntary movement from 1829, see Stewart J. Brown, 'Religion and the Rise of Liberalism: the First Disestablishment Campaign in Scotland, 1829–1843', *Journal of Ecclesiastical History* 48, no. 4 (October 1997), 682–704.
24. For discussion of these periodicals, see Perkins, *Women Writers*, pp. 247–66; Duncan, *Scott's Shadow*, pp. 299–300; Joanne Shattock, 'Periodicals and Newspapers', in *The Edinburgh History of the Book in Scotland. Volume 3, Ambition and Industry 1800–1880*, ed. Bill Bell (Edinburgh, 2007) pp. 353–6; Walter E. Houghton (ed.), *The Wellesley Index to Victorian Periodicals* 4 (Toronto, 1987), pp. 475–81.
25. CJ, '*Johnstone's Edinburgh Magazine*: The Cheap and Dear Periodicals', *Tait's Edinburgh Magazine* [TEM] 4 (January 1834), 490–500, at p. 490. All references are to old-style volume numbers.
26. CJ, '*Johnstone's Edinburgh Magazine*', 495–6; 'Union of Johnstone's and Tait's Magazine', *JEM* 1 (May 1834), 528–30; [William Tait], 'Advertising in Scotland', *TEM* 7 (March 1836), 198–200; James Bertram, *Some Memories of Books, Authors and Events* (Westminster, 1893), pp. 11–12.
27. See Michael W. Hyde, 'The Role of "Our Scottish Readers" in the History of *Tait's Edinburgh Magazine*', *Victorian Periodicals Review* 14, no. 4 (winter 1981), 135–40.

28. Houghton (ed.), *Wellesley Index*, vol. 4, p. 478; correspondence of Christian Johnstone and William Tait, 22 August 1840, NLS MS 1670 ff. 71–5.
29. Houghton (ed.), *Wellesley Index*, vol. 4, pp. 503 and 534 (editorial notes for articles 461 and 1430).
30. The attributions of the *Wellesley Index* have been generally accepted here.
31. Shattock, 'Periodicals and Newspapers', p. 355; Hyde '"Our Scottish Readers"', 139.
32. Tait, '*Johnstone's Edinburgh Magazine:* prospectus', TEM 3 (September 1833), 783.
33. Houghton (ed.), *Wellesley Index*, vol. 4, p. 478.
34. CJ, 'Publications of the Society for the Effusion of Useful Knowledge', TEM 1 (September 1832), 658–60.
35. CJ, 'The Modern Andrew Marvell', TEM 7 (December 1836), 795–9, at p. 798; CJ, 'Joseph Sturge, A Visit to the United States in 1841' and [CJ?] 'Postscript Political', TEM 13 (June 1842), 363–8 and 411–12.
36. CJ, 'The Spy System; or, Tis Thirteen Years Since', TEM 3 (May 1833), 198–222.
37. CJ, 'Memoirs and Trials of the Political Martyrs of Scotland persecuted during the years 1793–4–5', TEM 8 (January 1837), 1–20.
38. See *The Scotsman*, 29 April 1837, for Tait's role and John Johnstone's subscription to the fund (I am grateful to Dr Michael Taylor for this reference); Alex Tyrrell with Michael T. Davis, 'Bearding the Tories: The Commemoration of the Scottish Political Martyrs of 1793–4', in *Contested Sites: Commemoration, Memorial and Popular Politics in Nineteenth-Century Britain* (Aldershot, 2004), ed. Paul A. Pickering and Alex Tyrrell, pp. 25–56.
39. CJ, 'What is going on: Scenes in Edinburgh (No. 1)', TEM 5 (July 1834), 419–34.
40. CJ 'The Pry Bureau. – No V. Branch Establishment, Birmingham', TEM 6 (March 1835), 195–202; CJ, 'Tam Glen's Letters to Political Characters', TEM 6 (August 1835), 539–41.
41. CJ, 'The National Distress', TEM 13 (July 1842), 421–5.
42. CJ, 'The Condition of the Labouring Poor, and the Management of Paupers in Scotland', TEM 11 (November 1840), 681–96; CJ, 'Condition of the Labouring Poor and the Management of Paupers in Scotland [part 2]', 11 TEM (December 1840), 749–60, at p. 750 and 760.
43. [CJ?], '*Report* of the Poor Law Commissioners for Scotland', TEM 15 (July 1844), 409–13.
44. CJ, '*Report on the Sanitary Condition of the Labouring Population*', TEM 13 (October 1842), 649–60, at p. 649.
45. CJ, 'Lockhart's *Life of Sir Walter Scott*', TEM 8 (April 1837), 205–20, and subsequent reviews in TEM 8 (August 1837), 469–87; 8

(September 1837), 557–66; 9 (February 1838), 92–112; 9 (May 1838), 307–27.
46. CJ, 'Robert Nicoll's Poems', TEM 6 (November 1835), 747–52; CJ, 'Preface', Robert Nicoll, Poems and Lyrics, 4th edn (Glasgow, 1852), pp. 1–64; CJ, 'Ingliston: a Tale by Grace Webster', TEM 11 (May 1840), 278–88.
47. 'A Chapter of Scottish and English Poets and Poetesses', TEM 7 (September 1836), 590–6; 'Our Feast of the Poets for September', TEM 8 (September 1837), 566–75; 'The Feast of the Poets for September 1840', TEM 11 (September 1840), 566–75.
48. CJ, 'The Sabbath Night's Supper', TEM 4 (January 1834), 6–18; see also CJ, 'Slavery, Sabbath Protection, Church Reform', TEM 3 (April 1833), 30–2.
49. CJ, 'Literary Register', TEM 12 (April 1841), 398.
50. CJ, 'The Life and Times of the Rev. John Campbell', TEM 12 (October 1841), 654–66.
51. On Robert Hall, see: Schoolmaster 32 (March 9 1833), 152, and 38 (20 April 1833), 253; CJ, 'Monthly Register', TEM 1 (April 1832), 134–6; CJ, 'Works and Life of the Rev Robert Hall', TEM (March 1833), 773–89; on Adam Clarke, see 'The Life of the Late Adam Clarke', JEM 1 (December 1833), 229–43; 1 (January 1834), 292–9; 1 (February 1834), 357–68; on Rammohun Roy, 'Obituary', JEM 1 (November 1833), 212; on the Howitts, 'Howitt's History of Priestcraft', JEM 1 (September 1833), 14–16; CJ, 'Mary Howitt's Sketches of Natural History', TEM 5 (August 1834), 443–6; CJ, 'The books of the season', TEM 8 (November 1837) 679, 687–8; CJ, ' Howitt's Colonization and Christianity', TEM (August 1838), 527–34.
52. See note 25 above; see also CJ, 'Monthly Register', TEM 1 (April 1832), 130; CJ 'A New Remedy for the Distresses of Ireland', TEM 10 (March 1839), 150–1; CJ, 'The Modern Pulpit', TEM 13 (November 1842), 704–8.
53. CJ, 'Illustrations of Political Economy – No. 2, The Hill and the Valley', TEM 1 (May 1832), 253–55; CJ, 'Miss Martineau's Political Economy,' TEM 1 (August 1832), 612–18.
54. CJ, 'Traits and Traditions of Portugal', TEM 4 (January 1834), 421–30, at p. 421.
55. CJ, 'Hannah Lawrance's Historical Memoirs of the Queens of England', TEM 9 (April 1838), 257–63; CJ, 'Historical Memoirs of the Queens of England', TEM 11 (March 1840), 111–4; CJ, 'Literary Register', TEM 13 (April 1842), 265; CJ, 'Literary Register', TEM 13 (May 1842), 339–42; CJ, 'Literary Register', TEM 13 (May 1842), 265; CJ, 'Literary Register', TEM 13 (August 1842), 544; CJ, 'Literary Register', TEM 13 (October 1842), 686–90; CJ, 'Hannah Lawrance, History of Woman in England', TEM 14 (March 1843), 193–6; CJ, 'Literary Register' TEM 14 (April 1843), 264–7.

56. CJ, 'Miss Edgeworth's Works', *TEM* 1 (May 1832), 279–85.
57. CJ, 'Free Trade – A Scotch D'Eon', *Schoolmaster* 47 (22 June 1833), 392.
58. CJ, 'Violet Hamilton (ch xxi)', *TEM* 12 (June 1841), 386. This series ran in fifteen parts from January 1840 to November 1841.
59. CJ, *'The Art of Needlework, from the Earliest Ages'*, *TEM* (November 1840), 723; CJ, *'Lights and Shadows of London Life'*, *TEM* 13 (January 1842), 27–8; CJ, *'Laing's Notes of a Traveller'*, *TEM* 13 (March 1842), 176–7.
60. CJ, 'The Ventilators', *TEM* 1 (April 1832), 35–57.
61. CJ, 'Blanche Delamere', *TEM* 10 (January 1839), 40–51; (February 1839), 105–16; (March 1839), 177–92; (April 1839), 255–68; (June 1839), 355–64; (September 1839), 597–611.
62. CJ, 'Lady Morgan's *Woman and Her Master*', *TEM* 11 (June 1840), 390–7.
63. CJ, 'Mrs Hugo Reid's *Plea for Woman*', *TEM* 15 (July 1844), 423–8.
64. CJ, 'Abdy's *Residence and Tour in the United States*', *TEM* 6 (November 1835), 715–24, at p. 715.
65. CJ, '*France, Social, Literary and Political*, by Henry Lytton Bulwer', *TEM* 5 (November 1834), 649–58, at p. 649.
66. CJ, 'Laing's *Sweden* and *Norway*', *TEM* 10 (May 1839), 307–27; CJ, 'Laing's *Notes of a Traveller*', *TEM* 13 (March 1842), 169–83, at p. 169.
67. CJ, 'Bacon's *First Impressions in Hindostan*', *TEM* 8 (June 1837), 397–400, at p. 399; CJ, 'Wrongs of the Caffre Nation', *TEM* 8 (August 1837), 515–23, at p. 515; CJ, 'Spencer's *Travels in Circassia and Krim Tartary*; and the Chevalier Taitbout de Marigny's *Three Voyages to the Coast of Circassia*', *TEM* 8 (October 1837), 603–20, at p. 610.
68. CJ, 'Wrongs of the Caffre Nation', 515.
69. 'New Colony of South Australia and the Penal Colonies', *TEM* 9 (December 1838), 776–89; CJ, 'Quaker Missions to Australia', *TEM* 14 (April 1843), 218–24; CJ, 'British Emigrant Colonies: New South Wales', *TEM* 5 (July 1834), 401–19; CJ, 'Howitt's *Colonization and Christianity*', *TEM* (August 1838), 527–34; CJ, 'John Hood's *Australia and the East*', *TEM* 14 (September 1843), 586–99; CJ, 'A Summer at Port Phillip', *TEM* 15 (April 1844), 213–18; on this humanitarian reaction, see Alan Lester, *Imperial Networks: Creating Identities in Nineteenth Century South Africa and Britain* (London, 2001), pp. 23–35, 63–7.
70. CJ, 'Quaker Missions to Australia', *TEM* 14 (April 1843), 218–24.
71. CJ, 'Howitt's *Colonization and Christianity*', 527–34.
72. See Silvia Sebastiani, *The Scottish Enlightenment: Race, Gender and the Limits of Progress* (New York, 2013), ch. 5.
73. CJ, 'Anglo-Indian Society', *TEM* 6 (October 1835), 683–93; CJ, 'Mrs Postans' *Cutch; or Random Sketches of Western India*', *TEM* 10 (January 1839), 28–35.

74. CJ, 'Mrs Jameson's *Winter Studies and Summer Rambles*', *TEM* 10 (February 1839), 69–81.
75. CJ, 'Catlin's Adventures among the North American Indians on the Upper Missouri', *TEM* 12 (December 1841), 792–801, at pp. 799–800, and 'Travels and Sketches among the Red Indians (Part II, concl.), *TEM* 13 (February 1842), 106–17, at p. 106.
76. CJ, 'The Slave Trade: *Voyage to Western Africa*', *TEM* 2 (March 1833), 789–99.
77. CJ, 'The Abolition of Negro Apprenticeship – Sturge and Harvey's Tour in the West Indies in 1837', *TEM* 9 (March 1838), 135–48.
78. CJ, 'Brougham's Speeches on Slavery', *TEM* 9 (April 1838), 203–9; CJ, '*Speeches of Lord Brougham*', *TEM* 9 (August 1838), 475–90.
79. CJ, 'The Abolition of Negro Apprenticeship', 139; for discussion of the complexities of the 'civilising mission', see, from an extensive literature, Catherine Hall, *Civilising Subjects: Metropole and Colony in the English Imagination, 1830–1867* (Cambridge, 2002), Chapters 1–2 and pp. 316–23; Esther Breitenbach, *Empire and Scottish Society: the Impact of Foreign Missions at Home, c.1790 to c.1914* (Edinburgh, 2009), pp. 100–12.
80. CJ, 'British Emigrant Colonies: New South Wales', *TEM* 5 (July 1834), 401–19.
81. CJ, 'New Colony of South Australia and the Penal Colonies', *TEM* 9 (December 1838), 776–89; CJ 'Australian Emigration', *TEM* 10 (March 1839), 168–76; see also 'The Manager of the South Australia Company', *TEM* 10 (February 1839), 135–6.
82. CJ, 'The Affghan War and Lady Sale's *Journal*', *TEM* 14 (June 1843), 370–83; CJ, 'The Affghan War – Sir A Burnes – the Retreat and Captivity', *TEM* 14 (July 1843), 456–69; CJ, 'The Captivity of English Officers and Ladies in Afghanistan', *TEM* 14 (August 1843), 512–21, at p. 521; CJ, 'The Garbled Despatches of Sir Alexander Burnes', *TEM* 14 (August 1843), 521–5.
83. CJ, 'Alexander's *Discoveries in the Interior of Africa*', *TEM* 9 (November 1838), 727–39, at p. 728.
84. CJ, 'Moffat's *Missionary Labours and Scenes in Southern Africa*', *TEM* 13 (August 1842), 528–44 (September 1842), 597–604.
85. CJ, '*Memoirs of the Life of the Rev John Williams*', *TEM* 14 (June 1843), 385–90.

# 8

# Robert Mudie: Pioneer Naturalist and Crusading Reformer

*Eva-Charlotta Mebius*

Although no longer a familiar name, Robert Mudie was one of the most prominent nineteenth-century descendants of the Scottish Enlightenment. However one defines that Enlightenment – whether as a shared interest in human behaviour and social change,[1] or in terms of natural philosophy and natural knowledge,[2] or more broadly as the general culture of Scotland's literati[3] – Mudie stands as a representative heir. A polymathic writer, novelist, poet, editor, naturalist and reformer, his very range encapsulated the intellectual daring and untrammelled virtuosity and curiosity of the eighteenth-century Enlightenment. But he is also a more problematic figure. For, if he is known at all now in Scottish intellectual history, it is as the author of a venomously negative and sourly satirical account of early nineteenth-century Edinburgh's intellectual life, *The Modern Athens: a dissection and demonstration of men and things in the Scotch capital* (1825). For Mudie, a self-described 'modern Greek', the notion that late Enlightenment Edinburgh was the modern Athens, was, as we shall see, not so much a proud boast as something more pejorative, a telling index of the city's empty boastfulness. Confusingly for our purposes, Mudie was both an exemplar of Scotland's post-Enlightenment vigour and a trenchant critic of early nineteenth-century Scotland's supposed intellectual vitality.

This chapter seeks to illustrate how the work of Robert Mudie could be important for debates concerning, what Paul Wood calls, the 'temporal limits' and 'rival chronologies' of the Scottish Enlightenment.[4] After all, as Alexander Broadie notes, what exactly the Scottish Enlightenment's philosophical afterlife looked like, has yet to be fully explored by historians.[5] Mudie's wide-ranging writings won him a high profile in nineteenth-century intellectual life. Building on his background as a well-liked teacher in Dundee, Mudie became one of the first great popular educators in print. He wrote diligently and at times eloquently, about the most varied subjects, becoming a popular authority on anything from the bittern, mathematics, China, Australia, India, to astronomy and emigration, and his work seems to have been welcomed by an enthusiastic readership on both sides of the Atlantic, which included Dickens, Darwin, and the American landscape painter Thomas Cole. As such, Mudie might also be viewed, in the present post-Enlightenment context, as one of the last of the polymaths described in the introduction to this volume.

Mudie was born in Forfarshire in 1777 or 1780 to the weaver John Mudie and his wife Elizabeth Bany/Barry. He spent his early years as a shepherd in the Sidlaw Hills, and as an apprentice to his father. However, he was lured from the path that had been set out for him by being introduced to the *Encyclopaedia Britannica*, to which he would later contribute. According to Alan Lang Strout, Mudie then started out as a weaver in the Bucklemaker Wynd in Dundee, but soon left that occupation.[6] After about four years in the Forfar and Kincardineshire militia, during which time he spent all the money he could spare on acquiring books and learning, the self-taught remarkable Mudie became teacher of drawing and Gaelic at Inverness Royal Academy around 1802, despite not being able to even 'lisp a word of Gaelic'.[7] A few years later we find him teaching arithmetic and drawing at Dundee Academy in 1809. Aside from his teaching, it was in Dundee that Mudie began his writing career with the poem 'The Maid of Griban', published in 1810, and the novel *Glenfergus* (1820). Mudie would eventually go on to write a history of the city in *Dundee Delineated* (1822). It was also in Dundee that he started collaborating with R. S. Rintoul (1787–1858), his future fellow Scottish Londoner and founder of the weekly magazine *The Spectator*, and contributing to the latter's *Dundee Advertiser*, which the two used as a vehicle for advocating burgh reform.[8] However, after writing too many unrestrained verses satirising the members of the town

Council, Mudie is said to have made many enemies, among them Provost William Hackney. Ultimately the town council bandied together to oust Mudie from Dundee Academy. These efforts were successful, and he left his position in June 1816. Alan Lang Strout identifies a couple of particularly scathing speeches 'in connection with the celebration of laying the foundation-stone for the new harbour in October, 1815' as having sealed Mudie's fate.[9] Mudie seems to have remained in Dundee or Edinburgh for a few years following his dismissal, attempting to start two unsuccessful periodicals of his own, the *Independent* (1816) and the *Caledonian Quarterly Magazine* (1821), and putting together various courses of lectures in logic, rhetoric and moral philosophy. He finally left to pursue a literary career in London in 1820 or 1821. It was said that in 'London, he went among literary people, clever, and prone to laugh. He lectured about everything . . . The chief attraction, however, was the comic grandeur, the broad magnificence, and Doric simplicity of his noble dialect.'[10] Like his future admirer Dickens, Mudie in London began working as a reporter for the *Morning Chronicle*. In 1822 he was asked to cover George IV's visit to Edinburgh, which was published as *A Historical Account of His Majesty's Visit to Scotland* that same year.

Indeed, George IV's visit to Edinburgh provided the point of departure for Mudie's darkly burlesque *Modern Athens*. However, what Mudie perceived as genteel Edinburgh's abject sycophancy towards George IV during his visit to the Scottish capital in 1822 inspired deflationary bathos. Mudie's barbed account of Edinburgh life opens with an account of the processions, levees and other fooleries of the royal visit. But Mudie's treatment then switches focus – though without any marked change in tone or register – and begins to unmask the intolerable smugness of Edinburgh's literati. Edinburgh, it transpires, is a second-rate provincial city – 'a widowed metropolis'[11] – living off memories of its time as a proper national capital and then as the citadel of Scotland's intellectual golden age. But that golden age was very short-lived, he insists. To be sure, Edinburgh hosted two prominent arbiters of taste in its literary magazines – the *Edinburgh Review* and *Blackwood's Edinburgh Magazine*; but those very names disguised their shallow local roots. However, Edinburgh continued to live off its former glories, not least 'the sages of the succession of schools' which, shining forth from the modern Athens had 'dazzled and illuminated mankind'.[12] How could one expect that philosophical tradition to endure, queried Mudie the burgh reformer, when the philistines of the town council, who were responsible for the bulk of university appointments, were 'the most unfit patrons of a school of philosophy'?[13] Moreover, now the lawyers, not the philosophers, were dominant in the city where interest was always seen to conquer principle. Local pride in the achievements of eighteenth-century Scottish philosophy had turned into a perverse form of 'self-adoration', he argued.[14] Mudie stood appalled at the 'brazenfrontedness' of Edinburgh's ongoing 'self-idolatry'.[15] Notwithstanding Mudie's own polymathic range and autodidactic achievement, for him a short-lived Scottish Enlightenment was dead, surviving only as empty, vainglorious boast, a mirage, rather than a living body of philosophy.

Mudie's success in London owed much to his connection with the publisher Charles Knight (1791–1873). Reminiscing about his life as a young publisher in London in the 1820s, Knight wrote in his autobiography about the day a 'huge ungainly Scot' had walked in 'dressed in a semi-military fashion' wearing 'a braided surtout and a huge fur cape to his cloak; spluttering forth his unalloyed dialect, and somewhat redolent of the whiskey that he could find south of the Tweed'.[16] Despite his initial misgivings, the man 'at length interested me', Knight wrote. Out of the many schemes for possible books, Knight selected an urban theme, a volume about London picking up Mudie's earlier account of Edinburgh in *Modern Athens*. *Babylon the Great*, Mudie's tome about London, became a success, and the social criticism of its sequel *A Second Judgement of Babylon the Great* (1829) may even have inspired some plot elements of Charles Dickens's *Oliver Twist* (1837–9).[17] Admittedly, Mudie's writings on urban life were not immune to the prejudices of the time. In particular, his observations on society are seriously marred by unwelcome passages which exhibit the most horrific antisemitism. Mudie was enigmatic and erratic, his well-deserved reputation as a populariser of natural history and ornithology needs to be set against some unsettling prejudice, and other character flaws.

Mudie's stint as a parliamentary reporter introduced him to some leading political figures, including Henry Brougham. This appears to have led to Mudie's involvement in the Society for the Diffusion of Useful Knowledge, which the Edinburgh-born Brougham had instituted in 1826 'to promote good and cheap publications for the working class that had become a reading class'.[18] Allegedly, Mudie was chosen to write 'the first published number of the *Library for the People*, on Astronomy'.[19] The idea of a useful library was exported to America too as the American School Library, which included Mudie's *A Popular Guide to the Observation of Nature*. Mudie's American success supports Broadie's thesis that the Scottish Enlightenment 'might indeed be considered Scotland's chief export to America', and it is also a helpful example of what the legacy of the Scottish Enlightenment looked like in a nineteenth-century context.[20] The ethos of the Society for the Diffusion of Useful Knowledge arguably continued to guide Mudie's literary efforts in the decade that followed, which saw the publication of his most significant work in popular natural history in portable form.

From the 1820s onwards, Mudie was a prolific contributor to several fields of enquiry, including history, philosophy, zoology, agriculture and the introduction of machinery. One of his more notable contributions was a heartfelt appeal for the reform of the education of women in *The Complete Governess* (1826). However, his most significant and substantial work was done in natural history, in works such as *The Feathered Tribes of the British Islands* (1834) and *The Natural History of Birds* (1836), as well as his four-part portable series *The Heavens* (1835), *The Earth* (1835), *The Sea* (1835), and *The Air* (1835), and the companion series made up of *Spring* (1837), *Summer* (1837), *Autumn* (1837) and *Winter* (1837). Nor should we forget Mudie's *A Popular Guide to the Observation of Nature* (1832), a paean to observation and the exercise of one's mind. As Mudie wrote, it is

> always dangerous to slight little things, for little things are all beginnings; and in obtaining knowledge, and thence enjoyment, it is at the beginning only that we can begin. All those beginnings are in nature ... Any body too, who possesses the

organ of sense necessary for the purpose, and will exercise that organ, may know those beginnings; and then comes the proper exercise of man.[21]

Mudie went on to say that the 'neglect of small things is, indeed, the grand error, in consequence of which so many pass in ignorance and heaviness, that life which nature and art (for after all, art is merely the application of nature) are capable of rendering so intelligent and so full of happiness'.[22] This approach is exemplified in Mudie's brilliant disquisition on the egg:

> the wonderful part of the matter is, that a body of the form of a pebble, and consisting of a thin shell of lime, lined with a soft membrane, and having within it first a transparent and then a yellow jelly, should have the power, by the action of heat and air alone, of evolving a vast number of animal organs and substances, all differing from each other in different kinds of eggs ... A careful observer may indeed find that there is in one part of the transparent jelly a little portion which has more consistency than the rest; but still a stretch of fancy is needed before it can be called organization of any kind. So that, if a person were to be told that out of those jellies there were to be evolved bones, and muscles or organs of motion, and nerves for sensation ... and not only keep itself in perfect order and repair for its appointed time, but become the source of future beings of the same kind, without number and without end, excepting from the bar and hindrance of external circumstances: – if a person who was ignorant of eggs, and the results of hatching were to be told that, or even a small part of it, it would utterly shake his belief in the testimony of the narrator.[23]

Mudie's works on ornithology were much admired, not least for imaginative flights of this sort. His reflections – perhaps still unsurpassed – on the bittern were excerpted and anthologised.[24] Mudie's decorative volumes also benefited from the work of George Baxter, the 'first British colour printer on a commercial scale'.[25] As such, Mudie's books are not only educational, but works of art in themselves. Indeed, Mudie's book, *A Popular*

*Guide to the Observation of Nature*, is a rich, but almost completely overlooked, resource for the understanding of nineteenth-century landscape painting.[26] Harriet Martineau (1802–76) celebrated Mudie's works on natural history as 'true poems'. When the 'self-educated Scotchman ... wrote about things that he understood', she continued, referring in particular to his works in ornithology,

> he plunged his readers into the depths of nature as the true poet alone can do. He is another example, as White of Selborne and Audubon were before him, of the indissoluble connexion between a nice and appreciative observation of nature and the kindling of a spirit of poetry.[27]

It was as a populariser of science that Mudie truly excelled, according to his contemporaries. His writings on natural history were read by the landscape painter Thomas Cole, Charles Darwin and William Henry Hudson, among others.[28]

However, Mudie's range was not limited to natural history or the sciences. A series of popular works on philosophy and the place of humankind in society bore the stamp of Scotland's Enlightenment legacy: *Mental Philosophy* (1838), *Man, in His Intellectual Faculties and Adaptations* (1839), *Man, in His Relations to Society* (1840) and *Man, as a Moral and Accountable Being* (1840). Moreover, Mudie's *Natural History of Domestic and Wild Animals* (1839) went beyond the normal parameters of the naturalist to address specifically the influence of animals on human society. His work never lost sight of the, sometimes dizzying, interconnectedness and interdependence of living beings and their environments as he tried to encourage a new generation of British naturalists, indebted to the earlier works of the English physico-theologians William Derham (1657–1735) and John Ray (1627–1705).[29]

Mudie's works had an international reach, and enjoyed some celebrity in the United States.[30] Even so, there were already slights and insinuations about Mudie's achievement. One commentator lauded Mudie's oeuvre, for its 'vigorous originality, and long "trails of light"', but noted too, how it was 'obscured here and there by such obliquities of style as we have already adverted to, and which almost invariably characterise a self-educated writer'.[31]

Mudie's profile was a chequered one. He was recognised as a voluminous but rather undisciplined writer and thinker. Even in his own time, Mudie managed to remain something of an outsider. Some blame this on overwork or his drinking, while others draw attention to his financial troubles, or, again, seemingly point to the fact that he was self-taught. Others suggest it was due to his unclubbability. But, as already mentioned, Mudie was involved with the Society for the Diffusion of Useful Knowledge, as well as the Linnean Society of London, and he was also considered a notable member of St James's Ornithological Society, which was founded to establish 'a collection of water birds in the garden of St. James's Park'.[32] Indeed, Mudie was as much a populariser as he was an original thinker. Although his works influenced several of the most notable cultural figures of the nineteenth century, his achievement was largely pedagogic. Yet he remains an indispensable figure for understanding the wider effects and aftermath of the Scottish Enlightenment. Mudie's work is well worth revisiting in part because of its global impact, evidenced by the articles and obituaries that appeared on both sides of the Atlantic following his untimely death in 1842. In the longer run, however, his significance faded. Mudie ended up as a tragic anecdote in the writings of Virginia Woolf on Jane Carlyle (1801–66) and Geraldine Jewsbury (1812–80) in the essay 'Geraldine and Jane' (1929). An ill-timed attempt at reviving his reputation in the years before World War II by the American literature scholar Alan Lang Strout did little to aid Mudie's reintroduction to the canon of nineteenth-century letters.[33]

Yet what might have been remembered as an improbably glorious literary career, ended in tragedy. Broken by a few productive, but financially disastrous, years in Winchester, Mudie died destitute in Pentonville in 1842, leaving behind his wife, son and four daughters. *The Spectator* wrote: 'He is dead, and the grave has closed over the remains of a Scottish weaver, who in his time, triumphing over difficulties and obstacles, instructed and amused thousands.'[34] Fittingly, the tragedy of Mudie's surviving wife and children was played out in the pages of the periodical press, where an appeal was made on their behalf. This was further immortalised in the correspondence of the Carlyles, who were both involved in trying to find places for two of Mudie's daughters. Their exasperation with the Mudie girls may have contributed later to a slightly more negative view of the father's legacy.[35]

From the many varied testimonies of contemporaries – some tinctured with mythologising and exaggeration – it is difficult to glean a complete picture of Mudie and his accomplishments. Mudie, self-taught as he was, was apparently fluent in ancient Greek, and his knowledge of geometry supposedly managed to impress the Scottish mathematician and professor at Edinburgh University, John Playfair. Or was he merely a 'radical metropolitan hack', as David Allan refers to him,[36] a drunken hack to boot? The need for Mudie to move to London may partly have been a consequence of the demise of the Enlightenment in Scotland, but Mudie's two decades of success, however precarious, in the English capital also suggests that the Enlightenment did indeed live on in the 'murky atmosphere of London' rather than in what Mudie regarded as the deceptively transparent air of Edinburgh.[37] Perhaps one might best understand Mudie and his writings as a peculiar product not only of the Scottish Enlightenment, but of interdisciplinary enquiry in an era before specialisation and scientism took hold. Suspended between the eighteenth and nineteenth century, between Scotland and England, between Edinburgh and London, between Georgian and Victorian culture, between the Enlightenment and post-Enlightenment, Mudie's role was, above all, that of an intermediary.

## Notes

Research for this chapter was generously funded by the British Association for Romantic Studies and the Universities Committee for Scottish Literature.

1. Hugh Trevor-Roper, 'The Scottish Enlightenment', *Studies on Voltaire and the Eighteenth Century* 58 (1967), reprinted in *History and the Enlightenment* (New Haven, CT, 2010), pp. 17–33, at p. 20. Research for this chapter was generously funded by the British Association for Romantic Studies and the Universities Committee for Scottish Literature.
2. See Roger L. Emerson, 'Science and the Origins and Concerns of the Scottish Enlightenment' in *History of Science* 26 (1988), 333–66. Emerson emphasises the importance of the *virtuosi*, and their leader Sir

Robert Sibbald, to accounts of the Scottish Enlightenment. He also notes the continued relevance of Sibbald's work in the 1760s to John Walker and David Skene. Indeed, this continued even in the work of Robert Mudie, who was familiar with and drew on Sibbald's work in natural history.

3. Richard Sher, *Church and University in the Scottish Enlightenment* (1985: Edinburgh, 2015), p. 8.
4. Paul Wood, 'Defining the Scottish Enlightenment', *Journal of Scottish Philosophy* 15 (2017), 299–311, at p. 300.
5. See Alexander Broadie, 'Introduction', in *The Cambridge Companion to the Scottish Enlightenment*, ed. Alexander Broadie (Cambridge, 2003), pp. 1–8, at p. 7. The history of Scottish philosophy has begun to be addressed in, for example, Gordon Graham (ed.), *Scottish Philosophy in the 19th and 20th Centuries* (Oxford, 2015). Mudie is not yet included in accounts of Scottish philosophy. Others may pursue the question of whether he should be. For example, one might explore his *Mental Philosophy* (1838) and its relation to the work of the Scottish philosopher and Professor of Moral Philosophy at Edinburgh University, Dr Thomas Brown (1778–1820).
6. Alan Lang Strout, 'Robert Mudie, 1777–1842', in *Notes and Queries* (1937), 146–9, at p. 146.
7. Anon., 'The Late Robert Mudie', in *London Saturday Journal* 3 (11 June 1842), 281–3, at p. 281.
8. Strout, 'Mudie', 146.
9. Strout, 'Mudie', 147.
10. Cited in William Norrie, *Dundee Celebrities of the Nineteenth Century* (Dundee, 1873), p. 79.
11. Robert Mudie, *The Modern Athens: a dissection and demonstration of men and things in the Scotch capital* (London, 1825), p. 257.
12. Mudie, *Modern Athens*, p. 161.
13. Mudie, *Modern Athens*, p. 212.
14. Mudie, *Modern Athens*, p. 162.
15. Mudie, *Modern Athens*, p. 253. For Mudie's reflections on the Athens of the North, see especially David Allan, 'The Age of Pericles in the Modern Athens: Greek History, Scottish Politics, and the Fading of the Enlightenment', *Historical Journal* 44 (2001), 391–417.
16. Charles Knight, *Passages of a Working Life During Half a Century: With a Prelude of Early Reminiscences*, vol. II (London, 1864), p. 18.
17. See Eva-Charlotta Mebius, 'Robert Mudie and Dickens: A Possible Source for *Oliver Twist*', *The Dickensian* 115 (Summer 2019), 128–42.
18. William F. Kennedy, 'Lord Brougham, Charles Knight, and The Rights of Industry', in *Economica* 29 (1962), 58–71, at p. 59.
19. Anon., 'The Late Robert Mudie', in *London Saturday Journal*, p. 282.
20. See Broadie, 'Introduction', p. 7.

21. Robert Mudie, *A Popular Guide to the Observation of Nature* (London, 1832), p. 82.
22. Mudie, *Popular Guide*, p. 86.
23. Mudie, *Popular Guide*, pp. 360–2.
24. See the often-reprinted extract from the *Feathered Tribes of the British Islands*: Robert Mudie, 'The Bittern', in *Half-hours with the Best Authors. Selected and Arranged, with Short Biographical and Critical Notices by Charles Knight*, vol. 3 (London, 1847), pp. 55–62.
25. Bamber Gascoigne, *Milestones in Colour Printing 1457–1859: With a Bibliography of Nelson Prints* (Cambridge, 1997), p. 42.
26. For a rare exception and illuminating discussion of Mudie's possible influence on Thomas Cole, see John C. Riordan, 'Thomas Cole: A Case Study of the Painter-Poet Theory of Art in American Painting from 1825–1850' (Syracuse University PhD, 1970).
27. Harriet Martineau, *The History of England During the Thirty Years' Peace: 1816–1846* (London, 1850), II, pp. 696–7.
28. See Eva-Charlotta Mebius, 'Mudie, Robert', in *The Edinburgh Biographical Dictionary of Scottish Writers* (Edinburgh, forthcoming).
29. See also Robert Mudie, *The British Naturalist; or, Sketches of the More Interesting Productions of Britain and the Surrounding Sea, in the Scenes which they Inhabit; and with the Relation to the General Economy of Nature, and the Wisdom and Power of its Author* (London, 1830).
30. J. B., 'Modern English Literary Men', in *United States Magazine, and Democratic Review* 14 (May 1844).
31. Anon., 'The Late Robert Mudie', p. 282 But the writer also speculated that this was due to Mudie's habit of dictating his work to his wife, rather than writing it himself.
32. Anon., 'St. James's Ornithological Society', *The Analyst* 5 (1836), 314–15, at p. 314.
33. Alan Lang Strout was Professor of English at Texas Tech. See also his significant contribution in Robert Mudie, *Things in General*, ed. Alan Lang Strout (Los Angeles, 1939).
34. Anon., 'Mr. Robert Mudie', in *The Spectator* 15 (13 August 1842), 789.
35. For more on the puddlement of Mudieism in which the Carlyles found themselves, see Mebius, 'Mudie and Dickens'.
36. Allan, 'Age of Pericles', p. 392
37. Mudie, *Modern Athens*, p. 46.

# 9

# Theories of Universal Degeneration in Post-Enlightenment Scotland

## Bill Jenkins

The idea that in ancient times there existed a lost civilisation boasting both an ideal social order and profound knowledge of the natural world has an enduring appeal, from Plato's Atlantis in the fourth century BC to the popular pseudo-archaeology of Erich von Däniken and Graham Hancock in the late twentieth century.[1] It is not, however, an idea normally associated with the nineteenth century, an era often typified as having made a quasi-religion of progress. It was, after all, the age of the steam engine, the telegraph and the explosive growth of new industrial metropolises. As David Spadafora has written, '[d]uring the first three-quarters of the nineteenth century, in particular, the belief in progress was widespread and sometimes seemed virtually unchallenged'.[2] In this chapter I will show that belief in degeneration was in fact alive and well in the early nineteenth century in the very country that had been central to the development of the progressivist theories of conjectural history during the Enlightenment.

As Steven Shapin has pointed out, it was widely taken for granted by early modern people that 'the ancients had better knowledge, and more potent technology, than that possessed by the sixteenth and seventeenth centuries or than any modern human beings could have'.[3] In his classic account of degenerationism, Victor Harris has traced the idea that the history of the world was a story of decay and decline through the late sixteenth and early seventeenth centuries. According to Harris, '[t]he belief that the world is decaying, that man has reached the lowest point in his corrupt and sinful history, that the end of all is on hand, is almost universally accepted by the second or third decade of the seventeenth century'.[4] However, Harris also claimed that after around 1635 'the belief in the natural corruption of the world ceased to be significant'.[5] Spadafora dates the decline of degenerationism somewhat later, claiming that 'the extent of historical pessimism ... began to wane with the end of the Augustan age in the 1730s and diminished substantially after about 1760', as the idea of progress became 'the dominant element in the historical outlook of the high eighteenth century'.[6] However, degenerationism had not in fact disappeared forever, but lingered on into the late eighteenth century in Scotland before seeing a striking resurgence in the early nineteenth century. Most of the major figures of the Scottish Enlightenment who addressed the natural history of man in their writings were firm believers in progress. As Spadafora has chronicled, David Hume, William Robertson, Adam Ferguson, James Dunbar, John Millar, Adam Smith and Henry Home, Lord Kames, all espoused a broadly progressivist reading of universal history, notwithstanding the enduring influence of the cyclical schemes of corruption and renewal which underpinned classical republican theories of politics.[7] The one notable exception, in this as in many other ways, was James Burnett, Lord Monboddo, whose ideas we will come to later. Among the Scottish literati of the second half of the eighteenth century the progressive stadial model of the history of civilisation predominated. William Robertson, for example, wrote in his *History of America* (1777) that: 'In every part of the earth, the progress of man has been nearly the same; and we can trace him in his career from the rude simplicity of savage life, until he attains the industry, the arts, and the elegance of polished society.'[8] Ferguson concurred, albeit with serious reservations about the cultural consequences of progress, in his *Essay on the History of Civil Society* (1767), where he asserts that: 'Not only the individual advances from infancy to manhood, but the species from rudeness to civilization.'[9] Adam Smith, Ferguson, Millar and Kames all wrote works of conjectural history in which they proposed that human civilisation naturally progressed through three or, more usually, four stages. Although some cultures had not progressed beyond the earliest stages of development, this was still a universal model of progressive development through which all peoples would pass. Perhaps the clearest exposition of this model of the history of civilisation is given by Adam Smith in his 'Lectures on Jurisprudence': 'There are four distinct stages which mankind passes through: – 1$^{st}$, the Age of Hunters; 2$^{dly}$, the Age of Shepherds; 3$^{dly}$, the Age of Agriculture; and 4$^{thly}$, the Age of Commerce.'[10]

The belief in universal progress in the Enlightenment and post-Enlightenment periods rested on three principles. Firstly, the world was governed by divine Providence. The hand of a benevolent creator had designed the world in such a way that everything was ultimately for the best. Any apparent evil only appeared so as a consequence of our limited perspective. As Alexander Pope famously wrote in his *Essay on Man* (1732–4):

All Nature is but Art, unknown to thee;
All Chance, Direction, which thou canst not see;
All Discord, Harmony not understood;
All partial Evil, universal Good[11]

Secondly, the deity worked through the agency of natural laws, which were accessible to human reason. The world was therefore fundamentally comprehensible. The deity might sometimes act to suspend the laws of nature for some specific purpose, but such direct intervention was the exception rather than the rule. Thirdly, the natural laws tended to bring about progressive change and improvement in the world in accordance with the dictates of providence. Such improvement was strong evidence for an omnipotent and benevolent deity, while at the same time sitting uneasily with such specifically Christian doctrines as that of the Fall. As we will see, it was those elements of the Christian drama most dear to evangelical Christians that were later to cause the biggest problems for any system of universal progress.

The best-known exception to the optimistic progressivism of the stadial theorists among the philosophers of the Scottish Enlightenment was James Burnett, Lord Monboddo. In his *Antient Metaphysics* (1779–99), Monboddo wrote that man had 'changed from what he was in ancient times, in health, strength, and size of body, and as the mind is so intimately connected with the body, that the mind also is degenerated in these later times'.[12] He traced this decline at least as far back as the ancient Egyptians, who reached a pinnacle of civilisation never again equalled and who were 'once the fountain and seat of all arts and sciences, from which they were propagated all over the world'.[13] Although Monboddo was noted for his eccentric opinions even in his own day, he was not alone in his gloomy view of the history of civilisation. David Doig, a noted philologist, scholar and fellow of the Royal Society of Edinburgh, published two *Letters on the Savage State, Addressed to the Late Lord Kaims* in 1792 in response to Kames's magnum opus of stadial theory, *Sketches of the History of Man* (1774).

Doig, a devout Episcopalian who had studied at the University of St Andrews, based his critique of Kames largely on scripture. The 'advertisement' that prefaces his book makes his motivation clear, stating 'that if mankind were *originally savages*, the *Mosaic history* must unquestionably be false; and therefore the author was flattered with the hope, that his letters, of which the tendency is to overturn that hypothesis, might be of some use to the cause of revelation'.[14] Doig traces all human civilisation to an intellectually and morally advanced antediluvian race, claiming that

> there did exist, time immemorial, somewhere in the eastern parts of the world, a society of people who were never in the savage state; but retained the remembrance of the arts and inventions which had been known among their ancestors, previous to a general inundation which had swept away the rest of the human race.[15]

Doig denied that people in the 'savage state' could ever progress by their own effort, but only through contact with a more civilised people, or through 'a peculiar disposition of Providence' which furnished some chosen individuals with 'endowments almost supernatural, for the purpose of qualifying them for civilizing *a rude, unpolished world*'.[16]

There is some evidence that Monboddo and Doig were not entirely voices in the wilderness in eighteenth-century Scotland. In a piece published in the Edinburgh periodical the *Lounger* in

1785, the historian Alexander Fraser Tytler, Lord Woodhouselee, complained about

> a set of cynical old men, who are perpetually dinning our ears with the praises of times past, who are fond of drawing comparisons between the ancients and moderns, much to the disparagement of the latter, and who take a misanthropic delight in representing mankind as degenerating from age to age both in mental and corporeal endowments.[17]

As we shall see, the prophets of decline did not fall silent at the dawn of the new century, but continued to argue for degeneration using many of the same arguments as Monboddo and Doig well into the middle of the nineteenth century.

On Monday, 1 March 1841 John Stark stood up at that evening's meeting of the Royal Society of Edinburgh to read a paper 'On the supposed Progress of Human Society from Savage to Civilized Life'. Stark was a natural historian and printer who had been a friend of Dugald Stewart, the University of Edinburgh's late professor of moral philosophy.[18] The paper drew on the writings of Doig, who was cited as an early critic of Enlightenment stadial theory.[19] It was later published in the *Transactions of the Royal Society of Edinburgh*. Stark explicitly attacked the model of the development of human civilisation proposed by Smith, Kames and the other stadial theorists, asserting that:

> It is a general belief that Man, in his supposed progress from Savage to Civilized Life, has passed through three distinct stages or periods, each one leading a step forward in the road to social improvement. These stages are asserted to be, 1. *The Hunter State*; 2. *The Pastoral State*; and, 3. *The Agricultural State*. Allusions to these different stages crowd the pages of the historian, the philosopher, and the poet; and arguments are founded on, and deductions drawn from, these states of existence, as if they were ultimate truths, neither to be discussed nor dissented from. It is the object of this paper to question the existence of these separate states, their necessary connection with one another, and the end to which ultimately they are supposed to lead.[20]

Peter Bowler has noted that '[t]he Scottish model of social progress implied that all societies began as groups of primitive hunters, but such a view was regarded as distinctly unorthodox throughout the first half of the nineteenth century. Primitive tribes' views were generally regarded as indications of just how low mankind could sink when the gift of divine revelation was lost completely'.[21] This was certainly the view of Stark, who stated firmly that primitive hunters must have degenerated from a higher state of civilisation, for 'if man had been created a degraded being, procuring his scanty subsistence from the spontaneous produce of nature, he never could, by his unaided exertions, have risen above that state'.[22]

The first half of the nineteenth century had seen a revival of interest in degenerationist interpretations of universal history in Scotland. Robert Chambers, author of *Vestiges of the Natural History of Creation* (1844), wrote in that work that '[i]t has of late years been a favourite notion with many, that the human race was at first in a highly civilized state, and that barbarism was a secondary condition'.[23] While Doig was an Episcopalian, most of the degenerationists active in Scotland in the first half of the nineteenth century were evangelicals, for whom the rationalistic optimism of the Enlightenment literati was anathema. In the first half of the nineteenth century the evangelicals were engaged in a fierce struggle with the Moderate Party for the soul of the Church of Scotland, and indeed the Scottish nation. This conflict was to culminate in the Disruption of 1843, which tore the church apart and gave birth to the Free Church of Scotland.

For the evangelicals, the picture of fallen humanity in a world cursed by God, which could only be redeemed through divine intervention, sat ill with any vision of universal progress. At least until the advent of Christianity, the trajectory of sacred history seemed to point downwards, falling away from initial prelapsarian perfection. However, the knowledge and wisdom with which mankind was endowed by the creator was not believed by degenerationist thinkers to have been erased completely at the time of the Fall, but to have fallen away gradually over the succeeding centuries. Before the Deluge, and even in the first few generations afterwards, a level of civilisation existed that was incomparably higher than that of later ages. This advanced ancient civilisation was thought to have flourished in the Middle East, considered the cradle of humanity, and home to the relatively sophisticated later civilisations of Babylon and Egypt. These civilisations had been able for a time to retain some of the ancient knowledge.

Stark's hostility to the idea of progress appears to have been largely rooted in theological considerations. His religious affiliations are unknown, but the opinions expressed in his paper are strongly indicative of evangelical sympathies. It is certainly clear that he endorsed a literalist reading of scripture as 'the most ancient, the most rational, and the only true account of the early history of our race', and upheld the centrality of the Fall to the Christian interpretation of universal history.[24] He also shared the evangelical emphasis on the Fall and the subsequent moral and intellectual degeneration of the human race; in his paper for the Royal Society of Edinburgh he wrote that 'the Scripture teaches that man was, at his creation, not only endowed with all the physical perfections belonging to our race in the highest degree, but also with all the intellectual information necessary to the happiness and enjoyment of the most perfect human being' and that the subsequent history of civilisation was one of decline from this original state of perfection.[25] Stark considered that the decline of civilisation had been a relatively gradual one, so that even '[t]he state of society after the Deluge, may thus be considered as one in a comparatively high degree of civilization'.[26]

Proponents of degeneration such as Stark were keen to counter the influence of popular works of naturalistic progressivism, including the influential *Constitution of Man*, written by the phrenologist George Combe. Combe's book was first published in 1828. At first it only achieved relatively modest sales, but after the publication of a cheap 'People's Edition' in 1835 sales soared and Combe's book became something of a publishing phenomenon. By 1860 it had sold 100,000 copies in Great Britain, and another 200,000 in America.[27] Its influence was profound throughout the nineteenth century. In 1881 the Liberal politician John Morley could write that the principles expressed in Combe's work 'have now in some shape or form become the accepted commonplaces of all rational persons'.[28] Combe adopts a progressive view of the history of civilisation that clearly owes much to Enlightenment stadial theory. In the 'People's Edition' of the *Constitution* he wrote that:

> He [man] adopted savage habits, because his animal propensities were not at first directed by the moral sentiments, or enlightened by reflection. He next assumed the condition of the barbarian, because his higher powers had made some advance, but had not yet attained supremacy; and he now manufactures, because his constructive faculties and intellect have given him power over physical nature, while his avarice and ambition are predominant, and are gratified by such avocations.[29]

While Combe evidently believed that the latest stage in human progress was not accompanied by unalloyed moral improvement, he is clear that 'the civil history of man ... proclaims the march, although often vacillating and slow, of moral and intellectual improvement'.[30] This progressive model of history is set within a clear deistic framework. Progress is built into the fabric of the world because 'the Creator has bestowed definite constitutions on physical nature and on man and animals, and that they are regulated by fixed laws'.[31] His optimistic vision, however, caused serious problems for evangelical commentators, who saw it as conflicting starkly with the doctrine of the Fall, without which Christ's Atonement and the whole Christian drama were meaningless. Indeed, Combe sets himself up in conscious opposition to the evangelical opinion that, as he puts it, 'the world was perfect at first, but fell into derangement, continues in disorder, and does not contain within itself the elements of its own rectification'.[32]

William Scott, a lawyer, evangelical phrenologist and one-time associate of Combe was so alarmed by the progressive doctrines expressed in the *Constitution* that he wrote a book-length critique of it entitled *The Harmony of Phrenology with Scripture* (1836).[33] This book proved popular enough for the publisher to bring out a second edition the year after its first publication. Scott flatly denies that the history of civilisation was progressive:

> as far as any conclusion can be drawn from history, from the monuments of ancient art, and other remains of antiquity, we

are led irresistibly to the belief, that the most ancient nations have been as far, or farther advanced in moral and intellectual attainments, than those which succeeded them.[34]

In contradiction to the stadial model of human history he argues, like Stark, that progress from a 'barbarous' state is impossible, and that 'no instance can be adduced of any barbarous nation, which, by its own unassisted efforts, ever advanced a single step in the career of moral and intellectual improvement'.[35] The only exception to this grim picture of degeneration is provided by the influence of true religion, through which 'a great and rapid improvement has now been going on for centuries, and is still proceeding, in those countries which have been brought under the influence of Christianity'.[36] However, without the influence of true religion, the trajectory of human history would point unrelentingly downward.

The apostles of progress did not confine themselves to discussing the advance of human civilisation. Many, including Combe, considered nature to have been imbued from the beginning with the principle of progressive development by a benevolent creator. According to Combe, the world 'appears to be arranged in all its departments on the principle of slow and progressive improvement. Physical nature itself has undergone many revolutions, and apparently has constantly advanced.'[37] One of Combe's most important disciples was Robert Chambers, author of the evolutionary epic *Vestiges of the Natural History of Creation* (1844). It was *Vestiges* which did more than any other book in the mid-nineteenth century to provoke a reaction from the enemies of universal progress. Chambers considered there to be a universal law of progressive development which had been built into the world by the Creator:

> The inorganic has one final comprehensive law, GRAVITATION. The organic, the other great department of mundane things, rests in like manner on one law, and that is, – DEVELOPMENT. Nor may these after all be twain, but only branches of one still more comprehensive law, the expression of that unity which man's wit can scarcely separate from Deity itself.

As Paul Baxter has demonstrated, science became a key battleground for some within the Evangelical Party, including the natural historian John Fleming, the geologist Hugh Miller and the natural philosopher David Brewster.[38] These scientific Evangelicals were determined to claim modern science for the side of the angels. The development hypothesis was a particular object of their wrath, as for them it typified both bad science and bad religion. It also struck them as a resurgence of the rationalistic optimism of the Edinburgh literati of the previous century that they despised. As Miller wrote: 'Christianity, if the development theory be true, is exactly what some of the more extreme Moderate divines of the last age used to make it, – an idle and unsightly excrescence on a code of morals that would be perfect were it away.'[39]

Even before the publication of *Vestiges*, the progressivist vision of nature promoted by Jean-Baptiste Lamarck in his *Philosophie Zoologique* (1809) had incurred the wrath of Scottish degenerationists. Stark explicitly critiques Lamarck's theory of the progressive development of humans from apes in his paper for the Royal Society of Edinburgh, where it was mockingly summarised as follows: 'some species of the Quadrumanous animals, or Apes, may, from the exigencies of their situation, have given up their natural propensities, and learned to walk, and speak, and think, by some fancied necessity of a progressive development of faculties'.[40] However, it was Chambers's 'development hypothesis' that generated the most pronounced reaction.

Miller went so far as to write an entire volume, *Foot-prints of the Creator* (1849), to counter the insidious influence of Chambers's infidel but wildly popular book and the development hypothesis it advocated. In this work Miller suggested that the evidence of progress in the history of life revealed by the geological record was in fact only the result of the deity's repeated supernatural intervention to create new classes of living things, which then degenerated over time.

> The lower divisions of the vertebrata preceded the higher; – the fish preceded the reptile, the reptile preceded the bird, the bird preceded the mammiferous quadruped, and the mammiferous quadruped preceded man. And yet, is there one of these great

divisions in which, in at least some prominent features, the present, through this mysterious element of degradation, is not inferior to the past?[41]

He claimed that the fossil fish of the Old Red Sandstone, which he had studied intensively over many years, showed just such a pattern of degeneration. He went so far as to explicitly link the 'principle of degradation' in the natural world to the degeneration of human civilisation since the Deluge. According to Miller, the more recent but more degraded class of fossil fish

> appears in geologic history as does that savage state which certain philosophers have deemed the original condition of the human species, in the history of civilization, when read by the light of the Revealed Record, under the shadow of those gigantic ruins of the East that date only a few centuries after the Flood.

The Evangelical natural philosopher David Brewster painted a similar picture of the history of life in his blistering review of the fourth edition of *Vestiges*. Brewster damned Chambers's progressivist development hypothesis as 'poisoning the fountains of science, and sapping the foundations of religion'.[42] Using the same argument that Miller would use in *Foot-prints of the Creator*, he denied that there was any hint of progressive development in the fossil record, citing evidence that 'the oldest fossil fish with which geologists are acquainted, is actually one of the highest organization!'[43] Brewster later gave Miller's *Foot-prints of the Creator* a glowing review. In it he gave his vivid imagination free rein, going as far as to speculate that there may have existed creations before the present one inhabited by creature of a higher nature even than the human race:

> Another creation may lie beneath: – More glorious creatures may be entombed there. The mortal coil of beings more lovely, more pure, more divine than man, may yet read us the unexpected lesson that we have not been the first, and may not be the last of the intellectual race.[44]

While Brewster did not propose that we were the degenerate descendants of these beings, who belonged to a separate creation, their possible existence underlined the extent to which the history of the globe was emphatically not one of constant and universal progress.

Two factors conspired to bring about a resurgence of degenerationist interpretations of universal history in early nineteenth-century Scotland. The first was the evangelical revival and the polarisation of the Church of Scotland into opposing Evangelical and Moderate camps. This gave added prominence to specifically evangelical preoccupations with the Fall and Atonement, elements of the Christian drama that sat uncomfortably in a progressive universe. The doctrine that in a fallen world change for the better could only occur through divine intervention, never through humanity's own efforts, was also an important doctrine to the evangelicals. The second factor was the rise of popular progressivist philosophies, such as those embodied in the works of Combe and Chambers. The popularity of these ideas and the impressive sales figures of the *Constitution of Man* and *Vestiges* were bound to illicit a strong degenerationist reaction among Scottish intellectuals with evangelical sympathies.

After mid-century the declining influence of the evangelicals and the near hegemony established by progressivist interpretations of both human and earth history in the wake of the publication of the *Origin of Species* in 1859 meant that belief in universal degeneration and in the existence of a highly advanced civilisation in ancient times waned, without ever entirely disappearing. The apparent vindication of stadial theory resulting from new archaeological discoveries also mortally damaged their intellectual respectability.[45] One or two individuals, such as George Douglas Campbell, the 8th Duke of Argyll, and the astronomer Charles Piazzi Smyth, still championed degeneration into the 1860s and 70s, but they were largely isolated figures whose theories were not widely accepted.[46] While the idea of decline from a lost golden age of civilisation deep in antiquity has remained a staple of popular culture and pseudo-archaeological fantasies, it largely disappeared from serious debate on the trajectory of world history.

# Notes

1. See, for example, Erich von Däniken *Chariots of the Gods?* (London, 1969) and Graham Hancock, *Fingerprints of the Gods: The Evidence of Earth's Lost Civilization* (London, 1995).
2. David Spadafora, *The Idea of Progress in Eighteenth-Century Britain* (New Haven, CT, 1990), p. 2.
3. Steven Shapin, *The Scientific Revolution* (Chicago, 1996), p. 74.
4. Victor Harris, *All Coherence Gone* (Chicago, 1949), p. 129.
5. Harris, *All Coherence Gone*, p. 4.
6. Spadafora, *Idea of Progress*, pp. 16–17.
7. Spadafora, *Idea of Progress*, pp. 253–320; Istvan Hont and Michael Ignatieff (eds), *Wealth and Virtue: the Shaping of Political Economy in the Scottish Enlightenment* (Cambridge, 1983).
8. William Robertson, *History of America* (1777), *Works of William Robertson* (12 vols, London, 1817), IX, p. 30.
9. Adam Ferguson, *An Essay on the History of Civil Society* (1767: Basel, 1789), p. 2.
10. Adam Smith, *Lectures on Jurisprudence*, ed. R. L. Meek, D. D. Raphael and P. G. Stein (Oxford, 1978), p. 14.
11. Alexander Pope, *An Essay on Man* (1733–4: London, 1763), p. 28.
12. James Burnett, Lord Monboddo, *Antient Metaphysics* (6 vols, Edinburgh, 1779–99), IV, p. 8.
13. Monboddo, *Antient Metaphysics*, IV, p. 397.
14. David Doig, *Two Letters on the Savage State, Addressed to the Late Lord Kaims* (London, 1792), pp. vii–ix.
15. Doig, *Two Letters on the Savage State*, p. 48.
16. Doig, *Two Letters on the Savage State*, p. 68.
17. Alexander Fraser Tytler, 'To the author of the Lounger', *The Lounger* 19 (1785), 159.
18. Obituary of John Stark, *Tait's Edinburgh Magazine* 17 (1850), 200.
19. John Stark, 'On the supposed Progress of Human Society from Savage to Civilized Life, as connected mill the Domestication of Animals and the Cultivation of the Cerealia', *Transactions of the Royal Society of Edinburgh* 15 (1844), 177–210, at p. 179.
20. Stark, 'On the supposed Progress of Human Society', 177.
21. Peter J. Bowler, *The Invention of Progress: the Victorians and the Past* (Oxford, 1989), p. 31.
22. Stark, 'On the supposed Progress of Human Society', 183.
23. [Robert Chambers], *Vestiges of the Natural History of Creation* (London, 1844), p. 297.
24. Stark, 'On the supposed Progress of Human Society', 186.
25. Stark, 'On the supposed Progress of Human Society', 186.
26. Stark, 'On the supposed Progress of Human Society', 207.

27. John van Wyhe, *Phrenology and the Origins of Victorian Scientific Naturalism* (Aldershot, 2004), p. 128.
28. John Morley, *The Life of Richard Cobden* (2 vols, London, 1881) II, p. 93.
29. George Combe, *The Constitution of Man Considered in Relation to External Objects* (1828: Edinburgh, 1835), p. 4.
30. Combe, *Constitution of Man*, p. 3.
31. Combe, *Constitution of Man*, p. 8.
32. Combe, *Constitution of Man*, p. 4.
33. Anon., 'The late William Scott, Esq.', *The Phrenological Journal, and Magazine of Moral Science* 15, no. 70 (1842), 44–50.
34. William Scott, *The Harmony of Phrenology with Scripture: Shewn in a Refutation of the Philosophical Errors Contained in Mr Combe's 'Constitution of Man'* (Edinburgh, 1837), p. 9.
35. Scott, *Harmony of Phrenology with Scripture*, p. 9.
36. Scott, *Harmony of Phrenology with Scripture*, p. 33.
37. Combe, *Constitution of Man*, p. 2.
38. Paul Baxter, 'Deism and development: Disruptive forces in Scottish natural theology', in Stewart Jay Brown and Michael Fry (eds), *Scotland in the Age of the Disruption* (Edinburgh, 1993), pp. 98–112.
39. Hugh Miller, *Foot-prints of the Creator; or, the Asterolepis of Stromness* (London, 1849), p. 17.
40. Stark, 'On the supposed Progress of Human Society', 181.
41. Miller, *Foot-prints of the Creator*, pp. 178–9.
42. [David Brewster], Review of *Vestiges of the Natural History of Creation*, *North British Review* 3, no. 6 (1845), 471.
43. [Brewster], Review of *Vestiges*, 486.
44. [David Brewster], Review of *Footprints of the Creator: or the Asterolepis of Stromness*, *North British Review* 12, no. 24 (1850), 480.
45. See Van Riper, *Men among the Mammoths: Victorian Science and the Discovery of Prehistory* (Chicago, 1993) for an account of these developments.
46. See the 8th Duke of Argyll, *Primeval Man: An Examination of some Recent Speculations* (London, 1869) and Charles Piazzi Smyth, *On the Antiquity of Intellectual Man, from a Practical and Astronomical Point of View* (Edinburgh, 1868).

# 10

# Robert Knox: The Embittered Scottish Anatomist and his Controversial Race Science in Mid-Nineteenth-Century Britain

*Efram Sera-Shriar*

On the evening of Monday, 17 May 1847 a grizzled and middle-aged Robert Knox was getting ready for a public lecture at Exeter Hall in London. For days the British press had been promoting an 'extraordinary exhibition', where spectators would have an opportunity to see first-hand actual representatives of the San People from South Africa and learn about their culture and physiognomy from a leading expert in the emerging science of ethnology.[1] A large and excited audience of several hundred curious patrons paid two shillings for the show, and shortly after 8 p.m. Knox took to the stage and introduced himself as the 'infamous anatomist Dr Robert Knox'.[2] This was no passing remark, but a self-aware descriptor of a man who by the late 1840s was one of the more controversial figures within the British race sciences. While this event may give the impression that Knox was a successful science populariser by the middle of the century, in reality he was an outlier in the scientific and medical community. But things had not always been this way for Knox and during the opening decades of the nineteenth century he was one of the most highly regarded anatomists and race scientists in Britain.

Knox began his career during the 1820s as a leading anatomist in Edinburgh. However, after revelations in the press exposed his involvement with William Burke and William Hare in the West Port murders, Knox's reputation as a respectable man of science dwindled. Remembered today as one of the most notorious criminal cases in modern Scottish history, the West Port murders were a series of sixteen killings committed over a period of about ten months between 1827 and 1828 in Edinburgh. Burke and Hare murdered their victims and sold the corpses to Knox, who used them for dissection in his anatomy classes.[3] Knox never fully recovered from this scandal, and most Victorians saw him as a divisive figure. Yet amongst his more devoted former students, such as Henry Lonsdale, and some of the more extreme British race scientists of the mid-Victorian period, including James Hunt and Charles Carter Blake, he maintained a strong following. These men continued to praise Knox's abilities as a scientific observer and pedagogue, long after his death in 1862.[4]

There is a scarcity of surviving archival material relating to Knox's life and career. He destroyed most of his letters and manuscripts before his death in the early 1860s. Even the materials that Lonsdale used in writing Knox's biography are lost.[5] What remains is Lonsdale's account from 1870 and Knox's published works, which for the most part he wrote after 1842 when he left Scotland deeply embittered. Understanding Knox's ideas is further complicated because of the scattered and disjointed nature of his writings in the period after the loss of his medical career. During the 1840s and 1850s he barely lived above a level of pauperism, and he wrote most of his books in haste because of his desperate need for money.

As the chapter will show, although Knox had a brilliant career during the earlier part of his life as one of the leading anatomists in Britain during the opening decades of the nineteenth century, his involvement in the West Port Murders between 1827 and 1828, and the scandal that ensued, damaged his reputation, and led to his marginalisation within the scientific and medical communities. He became deeply embittered by these negative experiences, which influenced his ethnological writings. Living in poverty, Knox used controversy to earn money, but the science that he produced had long-lasting and negative consequences. Not only was he a vocal proponent of polygenesis, the belief in the multiple origins of races, but he was also a staunch critic of developmentalism and promoter of biological determinism. His contributions to ethnology and anthropology came to define the scientific racism of the late Victorian era. The maturation of these abhorrent racial ideas was eventually published in his infamous book, *The Races of Men: A Fragment* (1850).

Born to a middling-sort family in the area of North Richmond Street in Edinburgh in 1791, Knox's intellectual abilities were evident from a young age.[6] His father, Robert Knox Sr, was a mathematics and natural philosophy teacher at George Heriot's Hospital, and the young Knox was introduced to scientific and medical topics from an early age. In 1805 he entered Edinburgh High School, where he excelled in his studies and was a dux and gold medallist for his schoolwork. After graduation, he enrolled in the medical school at the University of Edinburgh, where he quickly rose in popularity with his medical peers becoming the president of the Royal Medical Society twice before his graduation as an MD in 1814.[7]

Despite these scholarly successes and immense popularity amongst his peers during his medical studies at the university, Knox failed his first examination on human anatomy; the subject in which he would become a leading authority by the mid-1820s, and which formed the foundation of his later ethnological research. It was under the so-called incompetence of the famed medical professor Alexander Monro III that Knox failed to initially acquire a thorough understanding of the physical structure of humans. Monro, or *Tertius* as he is often known, was the third generation of his family to hold a professorship in anatomy at the University of Edinburgh, after his grandfather and father both previously held it. Despite his illustrious family pedigree, Monro's classes were often described as uninspired, and even Charles Darwin who studied with him during the mid-1820s remarked that Monro 'made his lectures on human anatomy as dull as he was himself'.[8] To better prepare himself for his re-examination, between 1813 and 1814 Knox studied anatomy at John Barclay's extramural school in Edinburgh. Under the tutelage of the vastly superior instruction of Barclay, Knox mastered the subject, and in 1814 at his second attempt, he passed his medical exam at the university.[9]

After graduation, Knox undertook a further year of training in London at St Bartholomew's Hospital, where he worked with the surgeon John Abernethy. Upon completing these studies, he travelled to Belgium where he served as a field surgeon and attended the wounded from the Battle of Waterloo. The British

Army, impressed by his work, then sent Knox to South Africa to act as a surgeon in the Cape colony. But his time in South Africa was fraught with scandal, and after an altercation with his superior officer, which led to a duel, Knox was discharged from his military service and he returned to Edinburgh on Christmas day in 1820.[10]

Things improved quickly for Knox once he was back in Scotland. By 1823 he was elected as a Fellow of the Royal Society of Edinburgh. He also organised a plan to establish a Museum of Comparative Anatomy at the Royal College of Surgeons of Edinburgh, which was accepted, and Knox became its first curator. By 1825 as his star continued to rise within the Scottish medical community, he was offered a partnership by Barclay to join him at his anatomy school in Surgeon's Square, Edinburgh.[11] Knox's classes were immensely popular and student enrolment was high. He was renowned for his flamboyant teaching style, which was far more appealing than the dull lectures Monro was delivering at the university. After Barclay's death in 1826, Knox took over control of the anatomy school.[12]

In November of 1827, Knox's good fortunes would forever change when he purchased a corpse from the serial killers Burke and Hare. In total, over the course of a year, Knox acquired sixteen bodies from the pair, who were eventual captured by the authorities in late autumn of 1828. When the full details of Knox's involvement in their murders was revealed publicly, his reputation never recovered. Knox avoided prosecution but the medical establishment in Scotland was quick to ostracise him. After a series of personal attacks by various groups in Edinburgh, the Royal College of Surgeons pressured Knox to resign from his curatorship at their comparative anatomy museum, and several other sources of income stopped as a result of his role in the West Port murders. By the early 1830s even his school was struggling to attract students.[13] Things worsened so much for Knox that by the early 1840s he was forced to close his school forever. Out of work and unable to find employment elsewhere in the city, Knox left Edinburgh deeply embittered.[14] With his medical career in tatters, he turned his attention to race science, where he was still able to earn a modest amount of money through his touring lectures and publications. The reason Knox's race science garnered so much attention, however, was not because of its brilliance, but due to its highly controversial and extreme nature.

Knox's earliest encounter with extra-Europeans occurred between 1817 and 1820 when he was stationed as a military surgeon in South Africa with the 72nd Highlanders during the Cape Frontier Wars. Inside the field hospital Knox gained a sound knowledge of human anatomy and physiology, operating on European and African casualties of war.[15] Outside the hospital, he gained invaluable natural history experience. As Lonsdale explained in his biography, Knox's experience in Africa had a significant impact on his medical and scientific practices because it afforded him an opportunity to observe *in situ* natural history specimens. As Lonsdale explained, Knox 'looked beyond the confines of his hospital engagements' to explore the 'the entire natural history under his survey' in the Cape territory, and ethnology was central to this naturalistic research.[16]

Although he was actively serving as an army surgeon while in South Africa, there were often periods where his duties were light. Ever the opportunist, Knox seized the chance to observe a broad spectrum of people because several different ethnic communities from both Europe and Africa came into contact with each other in the Cape colony. Lonsdale argued that 'Early in his African experiences the ethnological faculty seemed strongly manifested in Knox', and he meticulously recorded the physical and cultural traits of the indigenous communities he encountered.[17] This material was incorporated into both his later lectures on race, such as his presentation at Exeter Hall in May of 1847, and his published work on ethnology. As Lonsdale wrote, 'a great deal of what he saw in Africa came to be worked up in magazine articles, whilst the anthropological *memorabilia* formed interesting details for his anatomical classes, and were afterwards woven in graphic colours with his "Fragment" on the Races of Men'.[18]

Knox examined at length the anatomy and physiology of the various peoples that populated the world in his *Races of Men*, and he also discussed different cultural practices that were specific to each group. The most significant aspect of his book, which separated him from other contemporary studies of human races, was that he based several of his racial descriptions on his own first-hand observations, collected in the field. For example, Knox substantiated his account of the Khoikhoi, or 'Hottentot' to use Knox's descriptor, with a mixture of data taken from his own primary experiences living in South Africa and from the testimonies of other travellers.[19] This was a considerable departure from the work of other ethnologists from the period, such as James Cowles Prichard (a Quaker from Bristol who took his medical degree at Edinburgh) and Thomas Hodgkin, who were solely reliant on the observations of travelling informants to supply them with ethnographic data for their investigations.[20]

Knox's theoretical perspective differed extensively from the Prichardian model, and for him race was everything. It not only shaped a person's physical appearance, but also their social behaviour. He recognised that such a stance positioned him in opposition to many of the leading ethnologists of the day and he wrote in his preface to *Races of Men* that:

> The 'Fragment' I here present to the world has cost me much thought and anxiety; the views it contains being so wholly at variance with long received doctrines, stereotyped prejudices, national delusions, and a physiology and philosophy, if it can be so called, as old at least as the Hebrew.[21]

While masked in a revisionist language that could appear to some as an attempt to forward a more progressive interpretation of human history, Knox was actually criticising the standard ethnological narrative of development as old-fashioned and obsolete.[22]

These contentious remarks were clearly designed to incite a response from his readers, and Knox stated that:

> The human character, individual and national, is traceable solely to the nature of that race to which the individual or nation belongs, [this] is a statement which I know must meet with the severest opposition. It runs counter to nearly all the chronicles of events, called histories; it shocks the theories of statesmen, theologians, [and] philanthropists of all shades.[23]

Knox was ruthless in his attack on traditional ethnological practice, and he referred to figures such as Prichard and the physician William Lawrence, who was also an important early progenitor of ethnological science, as 'hack compilers'. Knox argued that these scholars based their studies on travellers' accounts and not first-hand evidence. Thus, their mastery of the subject was only second-hand. He also argued that these ethnologists were committed to 'false doctrines' such as monogenesis – a theory postulating the single origin of humans. As one of the few self-proclaimed researchers to have both first-hand experiences observing extra-European races *in situ*, combined with being a chief promoter of polygenesis, Knox believed that his opponents would omit his divergent theories and accounts from their work because it would discredit their research.[24]

In his introduction, Knox presented a vastly different approach to the study of race by forwarding a polygenetic view heavily indebted to comparative anatomy and transcendentalism. He wrote that 'Of man's origin we know nothing correctly; we know not when he first appeared in space; [and thus] his place in time, then, is unknown.'[25] He continued by attacking the chronologies of naturalists who attempted to outline the course of human history, and he stated, 'how worthless are these chronologies! How replete with error human history has been proved to be.'[26] For Knox, origin theories were a secondary concern for any scientific study on humans. Instead, the primary aim for researchers was to observe and describe the current form of different races. French naturalism was therefore core to Knox's ethnological praxis.

In 1821 Knox had moved to Paris where he studied comparative anatomy with Georges Cuvier and transcendentalism with Étienne Geoffroy Saint-Hilaire. Knox's time in France was formative and shaped his theoretical and methodological frameworks. For Knox, comparative anatomy provided researchers with a practical method for organising humans into groups based on similarities and differences, while transcendentalism furnished them with a basis for all theories of race. In his book, *Great Artists and Great Anatomists* (1852) Knox praised the contributions of both Cuvier and Saint-Hilaire to medicine and science.[27] He wrote that Cuvier's comparative anatomy formed 'the basis of all zoological knowledge [or] in other words, to the science of organic beings'.[28] And this was further reinforced when Knox explained the centrality of anatomical training in many of his books. He wrote, for example, in his *Manual of Human Anatomy* (1853) that 'It is to the labours of the anatomy of adult forms that Medicine, Zoology, Geology owe their present positions, whatever that may be. For the Medicine which appeals not to Anatomy is empiricism; and the Zoology not based thereon is not a science.'[29] The same set of assumptions was extended to Knox's conception of ethnological science.

Transcendentalism was equally essential to Knox's race model, and he believed there was an underlying structural relationship between diverse groups of organisms in nature. His transcendentalism was a primary element of his theoretical paradigm for studying races and he wrote that 'transcendental anatomy, which alone of all systems, affords us a glimpse and a hope of a true "theory of nature"'.[30] Curvier and Saint Hilaire, therefore, both had an impact on Knox's writings regarding human variation. It was evident that the physical structure of different human groups was the cornerstone of Knox's ethnology. Knox wrote in *Races of Men* that 'The basis of the view I take of man is his physical structure', and he argued that 'To know this must be the first step in all inquiries into man's history.' All abstractions that ignored or underexplored this aspect of human variation studies was, in Knox's view, 'erroneous'.[31]

Equally important for studying different races, according to Knox, were the observational abilities of a researcher. Natural history training was useful, but to substantiate ethnological knowledge, one had to avoid basing their interpretations solely on *a priori* systems, which Knox claimed could 'misdirect' researchers. As he explained, so much attention was given to pressing students into memorising natural history taxonomies and terminologies at the expense of 'actual observation through the senses'. What anatomy instruction should prioritise was a pedagogic programme that aimed to enhance 'the powers of observation' and emphasise the importance of *prima facie* evidence as the surest source of knowledge.[32] Most importantly, however, Knox explained that the language of natural history was riddled with political implications.

Therefore, its application in ethnological discourse adversely affected the interpretation of human difference.

In *Races of Men*, Knox argued that 'Men are of various Races; call them Species, if you will; call them permanent Varieties; it matters not. The fact, the simple fact, remains just as it was: men are of different races.'[33] Whether one viewed race as a species or variety, so far as Knox was concerned, was unimportant. What mattered was that there was a visible difference and it was this difference that counted. Thus, the point to emphasise in ethnological accounts was racial distinction. Knox continued by attacking Prichard's taxonomy, which was based on the classification system of the German physician, Johann Friedrich Blumenbach.[34] Knox stated that early on in his career he 'examined the work of Blumenbach, of which the laborious writings of Dr. Prichard were an extension' and saw that it was 'an imperfect work'.[35] This criticism was significant, especially given the position Prichardian ethnology occupied in British scientific circles. Prichard's monogenetic paradigm for understanding racial diversity was the dominant model in Britain at the time, and many ethnological researchers viewed him as the figurehead for the budding discipline.[36] Knox's hypercritical attack was targeted and controversial, with the aim of stoking an outcry.

But Knox's aggressive critique did not end there, and he remarked that 'the philosophic formula of Blumenbach [and by extension Prichard] led to no results; explained nothing; investigated no causes'.[37] When anatomy was discussed it only focused on some areas, such as skull conformation. For Knox, this was insufficient. Moreover, because Blumenbach and Prichard devoted so much attention to a limited study of only certain aspects of human anatomy, they failed to suitably explore the importance of human physiology and its impact on shaping racial variations. This was a significant shortcoming according to Knox, and thus any conception of race based on Blumenbach's interpretive system for understanding human diversity was flawed and incomplete. As Knox wrote, Blumenbach's method 'left every great physiological question unanswered'.[38]

Knox wanted to promote a race theory which argued that all humans were biologically determined. All immaterial social attributes across different cultures were both secondary to, and dependent on physical conditions. Knox argued, for example, that if Africans were educated in Britain and enculturated into European society, their intellectual abilities and social position would never exceed the 'natural capabilities' of their race. Even if their immersion into a culture influenced their behaviour, he still believed they would ultimately remain biologically distinct. He wrote, 'If any one insists that a Negro or Tasmanian accidentally born in England becomes thereby an Englishman, I yield the point; but should he further insist, that he, said Negro or Tasmanian, may become also a Saxon or Scandinavian, I must contend against so ludicrous an error.'[39] Even for the 1850s, Knox's racial comments were extreme and clashed with the more moderate views of many of the leading ethnologists at the Ethnological Society of London, which was the primary scientific society devoted to race science in Britain at the time.[40]

Nevertheless, Knox's brash and extreme approach to race studies found a following with a new generation of race scientists who supported polygenesis. This was a growing community in the middle of the nineteenth century, and figures such as Hunt, who formed the Anthropological Society of London in 1863 in opposition to the more moderate research programme of the Ethnological Society of London, positioned Knox as a chief theorist for this alternative race science. Knox's emphasis on racial difference and biological determinism struck a chord with the more hard-line racism of these researchers.[41] However, even with this devout fan base, Knox's controversial writings did not go unchallenged, and reviews of his book *Races of Men* were highly critical.

Knox's *Races of Men* met with much scientific and public outcry in the British periodical press, and for the most part his methods and theories were denounced.[42] Many reviews emphasised Knox's disrespect for the British scientific and medical community, and in most cases, journals positioned his strong opinions as the ideas of an embittered 'madman' that were unsubstantiated and designed to stoke controversy. In 1850 the *Gentleman's Magazine* wrote that Knox 'repels us from a consideration of the great points of his work both by his abuse of all men and things which come in his way, and the dogmatism of his unsupported assertions'.[43]

The reviewer compared Knox's work to that of Prichard, and he stated that the subject was 'investigated by Prichard with laborious patience and acuteness'. But Knox's ethnological science was altogether a different story: 'How different is it in the hands of the present writer [Knox]. He rushes to the consideration of certain points . . . with a mind full of violent prejudices and in a rash presumptuous headlong spirit.'[44] This was a powerful criticism that delegitimised Knox's work as a politically motivated rant, while at the same time reinforcing the well-established and popular research programme of Prichard and his more moderate ethnological model.

The *Gentleman's Magazine* was not alone in finding Knox's attack on science and medicine overpowering and aggressive. In 1850, a reviewer for the *Literary Gazette* stated that 'a wild vein of political animosity' runs through Knox's *Races of Men* and his writing was 'more in the style of the triton among the minnows . . . than of a man who really must know something of the subject and who possesses real merit for his account'.[45] In accordance with the way in which the *Gentleman's Magazine* derided Knox's abilities as a scientific researcher, the *Literary Gazette*'s reviewer argued that *Races of Men* was an 'amusing book in many respects' because so many of its claims were unfounded, with almost no evidence to support its suppositions.[46] Moreover, the reviewer asserted that they pitied 'the poor beginner into whose hands [Knox's] book fell'.[47]

Another significant criticism levelled at Knox's *Races of Men* was how poorly the book was organised and structured. The confused nature of the text was partially the result of Knox having to publish it in haste. After his medical career fell apart in Scotland, he was constantly in desperate need of money. *Races of Men* was rushed because by the end of the 1840s he was living hand to mouth and he needed to get the book out as quickly as possible so that he could afford lodgings and food. However, as the reviewer for the *Literary Gazette* wrote, the findings in *Races of Men* were difficult for researchers to use. As a text, it was hard to read and to navigate the various chapters, as well as to identify important passages. As a reference source it had extremely limited value.[48]

In 1850, *Bentley's Miscellany* also included a disparaging review of Knox's *Races of Men*. The writer criticised the book because it challenged Prichard's monogenism and use of biblical theories, and historical data. The reviewer stated that Knox 'denied all that the Bible asserts as to the origin of man and the beginning of time, and calls chronology, sacred or profane, worthless'.[49] This, it was argued, cut to the core of ethnology's developmental foundations. For the reviewer, Knox's work was an offensive piece of research, which was purposefully outlandish and controversial, and designed to anger readers and stoke an emotive response. *Bentley's Miscellany* found little value in Knox's writings, and ended its review by stating, 'we must close our notice of this offensive book'.[50]

*Fraser's Magazine* also published a negative review of Knox's *Races of Men*. The reviewer recognised the embittered tone of the book and argued that 'Dr. Knox writes as a man who has a standing quarrel with all the world.' So resentful was Knox about his current social standing, especially within the scientific and medical community in Britain, that he could not 'take pen in hand without straightway getting into a passion, and placing himself towards all who have the audacity to entertain opinions different from his own, in an attitude most unfavourable to the perception and discovery of truth'.[51] Even when Knox situated his work within a more scientific analysis, his findings were questionable. For example, as the reviewer from *Fraser's Magazine* stated, Knox explained human variation through the 'application of the transcendental theories' of French naturalists such as Saint-Hilaire. However, Knox's commitment to these theoretical models was 'very exaggerated' and therefore misplaced.[52]

In 1852 Knox received a particularly scathing review from the *Athenaeum* that accused him of tainting the minds of youth with his attack on Prichard's ethnology:

> If he lectured as he writes, it may account for his popularity amongst young men entering on their professional career; since it is flattering to the vanity of the young to be told how their fathers have been led by the nose by great names, and what a rare opportunity they have of distinguishing themselves by the adoption of ideas altogether new to the world.[53]

This was clearly a reference to Knox's more devout following among the newer generation of race scientists in Britain. Figures such as Hunt and Blake embraced Knox's alternative ethnological model.[54] However, as the *Athenaeum* contended, a more experienced and knowledgeable reader would quickly recognise the great 'flaws' in Knox's work and understand it to be nothing more than propaganda attempting to challenge the established authority of the leading members of the British scientific and medical community. The *Athenaeum*'s reviewer wrote, 'The mature man finds out that he has been deceived: – and his warning to the rising generation may perhaps account for the fact of our meeting Dr. Knox so often now in literature.'[55] One of the main reasons that Knox was cited so frequently, according to the *Athenaeum*, was because his work was so controversial.

The *Athenaeum*'s reviewer went on to attack Knox's personal character, stating that 'Dr. Knox, in fact writes as a disappointed man; and so much that he says is evidently dictated by this spirit of disappointment, that his works can in no way be read as guides on the subjects which he professes to teach.'[56] The article was evidently referring to how Knox's career fell apart because of his connection to the Burke and Hare murders. It stated, that

> if Dr. Knox would calmly reflect on his own career and productions, he would feel that he has lived in a house of a kind of glass that would not bear the return of such very large stones as he has been freely throwing at the houses of others.[57]

By the end of the 1850s there was a growing divide within British ethnology. On the one hand, figures such as Hodgkin and Robert Gordan Latham continued to develop and refine the research field by basing their work on the well-established Prichardian model that was anchored in monogenism and historical developmentalism. On the other hand, a separate group of researchers following in the teachings of Knox argued in favour of a polygenetic model, based on racially deterministic theories. Reflecting on the closing years of the 1850s, Hunt, who had become a chief disciple of Knox, stated in his 1863 'Introductory Address to the Study of Anthropology' that 'Ethnology as now understood, has quite outgrown the narrow basis on which it was started. We must, therefore enlarge and deepen our foundations.'[58] Hunt continued by noting that 'An attempt has been made to divide all ethnologists into two parties, monogenists and polygenists: and each party is supposed to be bound to support the side to which they may be espoused.'[59] This evaluation of the state of ethnology in Britain by the start of the 1860s marked the beginning of an anthropological schism that nearly tore the discipline apart.

In a sense the division to emerge in British race science during the middle of the century was heavily influenced by the work of Knox. It represents one of his most significant and long-lasting legacies in the discipline. Knox's ideas ushered in a generation of researchers who were far more extreme and bigoted in their views than the more moderate generation that preceded them. While many of these first-generation ethnologists in the nineteenth century came from Quaker backgrounds and were committed to philanthropy and social and racial betterment, the second-generation ethnologists were far more irreligious and less concerned with social and racial improvement.[60] The root of this harsher ethnological model was, to a large extent, shaped by the aggressive and rancorous writings of Knox, which was the product of his bitterness after his failed medical career due to his involvement in the Burke and Hare murders in the late 1820s. As Knox became more desperate for money, he used controversy and racial extremism to gain attention and earn a living.

## Notes

1. Anon., 'Advertisement', *The Times* (13 May 1847), 1.
2. Anon., *Now Exhibiting at the Egyptian Hall, Piccadilly: The Bosjesman, or Bush People, from the Interior of South Africa, who First Appeared at the Exeter Hall, on Monday, 17th May* (London, 1847), pp. 1–2. See also Sadiah Qureshi, *Peoples on Parade: Exhibitions, Empire and Anthropology in Nineteenth-Century Britain* (Chicago, 2011), p. 1.
3. Anon., *An Account of the Life of William Burke, who was Executed on Wednesday the 28th Day of January, 1829, for Murder: With the Confession he Made while Under Sentence of Death* (Dunfermline, 1829); Anon., 'A Sketch of the Life and Writings of Robert Knox, the Anatomist,' *Examiner* 3279 (1870), 773–4; Isobel Rae, *Knox the Anatomist* (Edinburgh, 1964),

pp. 122–54; Henry Lonsdale, A *Sketch of the Life and Writings of Robert Knox, the Anatomist* (London, 1870), pp. 73–89; and Alan W. Bates, *The Anatomy of Robert Knox: Murder, Mad Science and Medical Regulation in Nineteenth-Century Edinburgh* (Eastbourne, 2010).

4. Knox's followers regularly promoted his importance for science and medicine even after his involvement in the West Port murders. For example, see Charles Carter Blake, 'The Life of Robert Knox, the Anatomist. A Sketch of his Life and Writing by Henry Lonsdale', *Journal of Anthropology* 1 (1871), 332–8; and James Hunt, 'On the Origin of the Anthropological Review and its Connection with the Anthropological Society', *Anthropological Review* 6 (1868), 431–42.
5. Evelleen Richards, 'The "Moral Anatomy" of Robert Knox: The Interplay Between Biological and Social Thought in Victorian Scientific Naturalism', *Journal of the History of Biology* 22 (1989), 377.
6. I am borrowing the term 'middling-sort' from E. P. Thompson, who convincingly argued that a recognisable 'middle class', comparable to our contemporary understanding, was still developing during the eighteenth century. A similar argument can be applied to middle-ranking society during the first half of the nineteenth century, of which Knox's family was a part. See E. P. Thompson, 'Patrician Society, Plebeian Culture', *Journal of Social History* 7 (1974), 382–405.
7. For general biographical information on Knox, see: Lonsdale, *Sketch*; Rae, *Knox the Anatomist*; and Helen J. Blackman, 'Knox, Robert (1791–1862)', in Bernard Lightman (ed.), *Dictionary of Nineteenth-Century British Scientists* (4 vols, London, 2004), III, pp. 1160–2. For a broader examination of Knox's career as a physician and anatomist, see Richards, 'The "Moral Anatomy" of Robert Knox', 373–436; and Ruth Richardson, *Death Dissection and the Destitute* (London, 1987), pp. 132–46.
8. Charles Darwin, *Autobiography: The autobiography of Charles Darwin 1809–1882* (London, 1958), p. 47.
9. Efram Sera-Shriar, *The Making of British Anthropology, 1813–1871* (London, 2013), p. 91. For more on extramural medical education in Edinburgh, see L. S. Jacyna, *Philosophical Whigs: Medicine, Science and Citizenship in Edinburgh, 1789–1848* (London, 1994), pp. 78–92.
10. Bates, *The Anatomy of Robert Knox*, pp. 39–40.
11. Sera-Shriar, *The Making of British Anthropology*, pp. 90–1.
12. Adrian Desmond and James Moore, *Darwin's Sacred Cause: Race, Slavery and the Quest for Human Origins* (London, 2009), pp. 40–1.
13. Lonsdale, *Sketch*, p. 21; Bates, *The Anatomy of Robert Knox*, p. 88; and Sera-Shriar, *The Making of British Anthropology*, pp. 90–1.
14. Bates, *The Anatomy of Robert Knox*, pp. 99–100.
15. Rae, *Knox the Anatomist*, pp. 14–15; Lonsdale, *Sketch*, p. 13.
16. Lonsdale, *Sketch*, p. 11.
17. Lonsdale, *Sketch*, p. 12.

18. Lonsdale, *Sketch*, p. 13.
19. Robert Knox, *The Races of Men: A Fragment* (London, 1850), pp. 156–7. See also Sera-Shriar, *The Making of British Anthropology*, p. 91.
20. For more on the use of secondary traveller accounts in nineteenth-century British ethnology, see Sera-Shriar, *The Making of British Anthropology*, pp. 71–7.
21. Knox, *Races of Men*, p. 7.
22. For more on Prichardian developmental historicism, see Efram Sera-Shriar, 'Human History and Deep Time in Nineteenth-Century British Sciences: An Introduction', *Studies in History and Philosophy of Science Part C: History and Philosophy of Biological and Biomedical Sciences* 51 (2015), 19–22, at pp. 19–20.
23. Knox, *Races of Men*, p. 7.
24. Knox, *Races of Men*, p. 8.
25. Knox, *Races of Men*, p. 9.
26. Knox, *Races of Men*, p. 9.
27. Robert Knox, *Great Artists and Great Anatomists* (London, 1852), pp. 1–5.
28. Knox, *Great Artists*, p. 2.
29. Robert Knox, *A Manual of Human Anatomy* (London, 1853), p. vii.
30. Knox, *Races of Men*, p. 20. For more on Saint-Hilaire and transcendentalism's influence on Knox's ethnology, see Knox, *Great Artists*, pp. 2–4.
31. Knox, *Races of Men*, p. 9.
32. Knox, *Great Artists*, pp. 6–7.
33. Knox, *Races of Men*, pp. 9–10.
34. Sera-Shriar, *The Making of British Anthropology*, pp. 35–7.
35. Knox, *Races of Men*, p. 11.
36. Sera-Shriar, *The Making of British Anthropology*, pp. 21–2. See also: George W. Stocking, 'From Chronology to Ethnology: James Cowles Prichard and British Anthropology 1800–1850', in J. C. Prichard, *Researches into the Physical History of Man*, ed. George W. Stocking (Chicago, 1973), pp. ix–cx.
37. Knox, *Races of Men*, 19.
38. Knox, *Races of Men*, 19.
39. Knox, *Races of Men*, 12.
40. For more on the Ethnological Society of London, see Sera-Shriar, *The Making of British Anthropology*, pp. 57–64. See also: George W. Stocking, 'What's in a Name? The Origins of the Royal Anthropological Institute (1837–71)', *Man* 6 (1971), 369–90; Zoë Laidlaw, 'Heathens, Slaves and Aborigines: Thomas Hodgkin's Critique of Missions and Anti-slavery', *History Workshop Journal* 64 (2007), 134–61; and Robert Kenny, 'From the Curse of Ham to the Curse of Nature: The Influence of Natural Selection on the Debate on Human Unity before the Publication of

the Descent of Man', *British Journal for the History of Science* 40 (2007), 363–88.
41. For more on Hunt and the Anthropological Society of London, including a detailed discussion on the more extreme race science of the period, see Stocking, 'What's in a Name?', 369–90; Sera-Shriar, *The Making of British Anthropology*, 109–45.
42. Anon., 'The Varieties of Man', *Bentley's Miscellany* 28 (1850), 393–5; J. Mitford, 'The Races of Men: A Fragment. By Robert Knox M.D.', *Gentleman's Magazine* (November 1850), 528–9; Anon., 'The Races of Mankind', *Fraser's Magazine for Town and Country* 44 (1851), 654–65; and Anon., 'Great Artists and Great Anatomists', *Athenaeum* 1297 (1852), 935–7.
43. Mitford, 'The Races of Men', 528.
44. Mitford, 'The Races of Men', 529.
45. Anon., 'Ethnology', *Literary Gazette* 1765 (1850), 855–7.
46. Anon., 'Ethnology', 857.
47. Anon., 'Ethnology', 857.
48. Anon., 'Ethnology', 857.
49. Anon., 'The Varieties of Man', 393–4.
50. Anon, 'The Varieties of Man', 394.
51. Anon., 'The Races of Mankind', 665.
52. Anon., 'The Races of Mankind', 665.
53. Anon., 'Great Artists and Great Anatomists', 935.
54. Sera-Shriar, *The Making of British Anthropology*, pp. 112–13.
55. Anon., 'Great Artists and Great Anatomists', 935.
56. Anon., 'Great Artists and Anatomists', 935.
57. Anon., 'Great artists and Anatomists', 937.
58. James Hunt, 'Introductory Address on the Study of Anthropology', *Anthropological Review* 1 (1863), 8.
59. Hunt, 'Introductory Address', 8.
60. For more on the anthropological schism of the 1860s, see Efram Sera-Shriar, 'Observing Human Difference: James Hunt, Thomas Huxley, and Competing Disciplinary Strategies in the 1860s', *Annals of Science* 70 (2013), 461–91; and Efram Sera-Shriar, 'The Scandalous Affair of the Anthropological Review: Hyde Clarke, James Hunt, and British Anthropology in the 1860s', in Bernard Lightman and Bennett Zon (eds), *Victorian Culture and the Origin of Disciplines* (Abingdon, 2019), pp. 135–57.

# 11

# Thomas Carlyle and the Scottish Enlightenment Concept of Sympathy

## Joanna Malecka

In *The Victorian Eighteenth Century* Brian Young noted that although Thomas Carlyle was 'the pre-eminent Victorian sage', he 'was not himself a Victorian, but a product of the closing years of the Scottish Enlightenment and of the international atmosphere of late Romanticism'. The eighteenth century, Young insisted, 'was the age with which [Carlyle] was most determinedly engaged with in his writings'.[1] This balanced appraisal challenges enduring depictions of Carlyle as an anti-Enlightenment figure dismissive of eighteenth-century thought.[2]

One of the first literary portrayals of Carlyle in terms of his estrangement from the Scottish Enlightenment comes from his early biographer James Anthony Froude (1818–94). Lionising Carlyle in imagery drawn from the Gospels and presenting him as a new spiritual leader and reformer,[3] Froude deliberately positioned Carlyle at a remove from what he perceived to be the despiritualised and predominantly secular discourse of the eighteenth-century Scottish intelligentsia. Froude's reading of *The French Revolution: A History* (1837) depicts Carlyle as a disgruntled auld licht Calvinist preacher, disgusted with wealth, progress and improvement.[4] Froude saw Carlyle, who admonished France for its recalcitrant Catholicism, as a mouthpiece for the millenarian and bitterly sectarian preaching of Edward Irving (1792–1834):

> France was the latest instance of the action of the general law. France of all modern nations had been the greatest sinner, and France had been brought to open judgement. She had been

offered light at the Reformation, she would not have it, and it had returned upon her as lightning . . . She had preferred to live for pleasure and intellectual enlightenment, with a sham for a religion, which she maintained and herself disbelieved.[5]

Elsewhere, however, Froude implicitly celebrates some of the main post-Enlightenment ideas in Carlyle's writing. In 'History: Its Use and Meaning' (1852), an article which ostensibly responds to Carlyle's *Past and Present* (1843), Froude catches the gist of Carlyle's meta-historiographical critique of the limits of human understanding and the need for breadth of sympathy in historical interpretation:

'The eye,' as Mr. Carlyle says, 'sees only what it brings with it.' Catholics, Protestants, Freethinkers, the superstitious and the sceptical, the conservative and the destructive, alike refer us to history, all for the confirmation of their own opinions: all, that is, to history written from their own point of view, compiled by their theory of evidence, interpreted by their theory of life.[6]

Without openly naming the Enlightenment concept of morality embedded in sentiment – derived, of course, from the works of Francis Hutcheson, Adam Smith and Hume – Froude presents Carlyle as its faithful nineteenth-century purveyor. He also portrays Carlyle as the inheritor of the Romantic concept of imagination seen as a creative power capable of bridging the gap between the natural world and spiritual reality:

History had driven away the imagination, and made the supernatural incredible; would it be possible for it to replace what it had destroyed, and reunite them again to reality? . . . The best English historians [sic], with the one exception of the writer whose honoured name we have placed at the head of this article – those most admired and read among us, Gibbon, for instance, and Macaulay – pretend to give us nothing but a picture of human things without God in them, without even the proper dignity of humanity in them; a picture of persons and of actions which leaves out love and hatred unaffected, our admiration without an object, emotion dormant, and imagination dead.[7]

Froude addresses here critically the theory of progress sponsored by the *Edinburgh Review* which regarded imaginative and spiritual language as out of place in serious historical writing. In 'Milton', which he published in the *Edinburgh Review* in 1825, Thomas Macaulay defined rational discourse as devoid of all imaginative and sentimental components: 'Hence the vocabulary of an enlightened society is philosophical, that of a half-civilized people is poetical.' The 'despotism of the imagination over uncultivated minds', according to Macaulay, in a civilised society must be replaced by a scientific and rational discourse:

> In an enlightened age there will be much intelligence, much science, much philosophy, abundance of just classification and subtle analysis, abundance of wit and eloquence, abundance of verses, and even of good ones, – but little poetry.[8]

The *Edinburgh Review*'s agenda was contested by *Blackwood's Magazine*, which stressed the role of feeling and imagination – derived from the Scottish Enlightenment's concepts of moral sense and sympathy – in interpreting society and culture. Carlyle enters these wider cultural and moral conversations via his criticisms of sectarianism and of a narrow definition of rationality; themes he identified as the unfinished projects of eighteenth-century historiography.

As early as 1829 in an essay on Voltaire, Carlyle pointed out the French philosopher's limitations as a historian. Voltaire's vision, Carlyle contended, was restricted by the narrowly polemical lens of his anti-Catholicism:

> [Voltaire] reads History not with the eye of a devout seer, or even of a critic; but through a pair of mere anti-Catholic spectacles. It is not a mighty drama, enacted on the theatre of Infinitude, with Suns for lamps, and Eternity as a background; whose author is God, and whose purport and thousandfold moral lead us up to the 'dark with excess of light' of the Throne of God; but a poor

wearisome debating-club dispute, spun through ten centuries, between the Encyclopedic and the Sorbonne. Wisdom or folly, nobleness or baseness, are merely superstitious or unbelieving.[9]

Carlyle rehearses here some of the key moments of the post-Burkean critique of the Enlightenment cult of reason. Burke sharpened Humean distrust of rationality until excessive faith in human reason emerged as 'a latter-day variety of enthusiasm'.[10] This shaped perception of such categories as enthusiasm, superstition, and sectarianism (all focal preoccupations of an Enlightenment concern for civility and sociability), which now came to be seen less as an expression of excessive religiosity than as a reflection of unchecked secularism. Speaking to this eminently post-Enlightenment sentiment, Carlyle presents Voltaire's irreligion as a secular reincarnation of the Enlightenment's chief enemy, religious sectarianism. Voltaire, we are told, had unknowingly perpetuated the demons he initially set out to extinguish. Enthusiasm was defined by Hume and others before him as the error of the Protestant faith, whereas superstition was traditionally associated with Catholicism;[11] but by reversing these traditional categories, Carlyle presents Voltaire's dismissal of the idea of the divine in Catholic religion as a case of secular superstition and narrowness of perspective. Here and elsewhere Carlyle calls for a broader definition of human rationality, which should allow spiritual reflection. Crucially, Voltaire is also criticised for his lack of what Carlyle elsewhere sees as the crowning achievement of Enlightenment thought – the Scottish concept of sympathy. Not only does Voltaire 'not chaunt any *Miserere* over human life', but even his humour lacks the more sympathetic notes of the Scottish Enlightenment: 'It grounds itself, not on fond sportful sympathy, but on contempt, or at best on indifference.'[12] By depicting Voltaire as a 'perfectly civilised man', Carlyle also registers a critique of the powers of civilisation to address humanity's deepest spiritual problems – the chief one being 'fellow-feeling for human sufferings'.[13]

Rationalised indifference devoid of sympathetic feeling on the one hand, and unenlightened religious enthusiasm on the other are themes that deeply concern Carlyle's early essays and literary fiction. The limits and strains of human sympathy are the thematic essence of *The French Revolution*, a work which, as Robert M. Maniquis has argued, is a profound re-examination of the Calvinist mentality, featuring the ultimate moment of deconstruction of the original Calvinist idea of fear as a moral force. *The French Revolution* also records the moment of literary and ideological death of the classical aesthetic category of the sublime in its political contexts, Maniquis claims persuasively: '[*The French Revolution*] records the death of the sublime as both a psychological and political category.'[14] By exploding these categories, Carlyle undermined the link between sublimity and terror.[15]

If Carlyle indeed deconstructs and explodes the Gothic sublime in his masterpiece, he offers by way of substitution a return to the original eighteenth-century categories of sympathy and benevolence conceptualised by the Scottish philosophical tradition. Both ideas are regarded by the Scottish Enlightenment thinkers as rooted in rationally examined sentiment and seen as fundamental in the universalist project of transcending the religious schisms and violence of the previous century. Carlyle's originality lies in linking a sympathetic re-examination of Scottish Presbyterianism to a more compassionate reconsideration of the French Revolution. In his sympathetic examination of the Scottish Presbyterian history Carlyle is preceded by an array of prominent Scottish Romantic writers: Walter Scott's portrayal of the Covenanters in *Old Mortality*, John Galt's *Ringan Gilhaize* (1823), and James Hogg's depiction of the tortured Calvinism in *The Private Memoirs and Confessions of a Justified Sinner* (1824). Another fundamental influence on Carlyle's sympathetic approach to Scottish Calvinism (and by extension of all humanity at its pompous heights of spiritual hypocrisy and its very lowest carnal bestiality) is the poetry of Robert Burns characterised by Carlyle in an essay published in 1828 as a poet who 'lives in sympathy'.[16] Carlyle recognises the universal appeal of Burns's poetry in his compassionate perception of all human emotions: 'He has a resonance in his bosom for every note of human feeling: the high and the low, the sad, the ludicrous, the joyful, are welcome in their turns.'[17] Burns's intimate portrayal of a spiritual communion with all creation anchored in the enlightened concept of sympathy

– distinct from the orthodox Calvinist perception of creation as irredeemably damaged – guides Carlyle's early Romantic texts. In particular, Burns's interpretation of the Book of Job in 'Address to the Deil' (1786) registers for Carlyle a crucial Romantic possibility of a less sectarian and more generous reading of Calvinism:

> This is worth several homilies on Mercy; for it is the voice of Mercy herself. Burns, indeed, lives in sympathy; his soul rushes forth into all realms of being; nothing that has existence can be indifferent to him. The very Devil he cannot hate with right orthodoxy![18]

Burns's reading of the Book of Job will feature prominently in *The French Revolution* which examines the French nation as a figure of suffering Job flooded with superfluous narratives spouting from his good-for-nothing comforters (chief among them, the British historians and the periodical press).

Carlyle's early publications in the *Edinburgh Review* reveal a sympathetic and mediating agenda which aimed to bridge the gap between contrasting political, religious and social demesnes. Not unlike later *Sartor Resartus* (a quirky mixture of Calvinist conversion narrative and German metaphysics)[19] his essay 'Signs of the Times' (1829) craftily navigates between the Whig terror of religious and political extremisms on the one hand and a sympathetic look at radical culture on the other. Published in the *Edinburgh Review*, 'Signs of the Times' is not only Carlyle's first major text addressed specifically at a Whig readership, but is also the outcome of his friendship and multiple intellectual exchanges with the *Edinburgh Review*'s editor, Francis Jeffrey (1773–1850). In short, in a rhetorical gesture similar to that used in 'Voltaire', we are told that the Whig intelligentsia inadvertently reproduces the demons of the French Revolution which they explicitly strove to extinguish. The cure is a radical re-examination of Enlightenment values, including an imaginative exploration of Scotland's own Calvinist past and of Calvinism's role in the Enlightenment project. 'Signs of the Times' features a sharp critique of the nineteenth-century Whig interpretation of Scotland's Enlightenment legacy. Carlyle creatively juxtaposes Jeffrey's succinct and balanced language with a Blackwoodian/Irvingite biblical style – such as famously utilised in *Blackwood's* 'The Chaldee Manuscript' (1817) satirising the Edinburgh Whigs – in order to mock Britain's assumed intellectual superiority over France.

The opening sentence suggests a commonsensical and anti-Burkean sentiment that the *Edinburgh Review*'s readers would have found a familiar ground: 'It is no very good symptom either of nations or individuals, that they deal much in vaticination.'[20] Cautiously Carlyle distances himself from the prophetic discourse closely associated with religious and political enthusiasm – a style for which he himself at various times during his life was admonished both by Jeffrey[21] and Macaulay, another major contributor to the *Edinburgh Review*.[22] Carlyle for his part described Macaulay as 'a spiritual Hippopotamus' whom 'we cheerfully let . . . shine as "the sublime of Commonplace"'.[23] Macaulay merits here a poetical payment in the kind from Carlyle for his lack of spiritual discrimination. As a heavy, awkward and out-of-place character in the spiritual realm, Macaulay is a poetic incarnation of the commonplace – as far as Carlyle was concerned, the unimaginative contemporary British psyche devoid of wonder and imaginative curiosity.

By openly rejecting prophetic language, then, Carlyle situates himself as a writer who endorses the Whigs' criticism of religious enthusiasm. In addition, he rehearses the Romantic anxiety that associated sympathy with the corruption of rational powers among the masses. Whereas sympathy was originally conceived within the Scottish Enlightenment as a force facilitating polite social interaction and a means of preventing the descent to enthusiasm, it had been redefined in Romantic discourse as a correlate of popular enthusiasm, leading to irrationality or even madness:

> Sympathy has been so rarely the Aaron's-rod of Truth and Virtue, and so often the Enchanter's-rod of Wickedness and Folly! No solitary miscreant, scarcely any solitary maniac, would venture on such actions and imaginations, as large communities of sane men have, in such circumstances, entertained as sound wisdom. Witness long scenes of the French Revolution, in these late times![24]

Here Carlyle noted the incendiary effects of sympathy and of imagination among the masses, with sympathy presented as a passion in need of rational examination. All this marks common ground with the Whig project of curtailing and controlling the dangers of popular imagination. In the same vein, for example, Jeffrey called for a less partisan and more objective reading of recent history. He proposed to draw from the Enlightenment tradition in order to paint large panoramic scenes capable of neatly balancing the causes and consequences of historical actions with a view to deciphering larger patterns of human behaviour:

> Nor can the story of any time be complete or valuable, unless it look before and after, – to the causes and consequences of the events which it details, and mark out the period with which it is occupied, as part of a greater series, as well as an object of separate consideration.[25]

In some of his more patronising moods, Jeffrey was also prone to gratuitously offer a post-factum advice to the French in a bet to teach them valuable moral lessons. By reinscribing the French Revolution in the history of the gradual progress of civic liberty modelled on British history, he presented the revolutionary violence as an easily foreseeable and avoidable occurrence, which – had only the French consulted Britain – would have been explained to them:

> As soon as an appeal was made to force, the decision came to be with those by whom force could at all times be commanded. Reason and philosophy were discarded; and mere terror and brute violence ... harassed and distracted the misguided nation, till, by a natural consummation, they fell under the despotic scepter of a military usurper. These consequences, we conceive, were obvious, and might have been easily foreseen.[26]

By the time Carlyle was writing 'Signs of the Times', this early Whig reading of Revolutionary violence as a regrettable and avoidable hiccup on the way to progress, gave way in the 1820s and

1830s to a more consistently utilitarian reading of Revolutionary terror as a deplorable but apparently unavoidable stage of civil progress.[27]

In 'Signs of the Times' Carlyle further inhabits the Whig language of progress, reform and religious toleration by ridiculing the conservative opposition to the repeal of the Test and Corporation Acts. In what follows though, he deconstructs this progressivist discourse by craftily juxtaposing the dangerous religious millenarianism with the *Edinburgh Review*'s cherished utilitarianism. Under the disguise of attacking the followers of Bentham and James Mill, Carlyle is addressing a Whig readership which he sees as the main perpetrators of utilitarian ethics:[28]

> At such a period, it was to be expected that the rage of prophecy should be more than usually excited. Accordingly, the Millenarians have come forth on the right hand, and the Millites on the left. The Fifth-monarchy men prophesy from the Bible, and the Utilitarians from Bentham. The one announces that the last of the seals is to be opened, positively, in the year 1860; and the other assures us that 'the greatest-happiness principle' is to make a heaven of earth, in a still shorter time.[29]

Far from remaining uninfected by the Continental enthusiasm and better placed to avoid revolutionary excesses than its European neighbours, Whiggism, we are told, contains within itself some of the seeds of British enthusiasm. Unknowingly, the *Edinburgh Review* is guilty of spreading an ideology which is a thinly masked body of superstition, black magic and fortune-telling – all suspect wizardry that no respectable Whig should stand by. In a Swiftian rhetorical move, Carlyle craftily shifts from a eulogy of Whig principles to a sharp critique of all prediction. The utilitarian calculation of the Whigs – seen as false pretension to divine foresight – risks undermining the Enlightenment legacy and exposing Britain to irrationality. Although presented by Mackinnon as defenders of due order against the irrationality of the lower classes, the commercial middle classes and the Whig intellectuals are in Carlyle's imagery victims of devilish wizardry, much in need of confronting their own demons.

Carlyle's satire on Whig ideology draws from another critic of Enlightenment thought and its shortcomings, Jonathan Swift, whose writing is one of the main influences during Carlyle's early creative years: *Sartor Resartus* is chiefly structured around Swift's imagery and rhetoric from *A Tale of a Tub*, while *The French Revolution* is in many ways a Gothic version of *A Modest Proposal*. 'Signs of the Times' provides Carlyle's answer to Swift's examination of 'mechanical' enthusiasm in the *Mechanical Operation of the Spirit*. Here Swift begins by providing a classical definition of enthusiasm as an excess of religious imagination expressed by 'ejaculating the soul, or transporting it beyond the sphere of matter or by uncontrolled passions' which results either in divine prophecy or devilish possession. Swift then adds a 'new' and uncharted type of enthusiasm which he terms 'mechanical' which he links not to an excess of imagination and feeling, but rather to their wilful suspension:

> But, the fourth method of religious enthusiasm, or launching out of the soul, as it is purely an effect of artifice, and mechanick operation, has been sparingly handled, or not at all, by any writer ... It is therefore upon this mechanical operation of the spirit, that I mean to treat, as it is at present performed by our British workmen.[30]

Just such unimaginative and soul-numbing effects of the mechanisation of human spirit are the hallmark of Carlyle's early writing. In 'Signs of the Times' in particular he sees the blind faith in civilisation's powers to answer humanity's deepest needs as the essence of British malady — to be cured by a vigorous awakening of the powers of sympathetic feeling via imaginative aesthetics. Carlyle challenges the British focus on Continental fanaticism, drawing attention instead to Britain's own homely version of enthusiasm. Again, we are reminded that attempts by progressive Whigs to exorcise enthusiasm merely reproduce it under a changed guise (akin to the short-sighted philanthropy of Dr Guillotine, who unknowingly constructs the means by which the revolutionary terror will multiply).

'Signs of the Times' is ostensibly a review of W. A. Mackinnon's *The Rise, Progress, and Present State of Public Opinion* (1828), in which Mackinnon rehearses the stadial model of society as progress towards more perfect forms of liberty originally developed by Adam Smith, William Robertson and Dugald Stewart. Mackinnon presents earlier civilisational stages and their moral values as incompatible with modern commercial standards. Carlyle instead proposes an alternative reading embedded in eighteenth-century discussions of moral sense and benevolence. In Carlyle's reading both rationality and irrationality are intermingled in human nature to the point where all attempts at exorcising evil are suspect and nefarious, symptoms of a 'justified sinner' mentality. In a Romantic reversal of Whig notions concerning the historical development of rationality, we are told that history teaches us that it is rational to expect regular outbursts of bestiality and fanaticism in society since the human proclivity for violence is ultimately inextinguishable:

> In this mitigated form, however, the distemper is of pretty regular recurrence; and may be reckoned on at intervals, like other natural visitations; so that reasonable men deal with it, as the Londoners do with their fogs, – go cautiously out into the groping crowd, and patiently carry lanterns at noon; knowing, by a well-grounded faith, that the sun is still in existence, and will one day reappear.[31]

Reversing the linear Whig reading of history, Carlyle proposes a re-examination of the past in order to draw spiritual and moral capital from it. By rejecting grand Enlightenment debates around 'the Metaphysical and Moral Sciences'[32] and narrowing its interests to institutional, or 'mechanical', control over human behaviour, Britain risks losing its moral compass. The solution is to return to the Enlightenment concept of the moral sense as a universal human trait, one with the capacity to bridge conflicting identities and agendas. Located by Hutcheson in the reflective – rather than purely emotional faculties – the moral sense was easily aligned with conscience, usefully for Carlyle's mediation between the moral, rational, and emotive powers.[33]

Carlyle further ridiculed naïve Whiggish explanations of society in terms of a calculus of causes and effects; such empty calculations reminded Carlyle of Hudibras, Samuel Butler's quixotic Puritan, and his comically overwrought attempts at explicating the universe: 'for every Why we must have a Wherefore. We have our little theory on all human and divine things.'[34] By replacing Enlightenment debates on the moral sense, and free will with an all-too-narrow focus on the institutional and legal aspects of human behaviour, Whigs risked imposing only a new set of ideological traps:

> By arguing on the 'force of circumstances,' we have argued away all force from ourselves; and stand leashed together, uniform in dress and movement, like the rowers of some boundless galley. This and that may be right and true; but we must not do it. Wonderful 'Force of Public Opinion'![35]

In Carlyle's reading, human behaviour is simply too complex to allow for such philosophical calculations. While embracing a view of humanity as free and ultimately unpredictable in its behaviour – forever poised between good and evil – might seem counterproductive to political philosophers, the alternative risked alienating humanity from an essential free will. The ideology of progress at its worst reduces humanity to its animalistic instincts:

> Political Philosophers deal exclusively with the Mechanical province; and occupying themselves in counting-up and estimating men's motives, strive by curious checking and balancing, and other adjustments of Profit and Loss, to guide them to their true advantage: while, unfortunately, those same 'motives' are so innumerable, and so variable in every individual, that no really useful conclusion can ever be drawn from their enumeration.[36]

Carlyle's own reading of history derived from Hume's scepticism of human understanding and causality. History is 'an ever-living, ever-working Chaos of Being, wherein shape after shape bodies itself forth from innumerable elements'.[37] Carlyle also followed Hume in presenting human action as 'based on Passion and Mystery',[38] not the dictates of reason. Historical narrative must eschew causal linearity, and instead present a multiplicity of conflicting narratives and warring passions. Witness the parodic chapter titles of Carlyle's *French Revolution*: 'Cause and Effect', 'Grilled Herrings', and 'Mumbo-Jumbo'. Carlyle openly interrogated any straightforward causal relationship between historical events: 'Alas for our "chains", or chainlets, of "causes and effects", which we so assiduously track through certain handbreadths of years and square miles, when the whole is a broad, deep Immensity.'[39]

Carlyle's verdict on contemporary Britain is pessimistic: far from being the most civilised of all nations, in the moral and spiritual spheres, it lingers far behind other nations:

> By our skill in Mechanism, it has come to pass, that in the management of external things we excel all other ages; while in whatever respects the pure moral nature, in true dignity of soul and character, we are perhaps inferior to most civilised ages.[40]

A return to the enlightened concept of moral sense, benevolence and sympathy is Carlyle's answer to Britain's current predicament, and by extension a sympathetic appreciation of France, including a recognition that the French Revolutionary moment had been a struggle for the fundamental dignity of every human being:

> France was the scene of their fiercest explosion; but the final issue was not unfolded in that country: nay, it is not yet anywhere unfolded. Political freedom is hitherto the object of these efforts; but they will not and cannot stop there. It is towards a higher freedom than mere freedom from oppression by his fellow-mortal, that man dimly aims.[41]

The solemn language introduced here in reference to France signals that Carlyle is beginning to work towards an epic depiction of the French Revolution, a project closely aligned, we should note, with his understanding of the Covenanter movement and the history of Scots Presbyterianism. Indeed, Carlyle criticised the failure of Scottish Whigs to construct an affirmative interpretation of the Covenanting past. Instead, Scottish Whigs embraced a heavily anglicised interpretation of their own history, which saw Scotland's Presbyterian past as a saga of bigotry, superstition and backwardness. Colin Kidd has persuasively argued that 'only among the Seceders did a full-blown Whig-Presbyterian historiography survive';[42] and it is telling that Carlyle, who came from a Seceding background, perceived that prevailing Whig norms allowed no place for an imaginative celebration of Calvinism and Scotland's Reformed legacy. When in his *Reminiscences* (1881) Carlyle bitterly criticised Francis Jeffrey's 'dead Edinburgh Whiggism, Scepticism, and Materialism',[43] arguably he was not only registering Jeffrey's rejection of the spiritual, but also referring specifically to their disagreement over Scotland's Presbyterian legacy. Indeed, he described Jeffrey as the 'man whom they have kneaded into the shape of an *Edinburgh Reviewer*, and clothed the soul of in Whig formulas'.[44] In total, Jeffrey wins only thirty-three pages in Carlyle's *Reminiscences* – compared to the hundred and thirty-four pages dedicated to Edward Irving, a Presbyterian clergyman and author of *Signs of the Times* (to which Carlyle's own 'Signs of the Times' is indebted).[45] Irving stands out as a heroic figure for Carlyle not only because of his Presbyterianism, which establishes him imaginatively in the tradition of the 'venerable . . . Old Seceder Clergy',[46] but also because of his early radical ideas and sympathetic association with the Glasgow Radical Weavers.[47]

The title of Irving's portentous sermon, which Carlyle borrowed, alludes to Matthew 16: 3: 'O ye hypocrites, ye can discern the face of the sky; but can ye not discern the signs of the times?' For both Irving and Carlyle, hypocrisy – mediated too in the case of Carlyle via Burns's Holy Willie's Prayer – looms large: Britain should direct its eyes at its own moral and spiritual problems before looking to criticise France. Moreover, Carlyle also imbibes Irving's emphatic message that the deplorable condition of the poor in Britain and Europe is a sign of moral and spiritual imbalance which cries for heaven's revenge. According to Irving, the French Revolution was an expression of divine judgement upon France for its treatment of the poor; and a similar fate awaited Britain if it continue to disregard the poor.[48]

Carlyle's friendship with another early philosophical radical, John Stuart Mill, led him to abandon a projected new ecclesiastical history of Scotland. In 1833 Mill had started a series of weekly articles in the *Examiner* attacking the Whig government. In response, in a letter to Mill written in 1833, Carlyle traced his critique of the major political and intellectual trends in a distinctly Presbyterian language:

> I recognised your criticism of the poor Whig Ministry almost at the second sentence. . . . Unbelieving mediocrity, barren, dead and death-giving, speaks itself forth more and more in all they do and dream. The true Atheist in these days is the Whig; he worships and can worship nothing but Respectability; and this he *knows*, unhappy man, to be – nothing but a two-wheeled vehicle! The Tory is an Idolater; the Radical a wild heathen Iconoclast: yet neither of them strictly are 'without God in the world': the one has an *infinite* hope, the other an infinite remembrance; both *may* be men and not gigmen.[49]

The political map that Carlyle draws here employs an unmistakably Presbyterian imagery: by presenting the radicals as dangerous iconoclasts, he aligns them closely with the figures of the leaders of Scottish and European Reformation, Luther, Calvin and John Knox. In his masterpiece Carlyle presents Knox as a Romantic hero, a radical iconoclast and a destroyer of the false depictions of the deity – as well as a symbolic Scottish patron of all sans-culottes:

> Scottish John Knox, such World-Hero, as we know, sat once nevertheless pulling grim-taciturn at the oar of French Galley, 'in the Water of Lore;' and even flung their Virgin-Mary over, instead of kissing her, – as 'a pented bredd,' or timber Virgin, who could naturally swim. So, ye of Château-Vieux, tug patiently, not without hope![50]

The sympathetic association of the French Revolutionaries with the Scottish Reformation leads to the portrayal of the sans-culottes as the true heroes of Carlyle's history, justified in their destruction of a political system which had lost sight of them.

Assessing Carlyle's agenda which looked to mediate between Scottish Presbyterianism, British radicalism and Whig principles,

Mill generously recognised in Carlyle a Romantic purveyor of human nature via a sympathetic mirroring of feelings:

> A deep catholic sympathy with human nature, with all natural human feelings, looks out from every page of these volumes; justice administered in love, to all kind of human beings, bad and good; the most earnest exalted feeling of moral distinctions, with the most generous allowances for whatever partial confounding of these distinctions, either natural weakness or perverse circumstances can excuse strength, no goodness or lovingness, passes unrecognized or unhonoured by him.[51]

Yet Mill, too, was aware that the philosophical concept of benevolence as defined by Hutcheson had become since the 1790s a suspect category, not least because of its associations with religious enthusiasm and political radicalism; and so he advises his readers to ignore Carlyle's political opinions and focus on the poetic qualities of his sympathetic language.

Carlyle's sympathetic portrayal of the masses in the *French Revolution* derives from his radical reappraisal of an Enlightenment legacy. The tradition of eighteenth-century Scottish moral enquiry underpinned his conception of sympathy and his larger cosmopolitan vision of what Britain shared with Europe. Yet Carlyle drew on the Scottish Enlightenment at a time when its legacy was deeply suspect; which serves to bring into sharper focus Carlyle's standing as a serious post-Enlightenment critic of progressive utilitarian nostrums.

## Notes

1. B. W. Young, *The Victorian Eighteenth Century: An Intellectual History* (Oxford, 2007), pp. 22, 26.
2. Francis O'Gorman and Katherine Turner (eds), *The Victorians and the Eighteenth Century: Reassessing the Tradition* (Aldershot, 2004), p. 2. For a discussion of the continuities between eighteenth and nineteenth centuries, see Murray Pittock, 'Enlightenment, Romanticism and the Scottish Canon: Cosmopolites or Narrow Nationalists?', in Gerard Carruthers and Liam McIlvanney (eds), *Cambridge Companion to Scottish Literature* (Cambridge, 2010), pp. 86–102. More recently critics such as

Ralph Jessop, *Carlyle and Scottish Thought* (London, 1997) and Jessop, 'Resisting a Dangerous Legacy of the Enlightenment: Carlyle, Hamilton, and James on the Mechanization of the Human Condition', *History of European Ideas* 39 (2012), 631–49, have further explored the Scottish Enlightenment roots of Carlyle's writing by convincingly arguing for the continuation of some of the main Enlightenment philosophical discussions in Carlyle's thought; whereas Alexander Jordan, 'David Hume Is Pontiff of the World: Thomas Carlyle on Epicureanism, Laissez-Faire, and Public Opinion', *Journal of British Studies* 56 (2017), 557–79, has also pointed out that Carlyle's early fascination with Hume gave way later to a more conventional nineteenth-century appraisal of his legacy.

3. Compare Froude quoting Christ's words from the Gospel of Matthew 5: 17 in reference to Carlyle: 'He had not come (so far as he knew his own purpose) to destroy the law and the prophets, but to fulfil them, to expand the conception of religion with something wider, grander, and more glorious than the wildest enthusiasm had imagined.' James Anthony Froude, *Thomas Carlyle: A History of the First Forty Years of His Life, 1795–1835* (2 vols, London, 1891) II, p. 4.
4. James Anthony Froude, *Life of Carlyle*, ed. John Clubbe (Columbus, OH, 1979), p. 76.
5. Froude, *Life of Carlyle*, p. 331.
6. James Anthony Froude, 'History: Its Use and Meaning', *Westminster Review* 62 (1854), 420–48, at p. 420.
7. Froude, 'History: Its Use and Meaning', 444.
8. Thomas Babington Macaulay, 'Milton', *Critical and Historical Essays contributed to the Edinburgh Review* (5th edn, 3 vols, London, 1848), I, pp. 1–62.
9. Thomas Carlyle, *Critical and Miscellaneous Essays* (2 vols, London, 1888), II, pp. 14–15.
10. Jon Mee, *Romanticism, Enthusiasm, and Regulation: Poetics and the Policing of Culture in the Romantic Period* (Oxford, 2005), p. 7.
11. Mee, *Romanticism*, p. 6.
12. Carlyle, *Critical and Miscellaneous Essays*, pp. 24, 42.
13. Carlyle, *Critical and Miscellaneous Essays*, p. 12.
14. Robert M. Maniquis, 'Filling up and Emptying Out the Sublime Terror in British Radical Culture', *Huntington Library Quarterly* 63 (2000), 369–405, at p. 404.
15. For an examination of Carlyle's use of Gothic in *The French Revolution*, see Mary Desaulniers, *Carlyle and the Economics of Terror: A Study of Revisionary Gothicism* (Montreal, 1995).
16. Carlyle, *Critical and Miscellaneous Essays*, I, p. 212.
17. Carlyle, *Critical and Miscellaneous Essays*, I, p. 212.
18. Carlyle, *Critical and Miscellaneous Essays*, I, p. 212.
19. For a discussion of *Sartor Resartus* as a Calvinist conversion narrative see,

Ian Duncan, *Scott's Shadow: The Novel in Romantic Edinburgh* (Princeton, 2016), p. 308.
20. Carlyle, *Critical and Miscellaneous Essays*, II, p. 100.
21. Compare Francis Jeffrey's dismissal of Carlyle's metaphysics as 'mystical jargon', *Letters of Francis Jeffrey to Thomas and Jane Welsh Carlyle*, ed. William Christie (London, 2008), p. 21.
22. Sorensen, 'Macaulay', in Mark Cumming (ed.), *Carlyle Encyclopedia* (Madison, 2004), p. 300.
23. Thomas Carlyle to John A. Carlyle, 20 December 1851, *The Collected Letters of Thomas and Jane Welsh Carlyle*, ed. Charles Richard Sanders et al. (42 vols, Durham, NC, 1970–), XXVI, pp. 273–5.
24. Carlyle, *Critical and Miscellaneous Essays*, II, p. 98.
25. Francis Jeffrey, 'A History of the early Part of the Reign of James the Second', *Edinburgh Review* 12 (July 1808), 271–306, at p. 285.
26. Francis Jeffrey, 'Mémoires de Bailly', *Edinburgh Review* 6 (April 1805), 137–61, at p. 142.
27. Most notably in Macaulay's 'Milton'.
28. 'Utility', according to Carlyle, was a concept employed by 'Editors of Whig newspapers'. See: Thomas Carlyle to John A. Carlyle, 10 August 1824, *The Collected Letters of Thomas and Jane Welsh Carlyle*, III, pp. 120–4.
29. Carlyle, *Critical and Miscellaneous Essays*, II, p. 100.
30. Jonathan Swift, *Works*, ed. John Nichols (19 vols, London, 1801), II, p. 254.
31. Carlyle, *Critical and Miscellaneous Essays*, II, p. 99.
32. Carlyle, *Critical and Miscellaneous Essays*, II, p. 103.
33. Cf. Mee, *Romanticism*, p. 45.
34. Carlyle, *Critical and Miscellaneous Essays*, II, p. 113.
35. Carlyle, *Critical and Miscellaneous Essays*, II, p. 112.
36. Carlyle, *Critical and Miscellaneous Essays*, II, pp. 107–8.
37. Carlyle, *Critical and Miscellaneous Essays*, II, p. 172.
38. Carlyle, Critical and Miscellaneous Essays, II, p. 172.
39. Carlyle, *Critical and Miscellaneous Essays*, II, p. 172.
40. Carlyle, *Critical and Miscellaneous Essays*, II, p. 111.
41. Carlyle, *Critical and Miscellaneous Essays*, II, p. 117.
42. Colin Kidd, *Subverting Scotland's Past* (Cambridge, 1993), p. 200.
43. Thomas Carlyle, *Reminiscences*, ed. Ian Campbell, K. J. Fielding (Glasgow, 2009), p. 362.
44. Carlyle, *Reminiscences*, p. 342.
45. Carlyle admitted the debt to Irving's prophetic sermon in a letter to his brother: 'I have written to Irving, explaining his share in that "Signs of the Times," and saying all manner of mystic things.' See: Thomas Carlyle to John A. Carlyle, 19 March 1830, *The Collected Letters of Thomas and Jane Welsh Carlyle*, V, p. 81.

46. Carlyle, *Reminiscences*, p. 184.
47. Carlyle, *Reminiscences*, p. 219.
48. Irving's strong language and deep concern for the plight of the lower classes make him a likely prototype for another fictional revolutionary in Carlyle's *Sartor Resartus* (1833–4), Professor Teufelsdröckh who shares Irving's radical politics and Presbyterian imagination.
49. Thomas Carlyle to John Stuart Mill, 28 October 1833, *The Collected Letters of Thomas and Jane Welsh Carlyle*, VII, pp. 22–3.
50. Thomas Carlyle, *The French Revolution: A History*, ed. David R. Sorensen and Brent E. Kinser (Oxford, 2019), p. 310.
51. John Stuart Mill, 'Carlyle's *French Revolution*', in *Collected Works of John Stuart Mill*, ed. John M. Robson (33 vols, Toronto, 1963–91), XX, pp. 132–67, at p. 163.

# 12

# Covenanting and Enlightenment in Nineteenth-Century Reformed Presbyterian Political Theory

*Valerie Wallace*

The achievements and later sufferings of the seventeenth-century Covenanting movement were for two centuries or more a core element of Scottish national identity: a pre-Enlightenment phenomenon which retained relevance and a high profile in post-Enlightenment Scotland.[1] The movement emerged when Alexander Henderson and Archibald Johnston of Wariston drew up the National Covenant of 1638 in protest at Charles I's attempt to bring the Kirk into conformity with the Church of England. During the British civil wars of the 1640s, a further measure, the Solemn League and Covenant of 1643, served as an alliance between Scots Presbyterians and the Long Parliament. During the Interregnum and Restoration, the movement dwindled and fragmented, though the later Covenanters launched unsuccessful uprisings against Charles II and James VII and II, which led to further persecution by the Stuart regime.[2] Scholars have explored Covenanting political thought in considerable depth, unpacking the biblical precedents, ideas of social contract, popular sovereignty, and the right of resistance to tyrannicide which underpinned their public declarations.[3]

Covenanting survived into the eighteenth century. Those who claimed a Covenanting identity included not only the movement's formal successors, the United Societies – also known as the Cameronians, or, later, Reformed Presbyterians – but also the much larger denomination of Seceders, who broke away from the Kirk in 1733. Dissatisfied with the Revolution settlement of 1690, the Union of 1707 and agrarian change, the United Societies threw down dykes, engaged in smuggling and threatened to rebel alongside a group of Jacobites, equally disgruntled but for different reasons.[4] Covenanting was pushed further to the margins during the Enlightenment, as the Moderate literati within the Kirk sought to play down the militancy of Presbyterianism's violent past.[5] While the example of the Covenanters provided a measure of inspiration to Scottish and Irish radicals in the age of revolutions, as John Brims and Ian McBride have respectively argued, their uncompromising rigidity proved unconvincing for the polite mainstream of Presbyterian society.[6]

Nevertheless, Covenanting proved remarkably resilient. Active Covenanting remained politically relevant in nineteenth-century Ireland and the United States where, as Joseph Moore and others have shown, it infused political struggles against slavery – a campaign which Covenanters in Ireland and Scotland supported – and constitutional struggles to reform the American republic's secular foundations.[7] Nineteenth-century Canada likewise felt the Covenanters' influence, as did Vanuatu (known then by colonists as the New Hebrides) where Covenanter missionaries strived simultaneously to abolish the Pacific labour trade and establish a 'Christocracy' under Britain's flag.[8] In the nineteenth century Covenanting was a vibrant transatlantic – and global – phenomenon.[9]

In Scotland – a crucial node within this Covenanting network about which we know comparatively little – the 'anti-government men', as they were nicknamed by their critics, remained a potent force.[10] Like their brethren in Ireland and North America, Scottish Covenanters remained committed to the centuries-old Covenants. By the end of the eighteenth century, members of the church had come round to paying taxes to an uncovenanted, Erastian state, and to engaging with its civil and criminal courts, but they still refused to acknowledge that state's legitimacy. Nations fortunate to enjoy the light of revelation and the ordinance of civil government were under an obligation, it was argued, to frame their constitutions according to God's will. If not, then Covenanting theories justified civil disobedience towards such ungodly and defective regimes.[11]

The Covenanters' political ideology was riddled with ironies and, from our vantage point, inconsistencies. They testified against slavery – 'hostile to the rights of common humanity, contrary to moral justice, and at variance with the maxims of revealed religion'[12] – and supported near universal suffrage (though their position on women's voting rights was not explicit), yet they argued that Catholics were 'morally disqualified' from sitting in parliament or holding government office.[13] They approved of Chartism but as a means to achieve a *third* reformation following which only the faithful would be saved.[14] The Rev. Peter Macindoe (1794–1850), a chief apologist for the Covenanters, argued forcefully that electing rulers was 'a *duty* enforced by moral obligations',[15] yet – until 1863 – the church banned its members from exercising the vote which, following the Reform Act in 1832, many of them acquired for the first time.[16]

Victorian Covenanters seemed to observers to occupy a kind of time capsule. As Moore has argued, they 'displayed a remarkable continuity across time and space'.[17] As far as the Covenanters were concerned, the Covenants were 'binding not only on the original Covenanters but on their posterity, who were represented by them, until such time as the object for which they were formed has been accomplished'.[18] In 1834, a contributor to the *Scottish Advocate*, a Scottish Covenanter periodical, explicitly compared the modern Whigs with the 'Reformers' of the sixteenth and seventeenth centuries and found the former wanting. Though the Whigs had extended the franchise, reformed the national churches, reduced taxation and abolished monopolies, they had failed to abolish church patronage, institute a system of scriptural education, or base policy on biblical precepts. Some MPs were professed deists, while cabinet dinners were held on the sabbath. The seventeenth-century reformers on the other hand, who had in the Solemn League and Covenant pledged the 'extirpation of popery and prelacy', deserved to be honoured for their political piety.[19] Looking back in 1840 on the effects of Catholic emancipation – the alleged threatening advance of Catholicism at home and abroad – the Covenanters declared Britain's safety to lie 'in retiring back upon the principles of 1638'.[20] The habits of mind of the Covenanters, who engaged in a centuries-old ritual of publicly testifying against the state, through Covenant renewal and fasting, are, it might be argued, key to understanding their political ideology. In 1868, the Rev. Alexander Moore, a Covenanter missionary from Belfast to Geelong, Victoria, was described by one critic as 'a perfect Rip Van Winkle, who has slept for, not one, but two centuries, and has let the development of human thought pass over him in vain'.[21]

But were the nineteenth-century Covenanters really so unchanged? While in certain obvious ways they clung to the past, in other ways their thought was decidedly modern. A subculture with seventeenth-century roots, Covenanting was sustained by engagement with, and refutation of, Enlightenment thinking. Peter Macindoe's key treatise, *The Application of Scriptural Principles to Political Government* (1831), on which this chapter will largely focus, engaged with the leading thinkers of Enlightenment Scotland, England and beyond: Ferguson, Smith, Montesquieu, De Lolme, Blackstone, Stewart, Mackintosh, Paley and Bentham, to name a few. Perhaps surprisingly, several modern thinkers from the Enlightenment era are prominent in Macindoe's text, while early Covenanting theorists like Samuel Rutherford or Restoration polemicists like Alexander Shields do not appear at all.

According to Caroline Erskine, Restoration Covenanters like Shields wrote for a persecuted minority rather than for the broader commonwealth. The political theory of Restoration Covenanting was intellectually weak, wild and eccentric, Erskine contends – a 'closed system', a 'dead end' – which had little appeal in the eighteenth century beyond Covenanting circles.[22] In the early nineteenth century, the system was more open, as Macindoe consciously directed his treatise to the political community beyond the Covenanter church. Macindoe employed the language of 'enlightenment' in his text thirty-seven times, which did not then have its present associations; but in a further complication and to ensure his ideas obtained 'a fair hearing', he peppered his work with extracts from 'some of the most distinguished divines, moralists, and civilians' from the period.[23] Macindoe primarily emphasised the illumination of the 'better light of Revelation',[24] yet, ironically, did not entirely exclude what we now think of as the Enlightenment, though it played a secondary role in his thinking. No one, said Macindoe, is permitted to follow the feeble glimmering light of nature instead of the full blaze of revelation ... however copious his intellectual acquirements, and however well qualified to explore the interesting regions of natural science, with the lamp of genius, and the light of observation, he has no right to elevate his fallible judgement above the unerring Mind of the Deity, or to prefer the crude notions suggested by natural reason, to the certain truths developed in the oracles of inspiration.[25]

Macindoe disdained rationalism, but also utilised Enlightenment arguments from the spheres of political and economic thought on behalf of a strangely intolerant form of liberty.

Nineteenth-century Scottish Covenanters, now known as Reformed Presbyterians, were not a large body. The Reformed Presbyterian Church was most popular in the south-west and west-central regions and by the mid-nineteenth century had thirty-seven ordained clergymen in six presbyteries ministering to just under 7,000 communicants.[26] But the size of the RP church belies its influence. The 1838 report of the commissioners of religious instruction in Scotland suggests that there were undoubtedly more hearers in the church than there were official members. It recorded that a new RP congregation had been established in Dundee in 1831. While there were only fifty-two communicants, between 200 and 250 people attended the church on average (while about 7,000 attended the local Kirk). The congregation currently met in the hall of the masonic lodge, but a new place of worship with space for 650 people was in the process of being built. In Stirling, around 400 people were in the habit of attending the RP church of the Rev. William Stevenson. The congregation had been established in 1775 but its numbers had grown by about one third since 1832. The bulk of hearers came from the 'poor and working classes' and travelled to attend from as far away as Comrie, a distance of about twenty-five miles.[27] The Rev. William Symington, RP minister in Stranraer and then Glasgow, was also popular; people queued outside to hear him preach. Owing to 'increasing demands for seats in the Meeting House' in Glasgow, which in 1814 held 600 people, a new church with space for 1,100 people was built in Great Hamilton Street (now London Road).[28]

The church had its own theological seminary which Peter Macindoe began attending in 1814 after he graduated from the University of Glasgow with an MA. He studied there until 1817 under the Rev. John Macmillan. Students at the hall attended four or five sessions, each lasting seven weeks. A typical formal teaching day lasted for six hours: students were quizzed on the professor's lectures, read scripture in Greek and Hebrew and wrote a weekly essay.[29] Like his fellow RP minister in New York, the Rev. Alexander McLeod (1774–1833), Macindoe was well-educated and 'intellectually refined' and thus had broader appeal than some of his peers.[30] He emerged as one of the church's most articulate defenders. In 1819 he became RP minister of Chirnside – close to Ninewells House, the childhood home of David Hume – and later Kilmarnock. He edited two of the church's periodicals – the *Scottish Advocate* and the *Scottish Presbyterian* – and published several pamphlets in defence of the church's position.

Macindoe's major publication, *The Application of Scriptural Principles to Political Government Essential to the Piety, Virtue, Order, Freedom, and Prosperity of Christian States*, was published in Edinburgh in 1831 by Thomas Nelson and Peter Brown. Macindoe was writing the book in September 1831 just as the House of Commons was passing a second parliamentary reform bill and he finished it in November. Macindoe's timing suggests that he intended his treatise to be an intervention in the reform debate. As a religious minister, Macindoe saw himself as a political actor. All citizens, he wrote, 'are bound to remonstrate with their rulers on the evils they commit'. But religious ministers, as the 'guardians of divine truth, pure morality, and rational liberty', had a particular obligation.[31] Max Skjönsberg has recently called on historians of political thought to pay greater attention to political action – to parliamentarism, in particular.[32] But historians of political thought must pay attention to religious contexts and religious actions as well. Sermons, denominational magazines, church testimonies and ecclesiological treatises were political as well as religious texts; sacred Covenants and fasts – accompanied by printed declarations against the wrongs of the commonwealth – were political as well as spiritual rituals.[33] For Macindoe (and others) politics were intrinsically religious. Like many of his contemporaries Macindoe was intent on ensuring that parliament properly mirrored the nation, but parliamentary reform was not an end in itself.[34] His chief concern – and the concern of his many admirers – was strengthening the state's bond with the church and fostering morality as prescribed by the Bible.

Macindoe continued in the *Application* the Scottish Reformed tradition of 'intensive mining of the Old Testament'. Like the seventeenth-century Covenanters, Macindoe regarded the Bible – the *Application*'s key source – as 'the definitive sourcebook for Protestant politics'.[35] He drew inspiration too from his contemporary RP polemicists, particularly Alexander McLeod, as well as from the early leader of America's second great awakening, Timothy Dwight (1752–1817), a proponent of evangelical orthodoxy and the most frequently cited near contemporary in Macindoe's text. Like his seventeenth-century Covenanting forebears, Macindoe also relied on George Buchanan's seminal *De Jure Regni Apud Scotus* (1579). Macindoe sounded many of the same notes as his ancestors, dwelling in his book on favourite Covenanting themes: the moral foundations of civil government, popular sovereignty and the right of resistance to bad rulers. One can certainly discern traditional continuities in Macindoe's text.

Nevertheless, the content and structure of Macindoe's book were indebted not just to the Covenants, but to seventeenth-century theorists from the Whig canon – most notably, John Locke – and to late Enlightenment thinkers of a more progressive cast. He began his treatise with a chapter devoted to a prominent theme in enlightened thought – the importance of the diffusion of knowledge. Macindoe argued that all classes in society, even the lowest, had a right to access political information. Rebutting contemporaries who argued that the lower orders were too uneducated and mentally ill-equipped to merit the elective franchise, Macindoe declared that God had bestowed on every man the ability to understand politics: 'all men are born on an equal footing as to political rights . . . all have by nature the same original powers, intellectual, moral, and physical . . . the poor have minds as precious in the sight of God as those of which the rich can boast'.[36] Macindoe also remonstrated against the imposition of taxes on the press. If the free circulation of knowledge was restricted and the acquisition of knowledge discouraged, society risked regressing to 'those dark ages of stupid intolerance'. Macindoe berated rulers for not doing more in aid of the 'true enlightenment' of the people. It was their duty to remove all restrictions that 'fetter the powers of the mind'.[37]

The lower classes must be well-informed, Macindoe insisted, for they were integral to the political system. Categorically rejecting the 'dangerous dogma' of the divine right of kings, Macindoe, drawing on Buchanan, argued that government originated, under the Supreme Being, with 'mankind' (or, the 'people'), 'composing various ranks', who had an 'inalienable right to dictate the constitution, according to which they shall be governed'. As Mackintosh had convincingly demonstrated in *Vindiciae Gallicae* (1791) – a text which Macindoe lauded – the revolution of 1688–9 had cemented the right of the people to frame the government and bestow the Crown. The people had an inalienable right to elect their rulers.[38] Macindoe hinted that, like his brethren in the United States and his Cameronian ancestors, he preferred republican to monarchical rule – closer to his idea of the ideal popular government – pointing to the economical republican administration across the Atlantic.[39] But he dodged the question by stating that Britain was lucky enough to enjoy an *elective* monarchy.[40] Refuting Burke, who had maintained that 'the constitution of a country being once settled upon some compact, tacit or expressed, there is no power existing of force to alter it without the breach of the covenant', Macindoe, the Covenanter, unconscious of the irony, insisted that the people had the right also to amend and improve the constitution. Quoting Ferguson, who had proclaimed that 'men are destined to improve on their lot', Macindoe argued that 'laws made in darker times' should be accommodated 'to the altered circumstances of modern society'.[41]

Drawing on Mackintosh (as well as De Lolme and others), Macindoe argued that civil government should be divided between legislative, executive and judicial branches, providing the executive was cheap, had few prerogatives and was always subservient to the legislative branch. As Ferguson and Mackintosh had made clear, Macindoe wrote, the legislative branch was the supreme power in the state which collected the general will and to which people of every rank should have an active share. Historically, the monarchy and nobility had enjoyed too much political influence. The House of Commons, as Burke had argued, should express the feelings of the nation. It 'is the undoubted right of the community', Macindoe contended, 'to elect their representatives in the legislature'.[42]

How should this be achieved? Macindoe's views on representation may have been influenced once more by Mackintosh, who had argued that parliament should reflect the diversity of the nation's classes and interests. Similarly, Macindoe argued that the influence of property owners should be secured but that the interests of the labouring classes – who formed a significant proportion of RP congregations, according to the commissioners' report – should also be protected: 'Surely, if the legislature should represent all the elements of power in the kingdom, land, money, trade, learning, intelligence – is it just to exclude the physical strength, by which its wealth is created, its battles fought, and its honours upheld?' But Macindoe, unlike Mackintosh, was prepared to accept near universal suffrage – only excluding criminals, paupers and those he termed 'imbeciles'.[43] Seeking to counter arguments in favour of universal and uniform suffrage, Mackintosh had warned that the labouring classes were a 'perpetual majority'; if representation was 'proportioned to numbers alone', every other interest in society would be 'placed at the disposal of the multitude'.[44] Macindoe's view was different:

> we cannot but think, that population ought chiefly to regulate the number of representatives which any district delegates. Will any one argue, that five millions of active men – the working classes who have no other property than their labour – are of little value in the state? Will any one say, that their political rights deserve no protection, and their just wishes no deference?[45]

Macindoe seems to have been less fearful than Mackintosh of empowering the perpetual majority. Yet he too was apprehensive of unbridled democracy, though for different reasons. According to Macindoe, the sovereignty of the people was limited. The notion of popular sovereignty, Macindoe maintained, was 'often used to signify sovereignty uncontrolled by precepts of scriptural morality'. The 'modern notion' that 'any government which is approved by the majority of the inhabitants in a country is the moral institution of Heaven' was groundless. Public opinion was not infallible; it had to be amenable to divine revelation. The will of the people, another RP text stated, is 'bounded by moral limits, even in the exercise of the elective franchise. The absolutism of the few is not more to be dreaded, than the appalling despotism of the many.'[46] Macindoe, it could be said, here developed an idea first expressed in the Queensferry paper – a Cameronian document from 1680 – which had argued that government should be founded on the word of God rather than on 'a plurality of votes'.[47]

Macindoe insisted that, like public opinion, utility was a false standard – reducing moral questions in politics to calculations of expediency was unconscionable, in Macindoe's mind. The Bible was the true standard of political government. Nevertheless, Macindoe did not, like the authors of the Queensferry paper, aim at establishing a theocracy which executed biblical commands. Rather, he sought to reconcile the principle of utilitarianism with maxims from scripture. Indeed, he embraced Bentham's fundamental principle: 'We prefer', wrote Macindoe, 'the broad principle that the public good, or, in other words, the greatest possible happiness of the greatest possible number, is the legitimate object at which government should aim.' As Adam Smith had pointed out in the *Theory of Moral Sentiments*, noted Macindoe, historically princes had been arrogant and had ruled in their own interest. Thankfully, as Stewart's *Elements* had made clear, legislating had now been reduced to a science helping statesmen to understand how to govern wisely. On this Macindoe quoted directly from Bentham's *An Introduction to the Principles of Morals and Legislation*, volume I: 'the happiness of the individuals of whom a community is composed, that is, their pleasures and their security, is the end, and the sole end, which the legislator ought to have in view'. God, Macindoe maintained, had expressed the same view in Rom. 13: 4: 'He is the minister of God to thee for good.' The Deity, Macindoe insisted, willed 'the greatest possible happiness to his rational creatures'.[48]

When the government failed to achieve the ends for which it had been established, the people had the right to resist – in the first instance by petition and in the last by force and revolution. Indeed, it was the duty of the people to resist a government which had ceased adequately to perform the duties prescribed to it: 'when civil power degenerates into despotism', it was declared, 'it ceases to be the moral ordinance of God for good to man. The abuse of power, in certain cases, forfeits the use; and the people may justly plead exemption from allegiance to their sovereign when he daringly violates constitutional laws.'[49]

In stressing the right of the populace to resist, Macindoe sounded a familiar Covenanting refrain. James Stewart of Goodtrees had in *Jus Populi Vindicatum* (1669) argued that the populace – not just the 'inferior magistrates', or nobility, as Buchanan and Rutherford had argued – could resist even when their representatives in parliament chose not to. Members of parliament were merely trustees, and the people had the right to protect themselves when their MPs betrayed the commonwealth.[50] Macindoe, it might be said, echoed Stewart when he insisted that MPs were entitled to 'conscientious obedience' only when they governed with the consent and unbiased suffrages of the people. Otherwise, it was 'virtuous resistance' to throw back in their faces the 'legal fetters' that they had forged.[51]

Yet Macindoe did not cite Stewart or any Covenanting theorist when making his argument on the right of the populace to resist. Instead, he drew on Blackstone. The last auxiliary right which Englishmen possessed, Blackstone had declared, was the right to bear arms in their own defence. Legislation at the Revolution of 1688–9 had affirmed this right by underlining the 'natural right of resistance and self-preservation, when the sanctions of society and laws are found insufficient to restrain the violence of oppression'. Resistance was justified, Macindoe argued, when tyranny threatened liberty of conscience, discouraged the 'free circulation of knowledge', and dampened the 'ardour of scientific discovery, useful invention, and commercial enterprise'. It was also unconscionable to endorse rule that contravened the law of God. But when was force justified? Macindoe here drew on Locke, Robertson, Paley, Burke, Mackintosh and Thomas Brown to contend that this question was one of 'extreme delicacy'. Force could be justified only as a last resort – when tyranny was extreme, when gentler means had failed and when success – and thus little bloodshed – was likely. Even when government was executed immorally, the pious minority would testify against the regime in peace.[52] Macindoe was keen to disprove allegations that the RPs were disloyal to the Crown, and insisted on the peaceful and respectful nature of their protest against the government.[53] The Covenanters had evidently travelled far from the terrain of the mountain preachers of the 'killing time'. Was Macindoe really another 'Rip Van Winkle'? Hardly. His engagement in the *Application* with a range of enlightened thinkers demonstrates that Macindoe was wide awake.

When in 1826 the RP church launched its first periodical – the *Reformed Presbyterian Monitor* – an 'ill-natured student' scornfully 'dissected' the first issue in a Glasgow shop.[54] Another contemporary described the political values of the RP church as the 'most radical and revolutionary on earth'.[55] Clearly not everyone was a fan. Yet, when Macindoe's treatise appeared, it was generally well received by mainstream Presbyterianism. The *Presbyterian Review*, recently labelled 'one of the most important sources for Evangelical thought within the Church of Scotland before the Disruption',[56] described it as a 'valuable and seasonable treatise on a much neglected but most momentous subject';[57] while the *Edinburgh Christian Instructor*, another important evangelical organ initially edited by the Rev. Andrew Thomson, leader of the Evangelicals in the Kirk, called for its wide distribution.[58] The *Scottish Guardian* newspaper, meanwhile, which reflected middle-class Church of Scotland views, declared the RP church to be 'much better informed on the scriptural principles of governments and churches than the established Church'. The 'old true-blue Covenanters', it proclaimed, were 'once more taking the field – coming down from the hills where once they successfully fought the battle of religion and liberty, to our great manufacturing cities'.[59]

The RPs were certainly eccentric, yet, as the royal commission reported, they were becoming increasingly popular and increasingly respectable. Indeed, the late Georgian and early Victorian period was in many ways another Covenanting moment. In an age of rampant evangelicalism, many Scots became hugely attracted by the romanticised narrative of the seventeenth-century Covenanting past. Thousands of people attended the unveiling of monuments to the Cameronians of the so-called 'killing time'; this type of commemoration was now a 'multi-denominational and national activity'[60] when just over a century before the first monuments to the Cameronians had been the product and manifestation of fringe militancy.[61] The Enlightenment Kirk had done its best to detach itself from the Covenants, but they remained a significant influence in Scottish religious life. And now, many Evangelicals shared Macindoe's views on the moral foundation to civil government. Political discussion suffused religious debate; Scottish Presbyterians were keenly aware that parliamentary reform would have a direct bearing on slavery abolition, the reform of church patronage – a grievance which mobilised the Scottish Presbyterian population for around 150 years – and the future relationship between church and state. It was becoming increasingly difficult to distinguish Covenanting politics from those of the Presbyterian mainstream. When the bulk of the Reformed Presbyterian Church united with the Free Church in 1876, one member declared that in all important matters the principles of the two churches were identical.[62]

The Covenanters' resurgence, it might be said, demonstrates that the Enlightenment, to which, on the face of it, the RPs were seemingly impervious, had well and truly died. The popularity of the Covenanters might be regarded as a sort of bellwether, indicating the rise and fall of tolerant, enlightened thought. Yet, on closer inspection, it turns out that the thinking of the Covenanters, as expressed by their chief apologist, the Rev. Peter Macindoe, is indicative not of the Enlightenment's death but of its afterlife.

Indeed, in light of Thomas Ahnert's reassessment of the Scottish Enlightenment's moral culture, Macindoe's reliance on Enlightenment thinkers, which was not just strategic, is not so surprising after all. The Moderate literati at the Enlightenment's height, though they had rejected the need for doctrinal standards – a view which was anathema to Macindoe – still regarded scripture as a 'practical manual for regeneration' to aid in the reform of conduct. The literati had been, like Macindoe, sceptical about a natural religion of reason and believed that salvation was impossible and secular morality incomplete 'without some form of divinely revealed faith'. Macindoe drew on these ideas in his treatise. His contention that the Bible should constitute the moral standard of government was indebted to Dugald Stewart. As Stewart had shown, argued Macindoe, God had implanted in man a social principle and endowed him with moral sentiments; it was through political union that man cultivated his moral powers. Macindoe contended that God had prepared man for social union by providing a 'code of morals' in the Bible, the revealed law of God. The 'unrivalled superiority of the Christian morality', he pointed out, 'has been admitted even by some of the most determined infidels'.[63] There were, says Ahnert, continuities between the moral culture of Enlightenment Scotland and nineteenth-century views on the formation of character.[64] An analysis of Macindoe's treatise suggests that the Enlightenment's legacy continued to be felt in the evangelical age, even in the most unlikely of places.

## Notes

1. See, for example, Edward J. Cowan, 'The Covenanting Tradition in Scottish History', in Cowan and Richard J. Finlay (eds), *Scottish History: The Power of the Past* (Edinburgh, 2002), pp. 121–46; James J. Coleman, *Remembering the Past in Nineteenth-century Scotland* (Edinburgh, 2014).
2. Chris R. Langley (ed.), *The National Covenant in Scotland* (Woodbridge, 2020); 'Covenants and Covenanting', *Scottish Historical Review* 99, Supplement: no. 251 (2020).
3. See, for example, Hector Macpherson, 'The Political Ideals of the Covenanters, 1660–88', *Records of the Scottish Church History Society* 1 (1926), 224–32; Ian M. Smart, 'The Political Ideas of the Scottish Covenanters, 1638–88', *History of Political Thought* 1 (1980), 167–93; John Coffey, *Politics, Religion and the British Revolutions: The Mind of Samuel Rutherford* (Cambridge, 1997); Allan I. Macinnes, 'Covenanting ideology in seventeenth century Scotland', in Jane H. Ohlmeyer (ed.), *Political Thought in Seventeenth-Century Ireland: Kingdom or Colony* (Cambridge, 2000), pp. 191–220; John Coffey, 'George Buchanan and the Scottish Covenanters', in Caroline Erskine and Roger A. Mason (eds), *George Buchanan: Political Thought in Early Modern Britain and*

*Europe* (Farnham, 2012), pp. 189–203; Caroline Erskine, 'The Political Thought of the Restoration Covenanters', in Sharon Adams and Julian Goodare (eds), *Scotland in the Age of Two Revolutions* (Woodbridge, 2014), pp. 155–72; Neil McIntyre, 'Representation and Resistance in Restoration Scotland: The Political Thought of James Stewart of Goodtrees (1635–1713)', *Parliaments, Estates and Representation* 38 (2018), 161–74; Karie Schultz, 'Catholic Political Thought and Calvinist Ecclesiology in Samuel Rutherford's *Lex, Rex* (1644)', *Journal of British Studies* 61 (2022), 162–4.

4. Colin Kidd, 'Conditional Britons: The Scots Covenanting Tradition and the Eighteenth-century British State', *English Historical Review* 117 (2002), 1147–76; Valerie Wallace, 'Presbyterian Moral Economy: the Covenanting Tradition and Popular Protest in Lowland Scotland, 1707–c.1746', *Scottish Historical Review* 89 (2010), 54–72.
5. Colin Kidd, 'Constructing a civil religion: Scots Presbyterians and the eighteenth-century British state' in J. Kirk (ed.), *The Scottish Churches and the Union Parliament 1707–1999* (Edinburgh, 2001), pp. 1–21.
6. Ian R. McBride, *Scripture Politics: Ulster Presbyterians and Irish Radicalism in the Late Eighteenth Century* (Oxford, 1998); John Brims, 'The Covenanting Tradition and Scottish Radicalism in the 1790s', in Terry Brotherstone (ed.), *Covenant, Charter, and Party: Traditions of Revolt and Protest in Modern Scottish History* (Aberdeen, 1989), pp. 51–62.
7. Joseph S. Moore, *Founding Sins: How a Group of Antislavery Radicals Fought to Put Christ into the Constitution* (Oxford, 2015); Randolph A. Roth, 'The First Radical Abolitionists: The Reverend James Milligan and the Reformed Presbyterians of Vermont', *New England Quarterly* 55 (1982), 540–63; Daniel Ritchie, 'Radical Orthodoxy: Irish Covenanters and American Slavery, circa 1830–1865', *Church History* 82 (2013), 812–47.
8. Eldon Hay, *The Covenanters in Canada: Reformed Presbyterianism from 1820 to 2012* (Montreal/Kingston, 2012); Valerie Wallace, '"The Slave Trade in the New Hebrides": Covenanting Ideology, the New Hebrides Mission, and the Campaign Against the Pacific Island Labor Traffic', in W. H. Taylor and P. C. Messer (eds), *Faith and Slavery in the Presbyterian Diaspora* (Bethlehem, PA, 2016), pp. 231–50.
9. Joseph S. Moore and Jane G. V. McGaughey, 'The Covenanter sensibility across the long Atlantic world', *Journal of Transatlantic Studies* 11 (2013), 125–34.
10. On the Covenanters in this period see Matthew Hutchison, *The Reformed Presbyterian Church in Scotland: its Origin and History* (Paisley, 1893). On their defence against accusations of harbouring anti-government principles, see Peter Macindoe, *Vindication of the Reformed Presbyterian Church in Scotland, from the Various Charges Preffered Against Her on the Subject of Civil Government* (Edinburgh, 1830).

11. *Historical Part of the Testimony of the Reformed Presbyterian Church* (Glasgow, 1839), pp. 257–8.
12. 'The Immediate Abolition of Slavery in the Colonies of Britain', *Scottish Advocate*, issue 5 (1834).
13. William Symington, *Popery, the Mystery of Iniquity* (Glasgow, 1829); *Resolutions Adopted by the Synod of the Reformed Presbyterian Church in Scotland, met at Glasgow, April 22nd 1829, its First Meeting After the Bill, to admit Roman Catholics into Parliament, had passed in to a Law* (n.p., 1829).
14. 'On the Bearings of the Distinctive Principles of the Reformed Presbyterian Church, on the Present State and Prospects of Civil and Ecclesiastical Society', *Scottish Presbyterian*, May 1838.
15. Peter Macindoe, *The Application of Scriptural Principles to Political Government Essential to the Piety, Virtue, Order, Freedom, and Prosperity of Christian States* (Edinburgh, 1831), p. 329.
16. 'Report of Synod', *Scottish Advocate*, May 1834; 'On Elective Franchise', *Scottish Presbyterian*, January 1843. See also the Reformed Presbyterian Synod in Scotland, *Claims of the Divine Government Applied to the British Constitution and the Use of the Elective Franchise, vindicating the authority of Messiah against the encroachments of Antichristian power* (Edinburgh, 1843).
17. Joseph S. Moore, 'Covenanters and Antislavery in the Atlantic World', *Slavery & Abolition* 34 (2013), 539–61, at 540.
18. William Symington, 'The Nature and Obligation of Public Vows; With an Explanation and Defence of the British Covenants' in Ministers of the Reformed Presbyterian Church, Scotland, *Lectures on the Principles of the Second Reformation* (Glasgow, 1841).
19. 'The Reformers of the 16th and 17th centuries superior, in several respects, to the Reformers of the 19th', *Scottish Advocate*, August 1834.
20. 'Catholic Emancipation', *Scottish Presbyterian*, March 1840.
21. A. M. Moore, *"Shakesperian Readings," and Their Apologists: With Reply to the Rev. T. McKenzie Fraser's Attack on the Reformed Presbyterian Church* (Geelong, Victoria, 1868).
22. Erskine, 'Restoration Covenanters', pp. 165, 172. Neil McIntyre has recently contested Erskine's view in 'James Stewart of Goodtrees'.
23. Macindoe, *Application*, p. v.
24. Macindoe, *Application*, p. 84.
25. Macindoe, *Vindication*, p. 39.
26. *Cyclopedia of Religious Denominations: containing authentic accounts of the different creeds and systems prevailing throughout the world: written by members of the respective bodies* (London, 1853) pp. 151–8; Gordon J. Keddie, 'The Reformed Presbyterian Church of Scotland and the Disruption of 1863. I. Disruption and Recovery', *Scottish Bulletin of Evangelical Theology* 11 (1993).

27. *Sixth Report by the Commissioners of Religious Instruction, Scotland* (Edinburgh, 1838), pp. 115–17, 340.
28. Thomas Binnie, *Sketch of the History of the First Reformed Presbyterian Congregation: Now Great Hamilton Street Free Church* (Glasgow, 1888), pp. 92–5.
29. Andrew T. N. Muirhead, 'Reformed Presbyterian Divinity Hall (1802–1876)', *Dissenting Academies Online: Database and Encyclopedia*, Dr William's Centre for Dissenting Studies, November 2011.
30. Moore, *Founding Sins*, p. 66.
31. Macindoe, *Application*, pp. 371, 375.
32. Max Skjönsberg, 'The History of Political Thought and Parliamentary History in the Eighteenth and Nineteenth Centuries', *Historical Journal* 64 (2021), 501–13.
33. See, for example, *Act of the Reformed Synod for a Public Fast with a Summary of its Causes* (Glasgow, 1816).
34. On parliament as a mirror of the nation, see Gregory Conti, *Parliament the Mirror of the Nation: Representation, Deliberation, and Democracy in Victorian Britain* (Cambridge, 2019).
35. Coffey, 'Buchanan', p. 199.
36. Macindoe, *Application*, p. 11.
37. Macindoe, *Application*, pp. 12, 228.
38. Macindoe, *Application*, pp. 128, 130, 132–3, 139, 147.
39. Macindoe, *Application*, p. 209.
40. Elsewhere Macindoe denied that the RPs were secret republicans: Macindoe, *Vindication*, pp. 19–22.
41. Macindoe, *Application*, pp. 140, 142, 172.
42. Macindoe, *Application*, pp. 163, 165–7, 180, 183.
43. Macindoe, *Application*, pp. 182–3.
44. James Mackintosh, 'Universal Suffrage', *Edinburgh Review* 31 (1818), 186. On Mackintosh's views on parliamentary reform, see Conti, *Parliament*, pp. 18–23.
45. Macindoe, *Application*, pp. 182–3.
46. 'A Magistratical Catechism, on Christian Principles continued', *Scottish Presbyterian*, May 1836.
47. Macindoe, *Application*, pp. 153–6. For the Queensferry paper see Gordon Donaldson, *Scottish Historical Documents* (1970: Glasgow, 1999 edn), pp. 240–1.
48. Macindoe, *Application*, pp. 144–6, 165, 219.
49. 'Magistratical Catechism', *Scottish Presbyterian*, September 1836.
50. McIntyre, 'James Stewart of Goodtrees'; Smart, 'Political Ideas', 184.
51. Macindoe, *Application*, p. 181.
52. Macindoe, *Application*, pp. 35, 156, 383–92.
53. Macindoe, *Vindication*.
54. 'To correspondents', *Reformed Presbyterian Monitor*, April 1826.

55. *Statement of the Berwickshire Bible Society, read at its institution January 14th 1835* (Dunse, 1835); Peter Macindoe, *Defence of the Reformed Presbyterian Church from Attacks in 'Statement of the Berwickshire Bible Society'* (Edinburgh, 1835), pp. 6–7.
56. Daniel Ritchie, '"Justice Must Prevail": The *Presbyterian Review* and Scottish Views of Slavery, 1831–48', *Journal of Ecclesiastical History* 69 (2018), 557–84.
57. 'Critical Notice', *Presbyterian Review*, March 1832.
58. *Edinburgh Christian Instructor*, May 1832.
59. 'The Presbyterian Magazine and the Scottish Advocate 1832', *Scottish Guardian*, 11 December 1832; 'Editorial', *Scottish Guardian*, 26 December 1832. For the Kirk's admiration of the Covenanters, see also 'Critical Notices', *Presbyterian Review*, September 1831 and September 1836.
60. Alasdair Raffe, 'Who were the "Later Covenanters?"', in Langley (ed.), *National Covenant*, pp. 197–214, at p. 209. For Victorian commemoration of the Covenanting movement, see Coleman, *Remembering the Past*.
61. Valerie Wallace, 'Radical Objects: Covenanter Gravestones as Political Protest', *History Workshop Online*, April 2017 <https://www.historyworkshop.org.uk/radical-objects-covenanter-gravestones-as-political-protest/>.
62. Binnie, *Sketch*, p. 191.
63. Macindoe, *Application*, pp. 111–16.
64. Thomas Ahnert, *The Moral Culture of the Scottish Enlightenment, 1690–1805* (New Haven, CT, and London, 2014), pp. 13, 15–16.

# 13

# Andrew Lang and the Cosmopolitan Condition

*Catriona M. M. Macdonald*

> Now a quarrel with the world is always one-sided: the world is quite indifferent to all of us.
> 
> Andrew Lang, *Cosmopolis*, September 1896

Andrew Lang (1844–1912) said very little about the Scottish Enlightenment as such, but then again, few of his generation, writing long before W. R. Scott's invention of the term in 1900, considered the efflorescence of scholarship in Scotland in the eighteenth century as a single, coherent phenomenon. In his *Short History of Scotland* (1911) Lang acknowledged that, according to Voltaire, Scotland 'led the world in all studies, from metaphysics to gardening', and he elsewhere recognised the Moderate sceptics of these years as important challengers of stifling Presbyterian conventions.[1] But Lang, a man of 'jovial intelligence'[2] and 'sardonic and bantering manner'[3] – a 'droopy aristocrat'[4] – also emphasised Scotland's debt to intellectual influences from other countries and cultures, and traditions of sceptical humanism that predated the period of the Enlightenment.[5] His approach to the Enlightenment, as with much else, was ironic; his intellectual frame, cosmopolitan. Yet, this was a cosmopolitanism that was of its times – an age of popular journalism and mass literacy – and, while it bore some resemblance to David Hume's cosmopolitanism, it was not bound to a Whiggish narrative of progress or to an improving agenda.[6] It was, however, resolutely Scottish in origin and orientation – a 'rooted cosmopolitanism', in the words of Kwame Anthony Appiah – which, given Lang's multidisciplinary reach, productivity and ubiquity in journals with an international circulation, shaped European and transatlantic visions of the cosmopolitan condition at the *fin de siècle*.[7] This essay addresses Lang's ironic engagement with Scottish Enlightenment perspectives on history, scientific inquiry and literary 'tastes', and critically examines his contributions to cosmopolitan networks, his relentless evocation of cosmopolitan nostalgia, and his – Scotland-inflected – engagement with emergent 'world literatures'. From this, it will become clear that Scotland's contribution to modern globalised aesthetics at the turn of the twentieth century meant going well beyond the Enlightenment.

In his histories of Scotland, Andrew Lang demonstrated his indebtedness to Enlightenment authors and the limits of that legacy: they only appear fleetingly in his footnotes. Certainly, when it came to his treatment of the Stewarts, his approach to the Reformation, and his assessment of the Union of 1707, Lang followed in their wake, but (as in most things) he took their scepticism a step further, and was demonstrably influenced by the ways in which antiquarian research and the rise of the historical novel had, by the mid-nineteenth century, mediated approaches to Scotland's past.

Karen O'Brien has perceptively drawn attention to the ways in which various major Enlightenment historians – including Robertson and Hume – shared a cosmopolitan recognition that valid national histories and identities 'intersect with and complete each other'.[8] Their approaches demonstrate a 'detachment towards national prejudice ... and an intellectual investment in the idea of a common European civilisation.'[9] In these respects, and in their debts to irony and scepticism as essential features of an enlightened state of mind, Lang was their disciple.[10] More particularly, Lang benefited greatly from their pioneering research on Mary Queen of Scots, their critique of religious fanaticism and their literary narrative style. This can in part be demonstrated in his 1905 volume, *John Knox and the Reformation*, where Lang rejected Carlyle's 'platonically Puritan' assessment of Knox, and substituted insights from Lord Hailes and Hume.[11] For example, Lang quotes Hailes's criticism of Knox's account of the provincial council called by Mary of Guise in March 1559: '"exceedingly partial and erroneous ... no zeal can justify a man for misrepresenting an adversary'". Lang reflected: 'Bold language for a judge to use in 1769!'[12] Hume's critique of a 1560 letter from the Congregation to the Scottish Catholic clergy (addressed as 'the Generation of Anti-Christ, the Pestilent Prelates and their Shavelings') is also deployed (at least in a qualified sense). David Hume had remarked: 'With these outrageous symptoms commenced in Scotland that hypocrisy and fanaticism which long infested that kingdom, and which, though now mollified by the lenity of the civil power, is still ready to break out on all occasions.' Lang commented: 'Hume was wrong, there was no touch of hypocrisy in Knox; he believed as firmly in the "message" which he delivered as in the reality of the sensible universe.'[13]

Lang, an independent scholar and journalist, far less reliant on the largesse of Presbyterian patrons than most Scottish writers in the eighteenth century and more sympathetic to the Catholic cause, frequently went much further than his Enlightenment forebears in outbursts against Knox and the reformers. In January 1896 Lang referred to Knox as an 'uncommonly bad Christian'[14] and four months later noted: 'If the Reformers are now unpopular, it is because they were interested, blatant, wastefully mischievous (as all revolutionaries always are), fanatical, uncritical, and violently intolerant.'[15] Lang's late nineteenth-century audience was a public tutored on Scotland's past by novelists associated with the Kailyard school[16] and he was clearly not averse to adopting a deliberately unscholarly and unmeasured tone.[17]

That said, he also learned important narrative skills from historians like Robertson, modulated by the novelistic insights and expressive engagement with history offered by Walter Scott (whose Waverley novels he edited in 1893–4 as the Border edition, whose poems he edited and anthologised, in 1894 and 1910, whose biographer – John Gibson Lockhart – he biographied in 1896, and whose 'life' he wrote in 1906).[18] As O'Brien makes clear, Robertson wrote with 'stylish polish on an English model' and allowed himself (and thus his readers) 'bouts of retrospective affection for the occasionally virtuous nobility of the medieval and early modern periods'.[19] Even during the Enlightenment, a politically neutered nostalgia for the pre-Union past was permitted and proved useful in reinforcing the continued need for a historiography of a nation then boasting no seat of power (with the exception of the Kirk) within its borders. Sentiment and nostalgia also allowed a place for a more empathetic rendering of the life of Mary Stewart – the queen that would later beguile Lang. (Lang wrote many scholarly and journalistic articles on Mary, and two monographs: *The Mystery of Mary Stuart* (1901), and *The Portraits and Jewels of Mary Stuart* (1910).) Again, as O'Brien makes clear (and despite his status as Moderator of the General Assembly of the Church of Scotland) Robertson's authorial voice in his *History of Scotland* (1759) 'frequently aligns itself with Mary's perspective, and participates imaginatively in her suffering ... Robertson's Mary is passive, beautiful, the epitome of gentility, and always in tears.'[20] In ways such as this, Robertson showed it was possible 'to incorporate Jacobitism as a purely aesthetic attitude, redolent of an attractive but defeated nationalism, within a Whig and cosmopolitan sense of progress'.[21] Lang, again, would go further.

Lang did not share the largely unqualified support of Scottish Enlightenment historians for the Union of 1707. His position at times is equivocal. While, in a letter to Mrs Maxwell Scott in May 1896, he bemoaned 'that distressful Union of 1707', elsewhere he styled it as 'that complete union which nature herself seemed to desire', 'the least evil of the choices before them', and an expression of the 'subconscious commonsense of the country'.[22] In similar fashion, in one publication he referred to the 'assimilation' of Scotland to England, while in another, he referred to the 'very gradual harmonising of Scotland to England'.[23] Leaving such problematic nuance to one side, Lang's histories clearly accepted the historic logic of union without an attendant belief in the inevitability of progress or the adoption of Whiggish politics – neither of which he shared with his eighteenth-century forebears. Lang's cosmopolitanism was devoid of explicit political intent and did not consciously aspire to the improvement of his readers. Lang was an historian who questioned rather than endorsed philosophical presumptions regarding the inevitability of progress: in this he sought to take scientific principles to their natural conclusion.

Lang's paradoxical relationship with his eighteenth-century predecessors was rooted in his scepticism regarding their simultaneous insistence on evidence, empiricism and scientific method, and their reliance on conjecture. This was clearly evident in his observations regarding survivals (customs, traditions, behaviours, tales) from previous ages which disrupted the smooth sequencing of stadialist histories much beloved of Enlightenment historians such as Adam Smith and Dugald Stewart. It is also apparent in his criticisms of Hume's position on theism and miracles, which in turn were mediated by Scott's *Letters on Demonology and Witchcraft addressed to J.G. Lockhart* (1830) and his own pioneering interest in psychical research, folklore and anthropology.

Lang explained the similarity of folk tales around the world as primitive elements in the human psyche: 'residual elements in the psychology of the civilized'.[24] He was led to this reasoning by adopting a comparative approach to civilisations across the world – a truly cosmopolitan approach which rested on the acknowledgement of 'the underlying psychic unity of mankind'.[25] Explored in detail in *Myth, Ritual and Religion* (1887), this perspective had wide-ranging consequences across his writings. We even find traces of it in his approach to reviewing when, in 1887 he defended Rider Haggard against allegations of plagiarism by emphasising that 'all ideas are old'.[26]

Lang's comparative anthropological methods and his sympathies with psychical research (as an early member of the Society for Psychical Research and its chairman from 1911 to 1912), also led him to question Hume's suppositions regarding early man's incapacity to believe in a single creator god, and the nature of evidence held to be acceptable by the Scottish philosophes. In *The Making of Religion* (1898), Lang, by deploying his familiar comparative methodology (drawing on evidence from Australia and the Andaman Islands and elsewhere), clearly took aim at Hume's argument in *The Natural History of Religion* (1757) that monotheism grew out of polytheism, pointing as he did to a simple truth: that we do not know what early humans believed.[27] Lang also attacked Hume's conclusion in *Of Miracles* (1748): namely, that miracles were an ontological impossibility. In this regard, Lang characteristically called on wider European precedents and identified in Immanuel Kant a more scientific (and perhaps perversely more 'Scottish') Enlightenment approach. Kant at least had shown a genuine interest in the clairvoyance of Emanuel Swedenborg, and the 'physics of hallucination'.[28] In a passage on Kant's *Träume eines Geistersehers* (1766) that is as revealing of his own as of his subject's methodology, he identifies Kant's position on the supernatural as 'almost identical with that of Sir Walter Scott'.[29]

Lang, at once pursuing his scientific aspirations and following in the steps of Scott who used the supernatural to great effect in his novels, sought to expand the evidence base on which analyses of religion could be built, and showed himself receptive to the possibility of 'facts' and experimentation denounced as 'fraud and malobservation' by Enlightenment authors and contemporaries such as Lord Kelvin.[30] He was well aware of the irony in this approach, though also took mischievous pleasure in introducing perspectives against which conventional writers could muster little in the way of a response: in addition to evidence from psychical research, Lang even deployed facts derived from angling to critique the miracles of St Columba.[31]

As Julia Reid has shown, Lang's anthropological research infused his causeries in *Longman's Magazine*, where he articulated a literary populism.[32] For a time it must have seemed that Andrew Lang's opinions were everywhere: he also had regular review columns in the *Illustrated London News* [*ILN*] (at first tellingly entitled 'From a Scottish Workshop'), *Cosmopolis* and *Cosmopolitan*, and was a regular contributor to *Blackwood's*, *Chambers's* and the *Times Literary Supplement* (and many more titles besides). Just as Enlightenment authors had a clear vision of what constituted the highest forms of cultural achievement in a civilised society, and shaped the aesthetics of the eighteenth century to suit, so Lang – perhaps with much greater claim to the title when it came to the immediate dissemination and popular circulation of his views – was an arbiter of taste in the *fin de siècle* period. From this position as 'a dictator of letters', he drew on specific Enlightenment cultural aspirations – for example, Goethe's vision of a world literature – but rejected their instructional and educational intent.[33]

Lang's natural inclination towards cosmopolitan perspectives and comparative methodologies, his international status as a literary phenomenon, the circulation and translation of his various works, his awareness of and engagement with foreign (particularly French) writers and literature, and his resistance to jingoistic rhetoric, appear to mark him out as the perfect ambassador of Goethe's ambition that – in part through the evolution of widely circulating periodicals – nations 'shall grow aware of one another, understand each other, and even where they may not be able to love, may at least tolerate one another'.[34] Yet Lang's comparative methodology was always *so* acutely alert to the 'otherness' of foreign literary traditions (and open, as few Enlightenment figures were, to the insights of non-European cultures), and conversely, *so* deeply rooted in national (Scottish) and local perspectives that – even had he wished it (and he did not) – it would have militated against the cultural universalism which Kant's era of 'perpetual peace' demanded. In one respect, this is hardly surprising perhaps: as Iain McDaniel has shown, important Scottish Enlightenment figures such as Adam Ferguson and Lord Kames made strong claims about 'the permanence of national rivalship [sic] and antagonism'.[35] Lang's commitment to Romantic particularism, and his resistance to any political agenda made him at best an unreliable fellow traveller in pursuit of such enlightened goals of international entente, at worst (as some believed), an irresponsible dilettante implicated in the worst crass commercialism. This state of affairs is evident in successive editions of 'From a Scottish Workshop' in the *ILN* where Lang's antiquarianism, literary interests and psychical research merge with classical analogies, local colour, human interest and humour. There, for example, we learn that 'the Toltecs, I fancy, were a kind of fabulous race, like the Pechts in Scotland and the Cyclopes in Greece' (28 March 1896) and hear of the recent death of the coxswain of the Aberdeen lifeboat (30 May 1896).

The realisation of Adam Smith's dream of a free trading world facilitated modern cosmopolitanism. However, Lang's embrace of populism, and his uncompromising commitment to romance and to adventure stories – particularly the work of Stevenson and Rider Haggard (both correspondents and collaborators of his) – in an era of mass readerships, cut across the improving ethos that motivated other Enlightenment philosophes. Lang rejected hierarchies of taste and value that inferiorised popular culture. Rather, despite his polymathic expertise, his criticism of contemporary fiction was 'based on essentially non-literary, anti-intellectual criteria'.[36] With his strong aversion to theory, DeMoor emphasises how Lang 'stuck to an impressionistic criticism, guided by his own likes and dislikes'.[37] According to Lang, this taste for romance was linked to a primitive capacity for myth-making – a 'survival' that shattered artificial codes of discernment just as it evidenced the persistence of barbarism, coexisting alongside (or more controversially within) the 'civilised' state. Romance was but a conduit for primitive impulses, and Lang's defence of the genre clearly challenges ideas that cosmopolitanism is invariably an elite exercise or, indeed, an exercise striving for mutual self-betterment.[38] Lang abhorred 'a sermon travestied as a story', and in 1887 he made the plea: 'Do not let us cry that, because we are 'cultured', there shall be no Buffalo Bill.'[39]

Lang's aesthetic cosmopolitan sensibility engaged ironically and sceptically with the uniformities implied by British imperialism, on the one hand, and the cultural blindness of other more abstract idealistic universalisms, such as socialism. His exploration of cultural differences and similarities across civilisations was not subordinate to a vision of an essentialised whole; instead, humanity was in all things and in every age never more than the sum of its parts, to be understood by making connections. Far from a failing, differences between cultural traditions were viewed as the successful outcome of cosmopolitanism. As Calhoun has noted: 'Cosmopolitanism becomes richer and stronger if approached in terms of connections rather than (or in addition to) equivalence.'[40] But connections are always made from a particular perspective. Thus, as Turner has noted: while 'the ability to respect others requires a certain distance from one's own culture, namely an ironic distance ... Irony may only be possible once one has an emotional commitment to a place.'[41] Lang's tolerance, engagement with foreign cultures and his rootedness in Scottish identities identify him – in Turner's phrase – as a patriotic cosmopolitan.[42] His ability to inform and influence a far more extensive global cosmopolitan sensibility, however, relied on international networks and a modern commercial infrastructure which in turn influenced literary fashions.

The material conditions that facilitate cosmopolitan cultures are essential to understanding their operation, but they are not divorced from the individual.[43] Key to understanding this environment is an appreciation of transnational experiences that 'are structurally embedded but personally embodied'.[44] Lang's career illustrates this in a number of ways. His connection to the Longman publishing empire, for example, began with an Oxford friendship with F. W. Longman – the son of one of the partners – in 1870. Longman's published Lang's first book, and provided him with outlets for his reviewing, in *Fraser's Magazine* (edited from 1879 to 1881 by Principal Tulloch of Lang's first alma mater, the University of St Andrews) and later *Longman's Magazine*.[45] Lang also acted as a reader for Longman's, advising on which books the firm should publish.[46] Lang used his position, here and elsewhere, to promote the work of friends – many of them Scots – whose literary outputs he admired,[47] and also writers on Scottish topics (e.g. history) which rarely featured otherwise in the review columns.[48] Such was his reputation for log rolling and 'puffing' the work of friends, that it attracted the ire of many writers, among them, Marie Corelli. Her book, *The Silver Domino, or side whispers, social and literary* (1893) took issue with Lang's influence:

> His shrill piping utterance is even as the voice of Delphic oracles, pronouncing judgement on all men and all things. He is the Author's Own Patent Incubator. His artificial warmth hatches all sorts of small literary fledglings who might otherwise have perished in the shell.[49]

Corelli, born Mary Mackay, the illegitimate daughter of a Scottish journalist and songwriter, was ironically something of a cosmopolitan creation herself – a French-educated concert pianist turned journalist and popular novelist – but was not part of the Lang brood.[50] Her swipe at Lang – 'benighted Europe know thee not at all' – was intended to wound where it would hurt the most.[51]

As Stefano Evangelista has shown, Lang's contribution to the journals *Cosmopolis* and *Cosmopolitan* show his influence on literary cosmopolitanism both as an evocation of the 'politico-philosophical ideals of world citizenship inherited from the eighteenth century and filtered through Goethe's notion of world literature, and the fast developing new understanding of cosmopolitanism inflected by consumer culture'.[52] The magazines were very different in tone, reach and intent: *Cosmopolis* was a multilingual magazine published across five sites in Europe and New York, and promoted serious literary dialogue across cultures, while *Cosmopolitan* was an illustrated fashion-oriented publication for the mass market. Yet Lang's contributions to each would have been familiar to readers of his work in *Longman's* and the *ILN*. In the March 1896 issue of *Cosmopolis* Lang observed that 'the temples of Tadmor are in better preservation than the cathedral of St Andrews'.[53] In the May issue, his assessment of Irish author William Carleton leaned heavily on comparisons with Scott, Robert Burns and James Hogg; in September, he wondered whether pious Greeks of an earlier age 'look[ed] hopefully and gratefully to the crowd of minor deities, Lares, Nereids, the local Demeter, the local Dionysus, as the Catholic looked hopefully and gratefully to St Boswell or St Bride of Douglas'.[54] Counter to its splengairy reputation, Lang's contributions to *Cosmopolitan* could also be rather douce: he recorded Edward Caird's move from the Chair of Moral Philosophy at Glasgow (the Chair once occupied by Adam Smith and Thomas Reid) to be Master at Balliol in February 1894, and Saintsbury's occupation of the Edinburgh Chair in Rhetoric and English Literature (held first by Hugh Blair in 1760) in January 1896, not to mention the discovery of Stuart papers in a 'queer repository of rubbish at Dundee' in February 1896.[55]

Certainly, in the first edition of *Cosmopolis* Lang praised its avant-garde rival, the *Yellow Book*, but the first pages of *Cosmopolis* were given over to the serialisation of Stevenson's last novel, *Weir of Hermiston*: Lang was in familiar company. While reluctant to review Stevenson's work in the pages of the same magazine in which it appeared, Lang's reflections on the novel – incomplete on Stevenson's death – in the July 1896 issue of the magazine were modestly critical: he suggested Stevenson would have executed revisions to the draft had he lived longer.[56] It was in *Longman's* that he defended the work against critics who had condemned Scotticisms in the text and allegations that Scottish reviewers were invariably partial to Scottish writers. Tellingly, Lang returned to the Edinburgh of the late Enlightenment to take issue with one reviewer:

> He *must* have heard of Jeffrey's reviews of 'a poetic child' named Scott. Was Jeffrey – then 'the first of British critics' – 'partial, indulgent, and boastful' as regards Sir Walter? Nonsense! In fact no man is a prophet in his own country, a Scot least of all. San Francisco, not Edinburgh, has a memorial of Mr Stevenson.[57]

One had to read across the products of many international presses to appreciate Lang's opinions: he was not simply the carrier of one editorial vision.

Lang revealed in his sceptical attitude to the Scottish reformers and his receptiveness to psychical research a tolerance towards, indeed an embrace of, ideas that challenged cultural and intellectual norms. His historical insights also demonstrated that his cosmopolitanism involved an element of travel through time – a temporal cosmopolitanism – which demanded an appreciation of the classics and 'survivals' from less 'civilised' eras, while remaining cognisant of contemporary literary trends and commercial fashions. As William Donaldson has pointed out, tradition for Lang was 'a purifying and refining medium', quite different from the heirs of the Enlightenment who at times appeared in thrall to novelty.[58] Tolerance, however, did not invariably (or perhaps even regularly) result in empathy, and could run counter to modernist and modernising trends now often strongly associated with cosmopolitanism. Rather, Lang's cosmopolitanism most frequently resolved itself in nostalgia and a longing for eras less buffeted by change.

Lang was critical of the new journalism that was heralding the end of the influence of the journals which he commanded.[59] Lang, as Corelli also suggested, was less likely to cheer female writers than men, even when they were Scottish: sarcastically, she commented:

> We hate scribblers in petticoats, don't we, good Andrew? Yea verily! We loathe their verses, we abominate their novels; we

would kick them if we dared. We do kick them, metaphorically, whenever we can, in whatever journals we command; but that is not half as much as we would like to do.[60]

Lang was no fan of the 'New Woman'.

Lang also, in thrall to romance, was seen as being out of sympathy with realism – the school in which most new (and most respected) authors were being educated. Dostoevsky, Thomas Hardy, Henry James, Tolstoy, Zola: each came in for criticism. The Russians in particular provoked his languid dismay: 'Why should I quarrel with another gentleman because he likes to sadden himself o'er with the pale cast of Dostoieffsky [sic], or to linger long hours with Mr Tolstoi [sic] in the shade?'[61] Lang himself denied that he was averse to realism as a genre: 'What is good, what is permanent, may be found in fiction of every *genre*.'[62] Still, if the measure of a convincing reviewer is to anticipate taste and cultural values and celebrate contemporary literary craft, and one mark of a cosmopolitan is tolerance, one must concede that in some respects Lang's personal taste could at times overwhelm his professional and philosophical positions (although one suspects that much was at times simply the default position of a well-known contrarian).

Lang's comparative methodology, evident across many disciplines, and his position as a Scot in London, sceptical of the British imperial project (although a fan of Rudyard Kipling), had consequences for how Scottish culture contributed to the cosmopolitanism of the *fin de siècle*. We see this in his poetry, and it is particularly striking in relation to poetic form. As Lauren Goodlad has noted: 'form . . . [is] a medium through which transnational processes are encountered, figured and, to some degree, shaped'.[63]

Lang, alongside Austin Dobson, Edmund Gosse, William Ernest Henley and George Saintsbury, experimented with traditional French verse forms and, as a group, they came to be known as the English Parnassians.[64] Marion Thain has shown how, in the hands of the Parnassians the stanza structures of the ballade, rondeau, rondel, triolet, villanelle and chant royal came to be exquisitely crafted carriers of transnational aesthetics.[65] What was carried, however, is not always obvious. Thain rightly identifies a tension between the French ballade and English ballad traditions, and acknowledges an internal fault line in Britain between Scottish and English ballads. But she strangely identifies Lang with English traditions, alighting on 'Ballade to Theocritus in Winter' and 'Ballade of Cleopatra's Needle' – two poems by Lang set in London – to illustrate her point that the volume in which they appear (*Ballades in Blue China*, 1880) has a 'dual locus' – 'contemporary *England* and ancient France'.[66] Rather, a more comprehensive approach to Lang's oeuvre suggests otherwise. 'Ballade of the Tweed' and 'Ballade of the Royal Game of Golf (East Fifeshire)' both appear in *Blue China*, and in the four volumes of his *Poetical Works* (1923), published posthumously, one encounters 'Ballade of his own Country' as well as many other poems on Scottish themes.[67] Rather, the ballade was a form through which Scottish themes (as well as others) could be mediated without recourse to an intermediary Britishness, imperialism or any other national identity for that matter. The exercise was sublimely an artistic one, and – while demonstrating the interaction of national literary form (French) and content (say, Scottish) – could also refract nationhood a step further, to the local, to the personal, to dialect. It is a characteristic of Lang's work, confirmed by considering *Poet's Country* (1907) – a collection edited by Lang of poems by and reflections on a wide range of poets, in the context of the regions that inspired them.[68] As Appiah has noted: 'Nations, if they aren't universal enough for the universalist, certainly aren't local enough for the localist', but equally localism can be 'an instrument to achieve universal ideals, universal goals'.[69]

Lang's defence of a range of Kailyard authors (most of whom wrote romances and adventures) ought to be seen in this light. S. R. Crockett was repeatedly praised by Lang in *Cosmopolitan*,[70] and Ian Maclaren, J. M. Barrie and Neil Munro all benefited from Lang's support.[71] Lang's defence, however, spoke to more than clannishness: it reinforced cosmopolitan tolerance. For example, Lang responded angrily to the review of S. R. Crockett's *Cleg Kelly, Arab of the City* (1896) in the *Saturday Review* which deemed the works of Crockett (and Maclaren) merely the books of choice for Sunday afternoons among those who supported 'a pathetic revolt of humanity against seriousness'.[72] 'Are we not in danger of a kind of literary Calvinism?' Lang asked in the *ILN*, echoing suspicions seen elsewhere in his histories.

> This doctrine appeared to me very alarming. Only a little flock, it is plain, has 'got culture,' while the many thousand readers of Mr Crockett must perish in their sins, I myself going the darkling way with them. May we not put in a word for a genial universalism?[73]

Similarly, defending Fiona MacLeod and Neil Munro from a critical review in *The Speaker*,[74] Lang hit back at the 'styleful youth of today' who, 'with their tormented manner and their bleak little pessimisms, have no more humour than a Scotch cart-horse'.[75]

Reading across the academic disciplines to which he contributed and the journalistic endeavours in which he proved a leading voice, it is clear that Lang went well beyond the Enlightenment. It would be strange had it been otherwise. The ways in which he both defended and attacked the insights of that earlier age, however, are – as evidenced here – worthy of comment, not least as they identify the *new* spaces in a *new* academic and literary environment mediated by *new* modes of communication in which Scottish voices were heard and proved themselves alive to *new* priorities and *new* readerships. Lang's cosmopolitanism leads us to conclude that one needs to look again at conventions which style the nineteenth century a lost literary age for Scotland, and London Scots as somehow divorced from Scotland or, worse still, invariably inimical to the nation's global influence.[76] It also suggests that Scottishness was constitutive of cosmopolitan tastes that brokered literary production and reception in international contexts: Scottish history, Scottish criticism and the Kailyard, far from being behind or at odds with cosmopolitanism were constitutive of how it developed in a Western capitalist context at the end of the nineteenth century. Indeed, it leads one to wonder whether Corelli may have been on to something when she suggested that, at least for a time, Lang's influence on English critical practice came close to a system of 'Scottish censorship' executed from Mayfair.[77]

# Notes

1. Andrew Lang, *A Short History of Scotland* (New York, 1912), p. 323; 'Introduction', in J. Vyrnwy Morgan, *A Study in Nationality* (London, 1911), p. xix.
2. Nathan K. Hensley, 'Andrew Lang and the Distributed Agencies of Literary Production', *Victorian Periodicals Review* 48 (2015), 359–82, at p. 361.
3. William Donaldson, 'Andrew Lang: a world we have lost', *Studies in Scottish Literature* 43 (2017), 155–65, at p. 165.
4. John Gross, *The Rise and Fall of the Man of Letters: aspects of English literary life since 1800* (London, 1969), p. 134.
5. Lang, 'Introduction', p. xx. In particular, Lang records his admiration for the French Renaissance philosopher Michel de Montaigne (1533–92), who had been educated by George Buchanan (1506–82), the Scottish humanist scholar and historian, at the College of Guienne. See Lang, *Lost Leaders* (London, 1889), pp. 38–44.
6. See Hannah Spahn, 'Character and Cosmopolitanism in the Scottish-American Enlightenment', in Thomas Ahnert and Susann Manning (eds), *Character, Self, and Sociability in the Scottish Enlightenment* (New York, 2011), pp. 207–24, at p. 212.
7. Kwame Anthony Appiah, *The Ethics of Identity* (Princeton, 2005), ch. 6.
8. Karen O'Brien, *Narratives of Enlightenment: cosmopolitan history from Voltaire to Gibbon* (Cambridge, 1997), pp. 1–2.
9. O'Brien, *Narratives*, p. 2.
10. O'Brien, *Narratives*, pp. 7, 10.
11. Andrew Lang, *John Knox and the Reformation* (London, 1905), p. ix.
12. Lang, *Knox*, p. 100.
13. Lang, *Knox*, p. 116.
14. Andrew Lang, 'Literary Chronicle', *Cosmopolis*, January 1896.
15. Andrew Lang, 'Literary Chronicle', *Cosmopolis*, May 1896.
16. See Andrew Nash, *Kailyard and Scottish Literature* (Amsterdam, 2007).
17. Catriona M. M. Macdonald, 'Andrew Lang and Scottish Historiography: taking on tradition', *Scottish Historical Review* 94 (2015), 207–36.
18. See Mark Phillips, 'Macaulay, Scott and the Literary Challenge to Historiography', *Journal of the History of Ideas* 50 (1989), 117–33.
19. O'Brien, *Narratives*, pp. 97, 110.
20. O'Brien, *Narratives*, pp. 115–16. Hume is less forgiving when it comes to the unfortunate queen.
21. O'Brien, *Narratives*, p. 121.
22. National Library of Scotland, MS.1633, Andrew Lang to Mrs Maxwell Scott, 9 July 1909?; Andrew Lang, 'Scotland: III. Political History' in *Encyclopaedia Britannica* (Cambridge, 1911) xxiv. 429–57, at p. 429; Andrew Lang, 'A Romantic Plot Against the Union I', in P. Hume

Brown (ed.), *The Union of 1707: a survey of events by various writers* (Glasgow, 1907), pp. 75–83, at pp. 75–6.
23. Lang, *Short History*, p. 322; Lang, *A History of Scotland from the Roman Occupation* IV (London, 1907), p. 522.
24. Caroline Sumpter, 'Devulgarizing Dickens: Andrew Lang, Homer and the Rise of Psycho-Folklore', *English Literary History* 87 (2020), 733–59, at p. 375.
25. William Donaldson, 'Lang, Andrew (1844–1912), anthropologist, classicist, and historian', *ODNB* (2004), <https://www.oxforddnb.com/view/10.1093/ref:odnb/9780198614128.001.0001/odnb-9780198614128-e-34396>.
26. Andrew Lang, 'Literary Plagiarism', *The Contemporary Review*, 1 January 1887.
27. See Nathan Porath, 'The Hume/Tylor Genealogy and Andrew Lang: of miracles and marvels animism and materialism', *Anthropos* 111 (2016), 185–200.
28. Andrew Lang, *The Making of Religion* (London, 1898), pp. 28–31.
29. Lang, *The Making of Religion*, pp. 30–1.
30. Lang, *The Making of Religion*, p. 41.
31. Andrew Lang, *A History of Scotland from the Roman Occupation* I (London, 1900), p. 73. Lang was, famously, a keen fisherman: see Andrew Lang, *Angling Sketches* (London, 1891), and his edition of Izaak Walton's *Compleat Angler* (London, 1896).
32. Julia Reid, '"King Romance" in *Longman's Magazine*: Andrew Lang and Literary Populism', *Victorian Periodicals Review* 44 (2011), 354–76.
33. *Blackwood's*, October 1898.
34. As cited in Stefano Evangelista, *Literary Cosmopolitanism in the English Fin de Siecle* (Oxford, 2021), p. 193. Goethe particularly noted the contribution of the *Edinburgh Review* to this internationalisation of literature.
35. Iain McDaniel, 'Unsocial Sociability in the Scottish Enlightenment: Ferguson and Kames on War, Sociability and the Foundations of Patriotism', *History of European Ideas* 41 (2015), 662–82, at p. 681.
36. Oscar Maurer, 'Andrew Lang and *Longman's Magazine*, 1882–1905', *University of Texas Studies in English* 34 (1955), 152–78, at p. 168.
37. Marysa Demoor, 'Andrew Lang's "causeries" 1874–1912', *Victorian Periodicals Review* 21 (1988), 15–22, at p. 15.
38. Bryan S. Turner, 'Cosmopolitan Virtue, Globalization and Patriotism', *Theory, Culture and Society* 19 (2002), 45–63, at p. 61.
39. Andrew Lang, 'Literary Chronicle', *Cosmopolis*, January 1896; 'Realism and Romance', *Contemporary Review*, November 1887.
40. Craig Calhoun, 'Cosmopolitanism in the Modern Social Imaginary', *Daedalus* 137 (2008), 105–14 at, p. 113.
41. Turner, 'Cosmopolitan Virtue', 55.
42. Turner, 'Cosmopolitan Virtue', 59.

43. Calhoun, 'Cosmopolitanism in the Modern Social Imaginary', 100. See also Lauren M. E. Goodlad, 'Cosmopolitanism's Actually Existing Beyond: towards a Victorian geopolitical aesthetic', *Victorian Literature and Culture* 38 (2010), 399–411.
44. Goodlad, 'Cosmopolitanism's Actually Existing Beyond', 406.
45. Maurer, 'Andrew Lang and *Longman's Magazine*', 153.
46. Reid, '"King Romance"', p. 356.
47. Marysa Demoor, 'Andrew Lang's "Causeries" 1874–1912', *Victorian Periodicals Review* 21 (1988), 15–22; 'Andrew Lang's Letters to H. Rider Haggard: the record of a harmonious friendship', *Études Anglaises* 1 (1987), 313–22.
48. Reid, '"King Romance"', p. 356. For example, on Lang's recommendation, Stevenson's 'A Gossip on Romance' appeared in the first number of *Longman's Magazine*.
49. [Maria Corelli], *The Silver Domino: or side whispers, social and literary* (London, 1893), pp. 311–12
50. Katherine Mullin, 'Mackay, Mary [pseud. Marie Corelli] (1855–1924), novelist', *ODNB* (2004), <https://www.oxforddnb.com/view/10.1093/ref:odnb/9780198614128.001.0001/odnb-9780198614128-e-34742>.
51. [Corelli], *Silver Domino*, p. 322.
52. Evangelista, *Literary Cosmopolitanism*, ch. 4.
53. Andrew Lang, 'Literary Chronicle', *Cosmopolis*, March 1896.
54. Andrew Lang, 'Literary Chronicle, *Cosmopolis*, May 1896, September 1896.
55. Andrew Lang, 'The Month in England', *Cosmopolitan*, February 1894, January 1896, February 1896.
56. Andrew Lang, 'Literary Chronicle', *Cosmopolis*, January 1896. See also Gillian Hughes, 'Introduction', in Robert Louis Stevenson, *Weir of Hermiston* (Edinburgh, 2017), pp. xxvii–l.
57. Andrew Lang, 'From a Scottish Workshop', *Longman's Magazine*, 1 August 1896.
58. Donaldson, 'Andrew Lang: a world we have lost', p. 161.
59. Demoor, 'Andrew Lang's "Causeries"', p. 17.
60. [Corelli], *Silver Domino*, pp. 300–1,
61. Gross, *Rise and Fall*, p. 137; *The Contemporary Review*, November 1887.
62. *The Contemporary Review*, November 1887.
63. Goodlad, 'Cosmopolitanism's Actually Existing Beyond', 404.
64. Marysa Demoor, 'Andrew Lang's Letters to Edmund Gosse: the record of a fruitful collaboration as poets, critics and biographers', *Review of English Studies* 38 (1987), 492–509. The name was derived from the title of the French journal, *Le Parnasse contemporain*.
65. Marion Thain, 'Parnassian Cosmopolitanism: transnationalism and poetic form', *Victorian Poetry* 57 (2019), 463–87.
66. Thain, 'Parnassaian', 469–70, 472. [My italics.]

67. Mrs Lang (ed.), *The Poetical Works of Andrew Lang* (4 vols, London, 1923). Elsewhere Lang noted the power of the Tweed: 'it is odd how that river is a kind of Being to people born near it. I don't think the English know the feeling.' National Library of Scotland, MS.1632, Lang to Mrs Maxwell Scott, 22 May 1901.
68. Andrew Lang (ed.), *Poet's Country* (Philadelphia, 1907).
69. Appiah, *The Ethics of Identity*, pp. 239, 241.
70. Andrew Lang, 'The Month in England', *Cosmopolitan*, June 1894, November 1894, December 1894, August 1895, January 1896, March 1896.
71. See, for example, Andrew Lang, 'Literary Chronicle', *Cosmopolis*, January 1896 (MacLaren); 'Notes on New Books', April 1897 (J. M. Barrie); 'At the Sign of the Ship', *Longman's*, 1 August 1896 (Munro).
72. 'Reviews', *Saturday Review*, 11 July 1896.
73. Andrew Lang, 'From a Scottish Workshop', *Illustrated London News*, 8 August 1896.
74. A.T.Q.C., 'A Word with the Celt – II', *The Speaker*, 21 March 1896.
75. Andrew Lang, 'From a Scottish Workshop', *Illustrated London News*, 18 April 1896.
76. Macdonald, 'Andrew Lang and Scottish Historiography', pp. 213, 218.
77. Corelli, *Silver Domino*, p. 343.

# 14

# Criticism and Freethought, 1880–1914

## Colin Kidd

The legacy of the eighteenth-century Enlightenment occupied an ambiguous place in nineteenth-century Scottish life. Its stunning record of achievement remained vivid and inspirational, particularly in the sciences; but the culture of free enquiry which the Moderates had fostered during the second half of the eighteenth century sat awkwardly in the nineteenth with the more ostentatiously Calvinist – and informally repressive – norms of the surrounding culture. It was a cold climate for freethinkers. David Hume himself had been a conspicuous outlier in the Scottish Enlightenment: an open debunker of Christian metaphysics and the very idea of the supernatural, he was markedly out of step with his Moderate protectors in the Kirk. Hume's works nevertheless comprised an important part of eighteenth-century Scotland's bequest to the nineteenth, encouraging a mode of freethinking which was obtrusively at odds with the suffocating ecclesiastical norms of the Victorian era. Atheism, agnosticism and materialism were unwelcome weeds in a society whose prim, Presbyterian bourgeoisie prided itself on overt displays of godliness and Calvinist orthodoxy. It is remarkable, indeed, how many nineteenth-century Scottish freethinkers, were first awakened to irreligion in their homeland, but – whether because of stifling social pressures or blocked opportunities – pursued careers elsewhere, most often in London's more liberal environment, or abroad in the Empire or United States.

The most celebrated case, certainly in the United States, is that of Frances Wright (1795–1852), better known as Fanny Wright, who was born in Dundee and spent a crucial period of her youth with a great-uncle, James Mylne (1757–1839), Professor of Moral Philosophy at Glasgow. It was here in Glasgow that she developed an interest in the pagan philosophy of Epicurus, the subject of her first book *A Few Days in Athens* (1822). Wright made two trips to the United States, eventually settling there. In the States she became a prominent critic of organised religion, slavery and the compartmentalisation of women, as well as an outspoken champion of birth control and sexual freedom. Yet Wright, atypical as she was in several respects, followed an all-too-typical pattern: the nineteenth-century Scottish freethinker who makes his or her name at a remove from the narrow constraints of Scotland itself. Consider the medic Robert Willis, born in Leith and trained at Edinburgh University, who settled in London, where, in addition to his medical publications, he translated Spinoza and promoted his pantheistic ideas, as well as authoring studies of Calvin's persecution of Servetus and a pamphlet entitled *The Pentateuch and the Book of Joshua in the Face of the Science and Moral Senses of our Age* (1875). There was, of course, no single or uniform trajectory. William MacCall (1812–78) was educated at Glasgow University then at the Presbyterian seminary in Geneva, but lost his faith, becoming first a Unitarian minister in Bolton, then a Pantheist in London. Adam Gowans Whyte (b. 1875) was a science graduate from Glasgow who became a journalist, moving to London in 1898 where in addition to his journalistic work, he authored freethinking works, such as *Do we believe?* (1904) and *The Religion of the Open Mind* (1913) – sometimes under the pseudonym 'John Allan Hedderwick' – and was a director of the Rationalist Press Association. Sometimes the Empire stood proxy for the freedoms of the capital. John Stuart Mackenzie, a member of the Ethical movement – a moral alternative to Christianity – studied at Glasgow, where he held a fellowship, as he did at Edinburgh, but spent the rest of his career variously at Cambridge and the Owen's College, Manchester, before becoming Professor of Logic at University College, New South Wales. This is just a sprinkling of lesser-known examples of enforced or chosen exile.

Of more abiding intellectual interest, perhaps, are two Cambridge friends – Sir James Frazer and William Robertson

Smith. Frazer was educated at school in Helensburgh and then Glasgow University, before moving to Trinity College, Cambridge, where he became the dominant name in British anthropology and freethought with his massive deconstructive work of comparative religion and mythography *The Golden Bough* (1890). An innovative and ingenious biblical critic and pioneer in Semitic anthropology, Smith was tried for heresy by the Free Church and, on losing his chair at Aberdeen, moved to Cambridge where he became Almoner's Professor of Arabic. Although a believer, Robertson Smith advanced an interpretation of Semitic totemism which was rich in implication that the Eucharist was a survival of tribal totemic rites. By a different route, Frazer too, indirectly suggested that the story of Christ's crucifixion and resurrection was a variant of a primeval vegetation myth. However, the scholarly attention paid to Frazer and Robertson Smith, deserved as it is given their central contributions to anthropology, has overshadowed the careers of other Scots who were once as prominent in contemporary intellectual life.[1]

This chapter focuses on three further Anglo-Scots freethinkers of the late nineteenth and early twentieth centuries, who, like so many others, spent their formative years in Scotland, and then found free rein for their irreligious questioning in England: the polymathic leader of British freethought, John Mackinnon Robertson (1856–1933), the theatre critic William Archer (1856–1924) and the publisher and writer, William Stewart Ross (1844–1906), who achieved a degree of pseudonymous celebrity writing on freethinking topics under the name Saladin.[2] These freethinking writers are grouped together here, not only as rough contemporaries but because they shared much in common. Robertson and Archer were close friends both from Edinburgh days and in London, and the paths of Robertson and Ross criss-crossed in the milieu of Charles Bradlaugh – the leader of British secularism – and his periodical the *National Reformer*. Both Archer and Robertson enlisted in the cause of Henry Vizetelly, who was tried in 1888–9 for his translations of Zola's novels.[3] Moreover, all three shared an interest in literature and language, ranging from literary criticism to spelling reform[4] and elocution,[5] which raises the question of how far literary and linguistic criticism was linked to criticism of scriptural religion. Robertson and Archer were convinced, too, of the promise of the new discipline of sociology to dispel old bigotries, not only religious, but racist and nationalist, though Archer's progressivism in some of these areas was less advanced than Robertson's. Notwithstanding their careers in London, these men – Robertson especially – continued to reflect on Scottish culture. Both Robertson and Ross were Burnsians,[6] and Robertson, as we shall see, was keenly aware of Hume's achievement, though oblivious of the ways in which his own assertive and unquestioning brand of secularism diverged in register from Hume's diffident scepticism.

Robertson was born on the Isle of Arran, but moved to Stirling where he was educated, leaving school at the age of thirteen. He became a railway telegraph clerk, and then moved to Edinburgh where he worked variously as a law clerk and for an insurance company, before getting a start in the newspaper world. In 1877 he became acquainted with Archer, whose post as a leader writer on the *Edinburgh Evening News* he took, on Archer's own recommendation, in 1878 when Archer left for London. In the early 1880s Robertson was prominent in the Edinburgh Secular Society, becoming acquainted with figures in Scottish freethought such as Thomas Carlaw Martin, W. E. Snell, the English lithographer and polemicist Joseph Mazzini Wheeler, and John Lees, a rope and twine manufacturer, at whose home in Portobello the group met. The group favoured beards and velvet jackets: then the ultimate in radical chic. It was at Lees's house that Robertson met Hypatia and Alice, the daughters of Charles Bradlaugh. In 1884 Robertson headed to London to work on Bradlaugh's *National Reformer*, as assistant editor, becoming editor in 1891. In 1893 the *National Reformer* ceased publication, but Robertson started and edited a new journal the *Free Review*. He was involved with the Rainbow Circle discussion group, to which he delivered twenty-two papers between 1899 and 1923,[7] and lectured at the South Place Ethical Society. Robertson wrote prolifically on the identity of Christ, whom he deconstructed as a personification of a solar myth. As well as his freethinking writings, Robertson was a prolific author on Shakespearean questions and an eminent literary scholar. Indeed, Robertson's writings range across a broad set of themes including sociology, race and textual analysis. Although he lived frugally, he had a library of 12,000 volumes. Robertson was also active politically. He was ultra-radical in his politics, favouring republicanism (long closely associated with secularism), abolition of the House of Lords, and woman's suffrage. Free trade – the only guarantee of cheap food – was another of Robertson's hobby horses. He stood for parliament, unsuccessfully, as an independent radical liberal in 1895 at Northampton, Bradlaugh's old seat. However, in the Liberal landslide of 1906 he became MP for Tyneside, which he held until 1918, becoming Parliamentary Secretary to the Board of Trade between 1911 and 1915. In 1915 he became a Privy Councillor, and later became President of the National Liberal Federation.[8]

Archer was born in Perth to members of the Glasite sect, a separatist group of disaffected former Presbyterians who were opposed to clericalism, prelacy and the church-state connection. Because his father moved frequently to find employment, Archer's schooling was somewhat peripatetic, at Perth and Dollar academies and George Watson's in Edinburgh, as well as schools in England. In the course of these early travels, Archer also visited relatives in Norway, becoming fluent in Norwegian, which would later play a crucial role in his emergence as the leading British champion of the drama of Henrik Ibsen. Archer studied at Edinburgh University, after which he went to Australia for a year. Back in Edinburgh he wrote leaders for the *Evening News*, and published his first forays into reform of the theatre. Although he moved to London notionally to study for the bar and was called to the bar by the Middle Temple in 1883, Archer never practised law. Rather he became the most influential theatre critic of his time, variously for the *London Figaro* (1878–81), the *World* (1884–1906), the *Tribune* (1906–8), the *Nation* (1908–10) and the *Star* (1913–20), as well as contributing articles to a number of other outlets. Whereas Clement Scott, the drama critic at the *Daily Telegraph*, was the leading voice of conservatism in the theatre, Archer stood out as his most prominent liberal adversary, championing experimental drama and radical causes. Indeed, Archer is now best remembered for his promotion of Ibsen, about whom it is reckoned he authored 175 articles, as well as publishing multi-volume translations of Ibsen's oeuvre. He reconised Ibsen's *Hedda Gabler* as a plea for women's emancipation. Feminist causes, including birth control, known as neo-Malthusianism, were closely linked to secularism. Archer was also a doughty combatant against what he termed 'Ibsenoclasts', stodgy conservative critics who denounced Ibsen's depravity and vulgarity. His Ibsenism was of a piece with his freethinking, and Archer was an enthusiastic and combative participant in the rationalist movement, maintaining links for a while with the Edinburgh Secular Society and becoming an honorary associate of the Rationalist Press Association. He was also active on behalf of a range of other causes. In 1904 he and his fellow critic Harley Granville-Barker proposed the establishment of a National Theatre. Later, Archer also became secretary of the Simplified Spelling Society, set up in 1908 to champion spelling reform. Archer was married, but maintained in addition a relationship from 1891 until his death with the actress Elizabeth Robins, who was also a theatre reformer. After Archer's death Robertson edited and introduced – in tribute to his late friend – *William Archer as Rationalist: A Collection of his Heterodox Writings* (1925).[9]

Ross was born at Kirkbean in Dumfriesshire, the son of a farm servant. He first attended New Abbey parish school in Kirkcudbrightshire, then went to Hutton Hall Academy near Caerlaverock, where he also served as an usher and assistant teacher. Already he had begun contributing to the press. He moved on to Glasgow University with the aim of becoming a Presbyterian minister, but here he experienced a crisis of faith, turned aside from theology to literature, in particular Burns and Carlyle, and did not complete his divinity course. He moved to London at the invitation of the publisher, Thomas Laurie, and assisted in the publication of educational works, eventually setting up his own publishing firm W. Stewart and Co. in 1872. In London Ross became a follower of Bradlaugh, and contributed to his periodical the *National Reformer*; but in 1877–8 fell out with Bradlaugh over the publication of Charles Knowlton's neo-Malthusian pamphlet, *The Fruits of Philosophy*. The secularist movement was not without its fissures, and the question of birth control caused Ross to transfer his allegiance to a rival freethinking journal, the *Secular Review*, of which he became joint editor in 1880 with Charles Watts, later from 1884 its sole editor and proprietor. Another source of division among freethinkers lay in the difference between atheism and agnosticism. Tellingly, in 1889 Ross changed the name of the journal to the *Agnostic Journal and Secular Review*, and again later to the *Agnostic Journal and Eclectic Review*.[10]

In various ways – and in the interstices of their miscellaneous other projects – these men waged literary war on organised religion. Their views were, however, far from monolithic. Robertson and Ross not only diverged on questions of birth control and agnosticism, but also over the emergence of socialism. Whereas Robertson embraced an advanced socially inflected New Liberalism, Ross remained a pre-socialist radical of a vintage stamp, an opponent of women's suffrage and suspicious of wider democracy.[11] Moreover, major differences of emphasis marked their various critiques of organised religion.

Robertson perceived that the new science of anthropology had the potential to undermine long-established theological verities, and attempted to found a new intellectual discipline, which he called 'hierology': situated at the confluence of anthropology, comparative religion and mythology, but with a pejorative, debunking edge. In the field of 'hierology', Robertson latched on to the anthropological insights of Robertson Smith and Frazer, but by way of cherry-picking and misrepresentation turned whispered suggestiveness into outright anti-Christian polemic. In *Christianity and Mythology* (1900) Robertson found himself in part-agreement with Frazer's *The Golden Bough*; but whereas Frazer's line of argument led 'unavowedly' to the implication that Christ originated in an annually slain vegetation-god, Robertson was stridently insistent on the parallel derivation of the Christ cult from the idea of a sun-deity born at the winter solstice.[12] Similarly, in *Pagan Christs* (1903), the gospel story emerged as 'a symbolic modification of an original rite of human sacrifice', Robertson arguing, in a gross distortion of Robertson Smith, that 'the doctrine of sacramental communion with deity' had been a means of 'conserving and sanctifying systematic cannibalism at the hands of priesthoods'. Robertson also directly quashed the views of another Scots anthropologist, Andrew Lang, whose views were more easily married to the old orthodoxies. Whereas Lang surmised that primeval peoples had some conception of a quasi-monotheistic 'high god', Robertson held a strictly evolutionist view of the development of religion from simple animism to more sophisticated conceptions of deity. After religions had evolved to a monotheistic stage, the next step in their evolution, Robertson argued, was the emergence of a need for an intermediary deity, a 'nearer god', between humanity and a remote sovereign of the cosmos; thus secondary deities – Christ-figures – emerged to fill this human craving. 'Christ-making', Robertson argued, 'is but a form or stage of God-making, the Christs or Son-Gods being but secondary Gods.'[13]

By contrast with Robertson's quasi-anthropological 'hierology', Archer's freethinking interests were more directly focused on ecclesiastical tyranny in the present. Most famously, he took up the cause of 'the Spanish Dreyfus', Francisco Ferrer, executed in 1909 ostensibly as a revolutionary, but in reality because he was a freethinker. Investigating the case at the instigation of the American magazine *McClure's*, Archer saw Ferrer as a victim of clericalist-cum-militarist authorities, who had rigged Ferrer's trial in ways that offended natural justice.[14] Archer also produced a critique of theatrical censorship, resolutely opposing the existing system of control of the London theatre by the Lord Chamberlain.[15]

Although Ross appeared to flirt with agnosticism, this did nothing to inhibit the fierceness of his critique of the persecutions, tortures and cruelties which, he contended, had long cowed ordinary people into belief. In *God and his Book* (1887) Ross sneered openly at the very notion of the divine inspiration of scripture, condemning the Bible as a farrago of palpable absurdity and internal contradiction, and exposing the spurious claims to the very high antiquity of the Old Testament and the apostolic pedigree of the New. Worse still was the sheer immorality contained within the Bible. An attentive reading of the entirety of scripture – not skipping the bloodthirsty and salacious portions of the Old Testament (some of which were comparable to 'Boccacio in lasciviousness') – was more likely to make the reader a freethinker than a believer. Not that this was news to students of biblical criticism, indeed such things were 'among the trade secrets of the parsons'. Yet equipped with 'the loaded dice of quibble and paradox', the clergy were able to reconcile this subversive knowledge with the retention of their livings. Although it was not quite as old as it pretended to be, the Bible was 'the natural evolutionary product and index of a remote and half-barbarous time.'[16]

In his book *Woman: her Glory, her Shame and her God* (1894), Ross demonstrated that far from ennobling and purifying women, Christianity had degraded them. Pauline theology was born in misogyny, and women had suffered disproportionately from the witch craze of the early modern era. At the heart of the book, perhaps surprisingly given its title, was a furious assault on the ways in which Christianity – whether through its scriptures or the sermons of its ministers – had aided and abetted the barbarities of slavery. Christian slavery had been worse than its ancient pagan counterpart, but all that was now conveniently forgotten as late nineteenth-century Christians – so recently converted to abolitionism – swept from their common memory the cruelties of their forebears and explained away the plain words of both Old and New Testament which justified slavery. Modern women were now safely protected behind the 'ramparts of secularistic opinion', yet sadly, by comparison with men, they seemed less receptive to freethinking rationalism. Nevertheless, victory was at hand. Christianity was 'dismembered and dying', and shrivelling into hypocritical casuistry which tried to reconcile its former barbarities with modern propriety.[17] Elsewhere Ross unmasked the benign self-image of liberal Protestantism, charging that the modern Christian was 'tolerant only in proportion as he is not a Christian'. For not only was persecution an integral feature of the Christian tradition, it was nagging inner 'doubt' about the whole truth of Christianity which was the 'well-spring of toleration towards those whose tenets are different'.[18]

All three freethinkers were also literary critics, and largely of a reformist kind. This brings into play deeper questions about the interplay of literary and scriptural criticism. Certainly, there was a general recognition that biblical criticism had shown scripture to be defective, whether with regard to its scientific standing or its internal coherence as a text. In *God and his Book* Ross had explored at great length and in considerable detail the origins and transmission of the Bible in scribal error, textual corruption, forgery, plagiarism, misattributed authorship, blurred and untestable division between canonicity and apocrypha, internal discrepancy and the whims of collation.[19] As a rationalist, Robertson distrusted the idea of authorial genius as a mode of literary explanation: it savoured too much of a discredited supernatural world view. He preferred to relate works of literature to their cultural background. However, in the more problematic case of Shakespeare – an undoubted genius by any standard – Robertson adopted an unusual stance. Dissenting both from outdated 'Ptolemaic'[20] bardolatry and from revisionist unmaskings of Shakespeare as a front for Francis Bacon or Lord Vere, Robertson was a disintegrationist. That is, he dismantled the individual plays and poems of the Shakespearean canon into their component contributions, most by Shakespeare, but some revealed by close attention to text and metre the work of other contemporary writers. In addition, he put enormous emphasis upon the influence of Montaigne on Shakespeare. Within the field of criticism, Robertson and Archer were both boldly revisionist Shakespeareans – keen to update Shakespeare to meet contemporary standards of scholarship and drama.

Robertson, in particular, aspired to develop a science of criticism, a subject also explored – though more sceptically – by Archer. In his article 'Criticism as an Inductive Science', Archer recognised the siren temptation of a scientific criticism which eschewed 'arbitrary dogmatism in literary judgments', but exposed the hollowness of such a project. Ultimately any analogy between scientific investigation and aesthetic evaluation was nugatory; for whereas zoology or astronomy deals with phenomena, criticism was a matter not of things themselves, but with 'relations', relations that is between the work of art and 'certain ideas in the percipient mind'. Relationships of this sort were not capable of demonstration or mathematical proof. Taste was a matter of opinion, and incapable of equation with scientific observation. Of course, criticism involved to some degree the 'application of laws, canons, standards', but only 'the vaguest and most general of these' could claim 'anything like scientific necessity'. Rather they were 'mere conventions' and as such potentially transitory, 'accepted today, rejected tomorrow'. While a historical approach to criticism remained a possibility, this marked the limits of what the inductive approach might achieve; the aspiration to bypass the subjectivity of whim and caprice, while understandable, was quixotic at best.[21]

But his friend's doubts on this score did not deter Robertson, who determinedly sought a route to making literary criticism a science. Literary critics remained 'a good deal in the dark as to the scientific discrimination of literary merit'. Yet he identified the nineteenth century as 'specifically the century of criticism', an era marked by 'dissatisfaction with the debris of the old codes'. Eighteenth-century Scotland had taken a step in the right direction. Nevertheless, Lord Kames's *Elements of Criticism* (1762) had fallen short of its promise. What was 'really wanted' in literary criticism, Robertson contended, was that there should be a 'statement of data and process of proof' which corresponded to what had arisen 'generations or even centuries ago in the case of the physical sciences'. It was surely attainable, Robertson reckoned. The very fact that 'wide agreement' prevailed regarding aesthetic merit in literature provided 'a proof that there are bases for a criticism which shall be scientific, or reducible to connected steps of reasoning from verifiable data'. Literary analysis was not merely 'the random expression of an aberrant opinion'. Nor should it remain the province of whim and caprice. Criticism had the potential to become a kind of science.[22]

Yet Robertson's yardstick of literary achievement now seems crudely evolutionist. What somehow advanced literature according to the temper and the drift of the age was to be celebrated, and stagnation deplored. For instance, Robertson condemned the torpid progress of English drama in the centuries since Shakespeare, not least by contrast with the enormous strides made in prose fiction in the same period.[23]

Of the three freethinkers, Robertson was the one who reflected historically on the relationship and possible connections between the Enlightenment of eighteenth-century Scotland and the secularist movement of the late nineteenth and early twentieth century. Of course, nineteenth-century Scots did not use the expression 'the Scottish Enlightenment', whose first coinage was in 1900, and only came into common currency from the 1960s; but it is important to note that they were keenly aware of the phenomenon, albeit lacking the convenient shorthand term we now use to describe it.

Robertson endorsed the cyclical interpretation of the course of Scottish intellectual history advanced by the pioneering English sociologist H. T. Buckle (1821–62): a long night of the gloomiest, unrelieved theocratic darkness followed by an unexpected eighteenth-century enlightenment and then a return during the nineteenth century to the grim blackness of religious prejudice. Robertson, who also authored an admiring defence of Buckle from his critics,[24] added his own solution to the paradox of the Scottish Enlightenment. For two centuries from the mid-sixteenth-century, Scotland – stultified by the Reformation – produced 'no secular literature of the least value'. Yet by a strange irony once deistic influences began to seep into Scotland during the late seventeenth and early eighteenth centuries, their influence was 'intensified' by the 'very aridity' of Presbyterian life, and the fact that 'the bigoted clergy could offer little intellectual resistance'. Thus the major intellectual advances of Hume, Smith, Adam Ferguson and others had occurred 'in that part of the British Islands where religious fanaticism had gone furthest, and speech and thought were socially least free'.[25] According to Robertson, the Scottish Reformation 'absolutely suspended the evolution of Scottish literature for some two hundred years; so that when a new growth commenced, the inspiration had perforce to come from other countries'.[26] The Scottish Enlightenment, in other words, was a transplant from outside.

The clearest expression of Robertson's interpretation of the course of Scottish intellectual history came in a provocatively titled work, *The Perversion of Scotland* (1886), which was an account of the Scottish Reformation and its stultifying effects over the long haul on Scottish cultural life. In the late fifteenth and early sixteenth century, Renaissance Scotland had an emergent poetry and drama which augured well for Scotland's future as a nation 'enlightened, artistic and free from superstition'. But at the Reformation 'the iron of human dogma wholly entered the national soul' leading to 'dark results of intellectual and social perversion'. The country exchanged the porous, sieve-like tyranny of a lax Catholicism for a regenerated clerical regime dedicated to a dour asceticism in every corner of Scottish life. Its equation of 'the free play of the mind' – whether in literature, thought, art and science – with 'rank profanity' ensured the complete extirpation of 'all leanings towards intellectual light'. The immediate consequences for Scotland included almost two centuries of cultural desiccation. A 'joyless monotone of asceticism' prevailed between the Reformation and the intellectual renewal associated with Hume and Adam Smith. Robertson had no truck with any notion that the flowering of Scottish culture in the eighteenth century stemmed from deeper seventeenth-century roots. Mid-seventeenth-century Scotland had 'no other intellectual life whatever' beyond polemical divinity, 'a dreary delirium of words'. Nor when renewal came did Robertson endorse the view that the 'remarkable literary revival' of the eighteenth century should 'go to the credit of the church'. Principal Robertson was the leading figure in a Kirk whose 'prevailing temper' was 'so widely different from his own', that his endorsement of Catholic toleration in 1779 brought him 'in danger of his life from the raving populace, which was countenanced in its bigotry by the majority of the clergy'. Adam Ferguson and John Home, the author of the tragedy *Douglas*, had minimal or truncated clerical careers, and the term 'Moderation' remained even in the 1880s a term for which the brilliant nineteenth-century Scottish theologian, John Tulloch (1823–86), needed to apologise. The Moderates were an embarrassment to the Kirk, and notwithstanding that brief interlude of tolerance and intellectual achievement, in its aftermath 'the inherent reactionary bias of the ecclesiastical system . . . turned back the hands of the social clock'. Nineteenth-century Scotland was as hostile to the achievements of its native eighteenth-century enlightenment as it was to culture in general. There was no popular memory – beyond a small freethinking subculture – of the leading natural philosophers of the Scottish Enlightenment, Joseph Black, William Cullen or James Hutton. Nor was there any 'popular Scotch edition of the philosophical works of Hume'. Indeed, while Scots took pride in their educational prowess, such boasts were worse than hollow. Those who knew Scottish culture most intimately had 'our misgivings about the compliments sometimes paid to it'.[27]

After all, Robertson admitted, 'nowhere, perhaps, [was] Hume less read and honoured than in his native land'. 'In matters theological', especially, 'Hume has counted for little with the general Scotch community.'[28] Nevertheless, Robertson's frequent invocation of Hume was problematic. For while Robertson conserved what he took to be the godless results of Humean speculation, he did not absorb its sceptical spirit. Whereas it remains an open question whether Hume – vertiginously poised between a Pyrrhonian and Academic scepticism – was an atheist or a deist, Robertson – a much less complicated figure – was a rigid unbeliever: a dogmatic archbishop of atheism rather than a genuinely freethinking gadfly. Hume's quicksilver fluidity, subversive interrogation of the limits of human reason, and ecumenical lightness of tone were far removed from Robertson's strident and monolithic rationalism.

In 1889 Robertson wrote the introduction to a new edition of Hume's *Natural History of Religion*, in which he complained of the 'mutilation' of Hume's irreligion in nineteenth-century editions of his work: such bowdlerising was an index of Britain's unfortunate 'social and intellectual history since the French Revolution'. Not that Hume himself escaped Robertson's reproaches, for the former's ironic playfulness, Pyrrhonian suspension of judgement and resort to common-sense mitigations of scepticism in his oeuvre, the latter took to be but the philosopher's cowardly 'temporising' with the norms of his age. Hume, in Robertson's view, was too fond of sociability and creature comforts to risk ostracism or martyrdom; worse, indeed, he was 'a Tory by temperament', to whom 'outspoken rationalism' was uncongenial.[29]

The divergence between the sceptic and the ardent secularist came into sharper focus in Robertson's *Rationalism* (1912). For here Robertson challenged Arthur Balfour's *Defence of Philosophic Doubt* (1879). Balfour, an English-educated scion of a Scottish family and a future prime minister, questioned the watertight rationality of science. Humean scepticism as 'an engine of destruction', Balfour perceived, was equally subversive of both religion and the supposed philosophical underpinnings of science. Both, it transpired, were 'unproved systems of belief'.[30] Balfour – the religious belief of this fideistic sceptic notwithstanding – had, arguably, as good a claim as Robertson to the mantle of Hume. This was something that Robertson recognised, conceding that 'Balfour's nihilistic treatment of reason has a surprising sanction in Hume'. However, Robertson convicted Hume of 'frequent great carelessness' in his oeuvre, and concluded that a prolific Hume – who would have 'recoiled' from Balfour's 'religious irrationalism' – had in fact collapsed Balfour's distinction between reasoning and customary experience in the *Enquiry*.[31]

Robertson, Archer and Ross played a central role in the British secularist movement, contributing both to its head-on attacks on the historical veracity of scripture and to associated reformist initiatives, including the earthy realism of the new drama. They were also – in their different ways – integral members of the metropolitan literary establishment, Archer perhaps more centrally than the others. This brief account of their careers provides an additional freethinking strand to the familiar thesis that Scottish intellectual life was substantially provincialised in the course of the nineteenth century. Secularism is a complicating wrinkle in any straightforward account of a core-periphery relationship. Nor is the fact that these distinguished freethinkers left Scotland in any sense to overlook the existence of a freethinking movement in Scotland. The Edinburgh Secular Society and Glasgow Eclectic Society sat at the centre of a handful of local freethinking bodies – though rarely more than six at any time, with fluctuating memberships and somewhat intermittent existence – across Scotland's major towns and cities.[32] Freethinking in Scotland was no more than a fringe concern, which carried risks of social ostracism in a society whose dominant ethos was one of oppressive Presbyterian conventionality.

Robertson had some inkling of this ecclesiastical endarkenment which had followed Scotland's eighteenth-century Enlightenment. The controversial case advanced by Buckle was in substance a plausible one: the brief spasm of Enlightenment had been obliterated by a renewed religiosity, evangelicalism being but a modern variant of a centuries-old clerical authoritarianism. In the reflux of 'pietistic reaction' and 'the new ecclesiastical ferment' of the nineteenth century, the 'intellectual life' of Scotland was once again 'less free than in England'. Economic conditions reinforced religious pressures. 'Most of the innovating elements' in the Scottish population followed opportunities in England and the empire, their departure from Scotland 'leaving the rival churches' of Presbyterian Scotland in 'undisturbed possession'. Ironically, as Robertson recognised, many of the Presbyterian clergy were themselves educated, 'rationalistic' in orientation and far from enthralled to dogma or superstition, yet 'afraid to declare themselves against the conservative mass'.[33] The legacy of the Scottish Enlightenment was a culture of free enquiry, but also a culture suppressed, its proponents forced into emigration, self-censorship or tortured hypocrisy by the resurgent orthodoxy of nineteenth-century Scottish Grundyism.

But how far did the stifling effect of authoritarian Calvinism push freethinkers south, and how far was the drift to London a pull-effect, arising from dreams of literary glory which now only the metropolis could offer? The answer is unclear, but no longer did Edinburgh – its publishing industry and secularist subculture notwithstanding – offer the amplitude of London, either in terms of literary outlets or freedom to dissent from social norms. The high road to London remains an important motif in modern Scottish intellectual history. In the mid-1880s Robertson lamented the 'singular fact' that there was 'no Scottish writer or artist of European distinction', excepting perhaps the literary critic David Masson, then 'resident in Scotland'. 'Our best men, in art, letters and science', he bemoaned, 'seem to gravitate to England.'[34] It seems likely, moreover, that a desire for countercultural freedom compounded the effect of literary ambition.

## Notes

1. See, for example, Robert Ackerman, *J. G. Frazer* (Cambridge, 1987); Robert Fraser (ed.), *Sir James Frazer and the Literary Imagination* (Basingstoke, 1990); William Johnstone (ed.), *William Robertson Smith: Essays in Reassessment* (Sheffield, 1995).
2. Alastair Bonnett, 'The Agnostic Saladin', *History Today* 63 (February 2013), 47–51.
3. Katherine Mullin, 'Pernicious Literature: Vigilance in the Age of Zola', in David Bradshaw and Rachel Potter (eds), *Prudes on the Prowl: Fiction*

*and Obscenity in England, 1850 to the Present Day* (Oxford, 2013), p. 39; Odin Dekkers, *J. M. Robertson: Rationalist and Literary Critic* (1998: Abingdon and New York, 2018), pp. 197, 206.
4. Edward Royle, *Radicals, Secularists and Republicans: Popular Freethought in Britain, 1866–1915* (Manchester, 1980), pp. 223–4.
5. For example, William Ross, *A System of Elocution based upon Grammatical Analysis* (Edinburgh, 1869).
6. See, for example, Robertson, 'The Art of Burns' and 'Stevenson on Burns', both in Robertson, *New Essays towards a Critical Method* (London, 1897); Ross, 'Robert Burns', in Ross, *Isaure and other Poems*, 2nd edn (London, 1894), pp. 92–6; Ross, *Robert Burns: Was he a Christian?* (London, n.d.).
7. Michael Freeden (ed.), *Minutes of the Rainbow Circle 1894–1924* Camden 4th ser. 38 (1989).
8. Dekkers, *Robertson*; G. A. Wells (ed.), *J. M. Robertson (1856–1933): Liberal, Rationalist, and Scholar* (London, 1987); I. D. Mackillop, *The British Ethical Societies* (Cambridge, 1986), pp. 57–65.
9. Thomas Postlewait, *Prophet of the New Drama: William Archer and the Ibsen Campaign* (Westport, CT, 1986); Peter Whitebrook, *William Archer* (London, 1993).
10. Bonnett, 'Agnostic Saladin'; Royle, *Radicals*, pp. 101–2.
11. Royle, *Radicals*, pp. 112, 116, 193, 220, 227, 234, 237, 247, 249, 258.
12. John M. Robertson, *Christianity and Mythology*, 2nd edn (1900: London, 1934), p. 34.
13. John M. Robertson, *Pagan Christs: Studies in Comparative Hierology* (London, 1903), pp. xi, 12–13, 98, 420.
14. William Archer, *The Life, Trial and Death of Francisco Ferrer* (New York, 1911), p. viii.
15. William Archer, 'The Censorship of the Stage', in Archer, *About the Theatre: Essays and Studies* (London, 1886), pp. 101–71.
16. William Ross, *God and his Book* (London, 1887?), esp. pp. 13, 25–6, 37, 45, 66, 132, 141, 180, 241.
17. William Ross, *Woman: Her Glory, her Shame and her God* (2 vols, London, 1894), I, esp. pp. 187, 193. See also Ross, *Witchcraft in Christian Countries* (Stockport, 1882).
18. William Ross, *Christian Persecution* (London, n.d.), pp. 4–5.
19. Ross, *God and his Book*, esp. pp. 13, 66–7, 81, 171, 180.
20. Robertson, *The Problem of Hamlet* (1919: New York, 1920), p. 87.
21. William Archer, 'Criticism as an Inductive Science', *Macmillan's Magazine* (May 1886), 45–54.
22. John M. Robertson, 'Science in Criticism', in Robertson, *Essays towards a Critical Method* (London, 1889), pp. 1–148, esp. pp. 1, 10, 18–19, 105.
23. John Robertson, 'Evolution in Drama', *Our Corner* (May 1886), 275–83.
24. Robertson, *Buckle and his Critics* (London, 1895).

25. John M. Robertson, *A Short History of Freethought* (1899: New York, 1957), pp. 318–19.
26. John M. Robertson, *The Perversion of Scotland* (1886), reprinted in Robertson, *Miscellanies* (London, 1898), p. 209.
27. Robertson, *Perversion of Scotland*, pp. 144, 155, 159–61, 189, 202–3, 215, 218.
28. Robertson, *Buckle and his Critics*, pp. 158–9.
29. Robertson, 'Introduction', Hume, *The Natural History of Religion* (London, 1889).
30. Arthur Balfour, *A Defence of Philosophic Doubt* (1879: London, 1920), pp. 85, 320.
31. Robertson, *Rationalism* (London, 1912), pp. 40–1.
32. Royle, *Radicals*, pp. 69–71, 341–2.
33. Robertson, *Short History of Freethought*, p. 422.
34. Robertson, *Perversion of Scotland*, p. 222.

# 15

# Epilogue: The Afterlife of the Enlightenment in Scottish Criticism

## Gerard Carruthers

Three remarkable books were published in 1961, each of which in a different way had something striking to communicate about the place of the Scottish Enlightenment in the country's cultural history. Muriel Spark's novel, *The Prime of Miss Jean Brodie*, has a key scene where the eponymous schoolteacher guides her middle-class pupils through the insalubrious Grassmarket area of 1930s Edinburgh. Counterpointing the grimness of depression-era poverty, and implicitly also the Scottish nationalism of that decade, Brodie reminds her girls brightly that they are 'European' and that as Edinburghers they 'owe a lot to the French. We are Europeans.'[1] Partly this pro-European stance connects with Brodie's relish for the 'gay French Queen', Mary Queen of Scots, and her hatred for Mary's adversary, fiery apostle of the Reformation, John Knox.[2] It relates too, however, to the pull Brodie felt towards European Fascism, and particularly her admiration for the Italian dictator, Benito Mussolini, and it also derives from her conception of 'Edinburgh [as] a European capital, the city of Hume and Boswell'.[3] The discerning reader notes conflicting European currents in the Brodie world view: rebarbative totalitarianism (Knox as well as Mussolini, on the one hand), and freer cosmopolitan intellectual energies on the other (Mary as well as major eighteenth-century Edinburgh writers). Clearly, in espousing each of these strains Brodie is a culturally confused character – or, alternatively in a meta-reading, a suitably reliable, erratic compass. Her creator's point is that Scottish like European culture is ambivalent and contestable, deflating and inspiring, unsettled in general. Brodie, like Scotland the nation – the novel makes clear – has elements in her of both the autocratic indigenous Calvinist, Knox, and the Romantic European, Mary. Much of this character-terrain is of course stereotypical and Spark herself knows it, her stock-in-trade as a writer being to twist, mangle and recycle quotidian clichés, often making the reader work hard in determining which perspective, if any, is reliable.

Spark's book is inspired to a large degree by James Hogg's *The Private Memoirs and Confessions of a Justified Sinner* (1824), which is in turn deeply indebted as a dark psychological character-study to the Scottish Enlightenment and the interest of David Hume and other historians in religious 'fanaticism'. Also lurking in the background of Hogg's Gothic horror is Adam Smith's idea of 'sympathy' (in a very neutral sense), or putting oneself in the place of another. It features the repellent Robert Wringhim vouchsafed salvation as one of the predestined 'elect', whose 'self-assurance' deforms his personality and begets evil deeds, though this turn towards evil is implicitly countermanded by his conscience (or, in the idiom of Francis Hutcheson, his 'moral sense'). Wringhim's essential inner being is ultimately destroyed, annihilated by the tension between living as an antinomian without regard to moral consequences and a persisting intuited apprehension of moral causality. Hogg, like other Scottish historical novelists of the early nineteenth century, including Walter Scott and John Galt, responded to Scottish moral and social theories of the previous century.[4] The novels of Hogg, Scott and Galt all feature intensely focused Smithian sympathies, not least for the predicaments of the marginalised or of historical 'losers', including those on the Covenanting and Jacobite extremes of Scottish life. This conception of Scotland's strained, variegated, oppositional culture – underpinned in fiction by the historiographical and psychological approaches of the Scottish Enlightenment – persisted into the twentieth century. Witness most obviously Spark's deployment of Mary and Knox, representative avatars in the popular imagination of the extremes of Scottish identity. More slyly, Spark alludes to such division when she yokes together Hume (sceptical about the coherence of human identity) and Boswell, the inventor of modern biography (or character-documentation): incongruous components of a not-so-unitary Scottish Enlightenment.

By 1961 Hume belonged to the intellectual mainstream and was no longer an outlier in the narrative of Scottish Enlightenment. Hume, 'the great infidel', bête noire of the Kirk in his own day for his irreligion, had become more comfortably part of the general narrative of eighteenth-century Scottish 'thought'. The recent revisionist scholarship of Norman Kemp Smith played a significant part in Hume's rehabilitation. Kemp Smith's limpid clarity demystified Hume and made him more accessible to the literate public. Kemp Smith's revisionism underpinned George Davie's classic work of 1961, *The Democratic Intellect: Scotland and her Universities in the Nineteenth Century*. Amidst a battery of strident arguments, Davie's *Democratic Intellect* sought to emphasise the linkage between Hume and the more academically influential Common Sense school of philosophy associated with Thomas Reid and his disciples.[5] For Davie, 'Reid and his followers had very much the same conception of philosophy as Hume', which is to say they had a central interest in 'natural belief'.[6] Davie's conclusion here is broadly accurate, but is, at the same time, somewhat disingenuous given Reid's well-documented rebuttal of Humean scepticism. Davie's Scottish Enlightenment of Hume and Reid involves elisions just as much as Brodie's indiscriminate pairing of Hume and Boswell. What was at stake for Davie was not at bottom a matter of epistemology, or even the history of philosophy, but a concern to advance a version of the Scottish Enlightenment that was culturally cogent and which ran continuously from Hutcheson in the first half of the eighteenth century down to the thinking of J. F. Ferrier and William Hamilton in the 1840s and 1850s. Determined to assert an unbroken Scottish intellectual and cultural tradition, Davie saw the metaphysical temper of the Scottish Enlightenment as informed by what he calls 'the Presbyterian inheritance': the continuation of a supposedly distinctive attitude to education, first apparent in the parish schools and universities of Reformation Scotland, not least the latter's broad curricula. Above all, Davie's book is a paean of praise to Scottish 'generalism', in educational interest and outlook, which is for him broadly synonymous with Common Sense philosophy (a national tradition in which he is keen to implicate Hume – at least to some degree), and which stands in distinction to the perceived narrowness and undue specialisation of English education.

In *The Democratic Intellect* Davie was determinedly revisionist about two epochs in Scottish history, the Reformation and the Enlightenment, both of which had become increasingly problematic. Each was seen as hostile to indigenous Scottish culture, and as having perverted what *ought to have been* the true course of Scottish cultural history – according to a newly dominant nationalist outlook in criticism and the arts. The period between W. R. Scott's coinage of the term 'Scottish Enlightenment' in his biography of Francis Hutcheson in 1900 and the backlash against the supposed detrimental influence of the Enlightenment on Scottish culture is really rather brief.[7] By the 1930s Scottish literary criticism, of the generalist variety, had become almost entirely suspicious of both the Enlightenment and also the Reformation. The very notion that Scotland of the 1920s and 1930s was undergoing a literary 'Renaissance' was pregnant with negative assumptions: that Scotland's historical development was warped, its culture badly out of joint. Edwin Muir, one of the leading figures in the interwar Renaissance, identified Scotland as a cultural and creative vacuum. Since the sixteenth century the Scots language had been eroded and undermined, Muir contended, to the extent that now the people of Scotland, 'thought' in one language (English) and 'felt' in another (Scots). As a result, Scotland lacked a 'homogenous' language.[8] The absence of this idealised, should-have-been Scots literary and philosophical language meant that a proper Scottish literature – rounded in its intellectual and affective capacities – was incomplete, impaired, impossible even. Muir outlined these views in *Scott and Scotland: The Predicament of the Scottish Writer* (1936). Controversially, he argued that the achievements of Burns and Scott were hollow, for that was the logical consequence of the systemic failure that Muir adduced. Scotland's two greatest creative writers of the post-Union era, then, were brought crashing down and with them, implicitly, the Enlightenment to which they were so heavily indebted.

Muir's overdetermined thesis and his idealisation of homogeneity rest ultimately on post-Romantic notions of people and nationhood, particularly on the idea that an unbroken, holistic human tradition is the primary constituent of nationhood. Muir's argument faced violent denunciation from Hugh MacDiarmid (Christopher Murray Grieve), the pre-eminent poet and leading Scottish cultural activist of the interwar era, who recoiled from Muir's pessimistic conclusion that Scots was unable to function as a fully viable literary language. Yet ironically Muir's *Scott and Scotland* exemplified the very logic of the cultural nationalism that MacDiarmid had done so much to put in place. Muir's account chimed with MacDiarmidism in largely rejecting, because culturally harmful, the Anglo-Scottish, or British, movement of Scottish history. For Muir, like MacDiarmid, this long detour in Scottish history – encompassing moments such as the Reformation, the Union of the Crowns in 1603, the Union of Parliaments in 1707, and the subsequent eras of Enlightenment and Victorianism – perverted the organic, natural course of Scottish cultural development. Scotland should have been linguistically itself, politically independent, and perhaps might even, like Ireland, have resisted the Reformation and remained Roman Catholic. Although not completely explicit about all of these things, Muir was unequivocal about the guilty parties: Calvinist puritanism in the first instance, and the capitalism and imperialism which had beguiled Scotland with the promise of the material benefits which accompanied incorporation in a British superstate. However, the cultural nationalism of both Muir and MacDiarmid bore strange – and unacknowledged – tints of Anglocentricity. Both critics obviously disliked – but affirmed as largely true – the Whig Protestant view of Scottish progress within the United Kingdom, and accepted T. S. Eliot's sweeping valorisation of English cultural maturity.

David Craig's *Scottish Literature and the Scottish People, 1680– 1830*, the third of our books published in 1961, distilled much of Muir's hostility to the actual cultural history of Scotland. Like MacDiarmid, Craig looked at the ruined remnants of authentic Scottish culture, especially Scots, as providing some authentic (if, for Craig, rather marginal) value within an otherwise beaten and concussed nation. For Craig, Scottish literary life and Scottish society more generally were sadly contorted, suffering from anglicising, cultural pollution and the skewed priorities of capitalism and the British Empire. The Enlightenment in Scotland represented in Craig's words, an 'alienation from things native'.[9] This condition was due to an anglicising mentality of aspirational but aridly cosmopolitan emulation in architecture, literature and general culture. The Enlightenment was led by

> remarkably talented men . . . a conscious intelligentsia . . . [possessing] anxious awareness of a powerful culture near by, very different from their own yet appealing to them as a model civilisation — a culture less tied than their own to a backward country and one, too, which had a more articulate character and powers of expression.[10]

The narrative here of all-too-hurried cultural engineering in the Enlightenment includes such exemplary expression as the neoclassical New Town of Edinburgh, the cringing lists of embarrassing Scotticisms compiled by David Hume, James Beattie and others, and Hume's stylistically celebrated essays in their impeccably trained English prose. However, we might be aware here of simplistic elision by Craig and the critical tradition he represented. For instance, neoclassicism is read by him rather feebly as overall an attempt to follow English 'progress', rather than as part of a long-standing humanistic tradition: at once broadly European yet also impeccably Scottish. The Muir-Craig tradition also valorised what it took to be the earthy, demotic centre of Scottish culture. Here we see, then, a central feature of the twentieth-century Scottish literary-critical tradition which couples a very English idea of organic tradition with a preference for the common folk as enduring custodians of authentic Scottish cultural value. The Scots-language productions of Burns and his eighteenth-century contemporaries are read as essentially embodying the latter, thus ghettoised and drained of their full cultural import. Moreover, as a Marxist, Craig counterposed to the authentic strains of Burns and the vernacular poets the bourgeois, elitist and proto-capitalist expressions of blindly optimistic progress to be found in Scotland's Enlightenment thinkers.

This contrast is further explored in David Daiches' *The Paradox of Scottish Culture: the Eighteenth Century Experience* (1964). At this point in the 1960s, cultural critics resorted to a psychological vocabulary (for example, 'split personality') which was crudely applied to social phenomena: as if a nation, like a person, required a whole and consistent identity to be healthy. Daiches, like Craig, was wedded to the notion derived from Eliot of organic tradition, and he too elucidated a fatal split between enlightened culture in Scotland and 'vernacular' Scots poetry. For Daiches, obvious cultural bifurcation is to be detected most especially in a linguistic fault line where Scottish cultural expression in both English and Scots is infected by an inability to hit the proper mark: 'This can be seen in poetry: Scottish poetry, when written in English, was often (but not invariably) derivative and stilted, and when written in Scots was always in danger of being self-consciously humorous or low or "quaint".'[11] Daiches also painted the literary criticism of the Enlightenment – the work on rhetoric and belles-lettres of Hugh Blair, Smith and others – as inherently deficient in its programmatic (implicitly un-Romantic) formalism:

> Eighteenth-century Scottish literary criticism, which is almost entirely concerned with rhetoric, with the study of formal devices for stirring the emotions, is generally quite incapable of dealing with the subtle and impressive devices of combining rational and emotional appeal to achieve richness of expression and tends to mistake floridity for eloquence, pathos for tragedy, and sentimental declamation for poetry. The reception of Macpherson's *Ossian* is evidence of this or, to take a more particular case, Henry Mackenzie's review of Burns's Kilmarnock volume in *The Lounger*, which praised some of the weakest and most sentimental of Burns's stanzas as being 'solemn and sublime, with [. . .] rapt and inspired melancholy'.[12]

With Daiches we reach the twentieth-century high point of the overgeneralised charges against the literati of the Scottish Enlightenment as crass mismanagers of the nation's culture.[13]

Roughly contemporary with the literary criticism of Craig and Daiches, George Davie's project of defining and defending the Scottish Enlightenment also relied on a notion of a holistic or 'traditional' Scottish culture. He rightly pointed out, for instance, in a useful corrective, that many of the Scots poets contemporaneous with the Enlightenment were themselves 'university men'; this countered the simplistic post-Burnsian notion that such writers were sprung from the soil or to be equated simply with a lower-class urban locus. Davie points out – on a somewhat slender basis – that Robert Fergusson's poetry is thematically inspired on at least one occasion by the mathematical insight of the Scottish Enlightenment.[14] Moreover, Davie makes the potentially highly accurate observation that Burns 'assimilat[es] the detached philosophic spirit of the Common Sense school'.[15] Additionally though, he might have pointed out that one of Burns's favourite books was Adam Smith's *Theory of Moral Sentiments* and that Smithian sympathy animates the poet's promiscuously disposed emotions throughout his work.[16] The Enlightenment character of Burns's work was long resisted in Scottish literary criticism which clung to the ideas of unpropitious bifurcation and debilitating 'paradox': that seeming literary achievement was ultimately hollow when insufficiently anchored in a purported idea of Scottish nationhood.

However, Davie's *The Democratic Intellect* responded primarily to an earlier critique of the Scottish Enlightenment which had flourished in the nineteenth century. In particular, Davie sought to countermand what he labelled accurately as H. T. Buckle's 'extreme and doctrinaire' *History of Civilization in England* (1857–1861), the Scottish part of this work being produced exactly one hundred years before Davie's own book.[17] For the English sociologist Buckle, such was the 'ecclesiastical tyranny' within Scotland by the eighteenth century that 'certain principles are taken for granted [by the Scottish Enlightenment generally]; and, it being deemed impious to question them, all that remains for us is to reason from them downwards. This is the deductive method.'[18] According to Buckle, the alternative to that approach was 'inductive philosophy'; 'secular' and 'scientific', in the spirit of the Baconian philosophy of England, 'with its determination to subordinate ancient principles to modern experience, [which] was the heaviest blow which has ever been inflicted on the theologians'.[19] Buckle was highly influential within nineteenth-century historiography, not least in identifying a flawed Scottish intellectual tradition. However, his treatment built upon a series of earlier writers, as we shall see: Lord Byron, William Cobbett, John Gibson Lockhart and Thomas Carlyle among others, all of whom operate to a greater or lesser degree on the assumption of Scotland's intellectual incapacity.

Nevertheless, Buckle's *History of Civilization in England* was the main reason that Davie felt the need not only to defend the Scottish Enlightenment but also to rehabilitate Scottish Presbyterianism. Whereas Buckle detected intellectual timidity in the Scottish Enlightenment and stern theocracy in the Kirk, Davie advanced an alternative interpretation which emphasised the continuity of a Scots Presbyterian tradition of democratic intellectualism which stretched from the Reformation to the Enlightenment, and beyond.[20] Ironically enough, Buckle's version of Scottish cultural history was highly deductive, indeed in many ways resting upon cultural stereotypes which had come to the fore in the late eighteenth century and which had matured further during the Romantic era of the early nineteenth century. Buckle, in fact, shared with Davie an overdetermined discrimination between Scottish (and English) national 'thought'. Many examples can be adduced. For instance, Buckle, in discussing Francis Hutcheson (an Irishman as much as a Scot) conflated the idea of 'induction' with idealisation or even theoretical technicality shorn of observed experience. Buckle said of Hutcheson's ideas of people and politics:

> Experience is either shut out, or made subordinate to theory; and facts are adduced to illustrate the inference, but not to suggest it. So, too, the proper relation between people and their rulers, and the amount of liberty which the people should possess, instead of being inductively generalized from an historical enquiry into the circumstances which had produced most happiness, might in the opinion of Hutcheson, be ascertained by reasoning from the nature of government, and from the ends for which it was instituted.[21]

Similarly in the case of Smith, Buckle perceived a deductive modus operandi erasing rounded observation of 'human nature'. He saw this writ large in Smith's isolated treatments of sympathy and selfishness, respectively, in *Theory of Moral Sentiments* and *Wealth of Nations*.[22] However, with Hutcheson, Smith and others of the Scottish Enlightenment, Buckle practised a kind of sleight of hand where lack of anthropological realism (sympathy and selfishness being treated together in the one account, as he implied it ought to have been in Smith) was held to be a major shortcoming. In fact, Smith and his contemporaries were perfectly aware that they were engaged in matters of theory – isolating mechanisms of behaviour – rather than presenting a historical realist's account of actual human events. It was this kind of overwrought generalisation by Buckle that led Davie to his defensive emphasis upon an eighteenth-century Scottish intellect grounded in a world of reasoned realism. Of a piece here, is his positing of 'generalism' as part of this holistic, worldly outlook. Later, in an essay which in some ways is a clearer articulation of the central English-Scottish tension posited in *The Democratic Intellect*, Davie overdrives a national opposition between Joseph Priestley's associationist outlook on reality and Thomas Reid's Common Sense version of the same.[23] However, David Hume and others of the Scottish Enlightenment were as obviously interested in the association of ideas in human mentality as Priestley, and made important contributions to that brand of philosophy. A large part of the problem, in fact, as well as opposing nationalist flag-waving is a shared, insensitive secularism on the part of Buckle and Davie. For the latter, Priestley is seen all too readily as a suitable representative of English culture, when he is so really only for a marginal part of it. Priestley, the embodiment of Unitarian rational dissent, saw his laboratory wrecked by a 'Church and King' mob in the early years of the French Revolution. To be fair to Davie, however, he did consider Priestley 'a radical', but his specialist experimentation (as a chemist and in other areas) proved sufficient for Davie to label him a devotee of his country's 'specialisation'.[24] In fact, Davie was doing unto Priestley what Buckle had done unto Smith: failing to see Priestley in context and in the round, in relation to his wider set of scientific and religious beliefs.

Buckle's claims about the Scottish Enlightenment, deeply hostile to what he took to be its underlying Presbyterianism, followed in the wake of an earlier indigenous disdain for Scottish intellectual life. It was evident in Thomas Carlyle's celebrated essay, 'Signs of the Times' (1829), which opined that 'nobody now cares about either' the '[mechanical] school of Reid' nor Hume's 'bottomless abysses of Atheism and Fatalism'. Carlyle, who welcomed Romanticism and especially subjective intuition, painted Scottish philosophy of the eighteenth century generally as all too empirically realist.[25]

However, this negative attitude to the Scottish Enlightenment seems to have first emerged in the bruising and partisan reviewing culture of early nineteenth-century Edinburgh, and was expressed most forcefully by John Gibson Lockhart in *Peter's Letters to his Kinsfolk* (1819). Lockhart adopted the fictional-documentary method of Tobias Smollett in his epistolary novel, *The Expedition of Humphry Clinker* (1771). Just as Smollett had conveyed his views on his native Scotland by way of an ostensibly neutral mouthpiece, a Welsh squire, Matthew Bramble, so Lockhart's mouthpiece an imaginary antiquarian, Dr Peter Morris, conveyed Lockhart's verdict on Scotland by way of Morris's communications back to his family in Wales. But whereas Smollett described Edinburgh in the golden age of the Scottish Enlightenment as a 'hotbed of genius', Lockhart's persona, Morris, acidly describes a very different intellectual character in early nineteenth-century Scotland. Morris equated the 'democratic intellect' of Scotland's capital with a lack of literary cultivation and sophistication:

> The reading public of Edinburgh do not criticise Mr Wordsworth; they think him below their criticism; they know nothing about what he has done. Or what he is likely to do. They think him a mere old, sequestered hermit, eaten up with vanity and affectation, who publishes every now and then some absurd poem about a Washing-Tub, or a Leech-Gatherer, or a Little Grey Cloak. They do not know even the names of some of the finest poems our age has produced.[26]

In the background here was a culture war that had been rumbling on for over a decade. But the main axis of division was not between England and Scotland so much as it was ideological. Indeed, the ire and animus of *Peter's Letters* was directed at the Whig cadre led by Francis Jeffrey associated with the *Edinburgh Review*. Lockhart, the Tory son-in-law of Walter Scott and a connoisseur of the new Romantic taste in literature, responded robustly to the cavils of anti-Romantic Whig critics:

> A man of genius like Mr Jeffrey must, indeed, have found it an easy matter to succeed in giving this turn of mind among a people where all are scholars and so few are readers as is the case here in Scotland. Endowed by nature with a keen talent for sarcasm, nothing could be more easy for him than to fasten, with destructive effect of nonchalance, upon a work which had perhaps been composed with much earnestness of thought on the part of the author, and with a most sincere anxiety after abstract truth either of reasoning or of feeling ... His [the Edinburgh critic's] object is merely to make the author look foolish; and he prostitutes his own fine talents to enable the common herd of his readers to suppose themselves looking down from the vantage ground superior intellect upon the poor, blundering, deluded poet or philosopher who is the subject of the review.[27]

Lockhart was particularly incensed – as we shall see – at the *Edinburgh Review*'s failure to appreciate Romantic poetry, and under the guise of the genial Peter Morris, sought to identify the root of the journal's crassness. He found it principally in a key part of the Scottish intellectual tradition:

> One of the greatest curses of a sceptical philosophy is that by leaving no object upon which the disinterested affections may exercise themselves it is apt to cause the minds of mankind be too exclusively taken up about the paltry gratifications of the personal feelings.[28]

Here we have a crude summation of Hume's scepticism about objective reality and the primacy of the feelings. Implicit also throughout *Peter's Letters* is a distaste for the democratic iconoclasm of Presbyterianism. The 'sarcasm' that Jeffrey purportedly relayed to his readership, Lockhart under the guise of Morris, linked both to Hume's scepticism and to the demotic outspokenness he associated with Scottish Calvinism.[29] For Lockhart, the Whigs of the *Edinburgh Review* were also distasteful for being more progressively disposed towards reformist politics and the notion of an expanded electorate. They were also to some extent 'Whigs' in its traditional Scottish usage signalling the most dissenting, even anti-monarchical of Presbyterians, or the Popular or Evangelical faction within the Kirk, which in the matter of patronage opposed the rights of the landed to appoint church ministers, and wishing instead that this prerogative be restored to the people of the parish.

At this time, of course, Lockhart and his allies were engaged in the new project of establishing *Blackwood's Magazine*, a gathering point for Tories opposed to the Whiggery and non-Romantic aesthetics of the *Edinburgh Review*. The 'Maga' had stutteringly appeared from 1817, but was retooled prior to the appearance of *Peter's Letters* as a stylish cutting-edge publication, highly modern in literary affairs (publishing Shelley for instance), in an overt demonstration that it had its finger on the contemporary pulse. The political sensibilities of *Blackwood's* favoured a nostalgic vein of conservatism: opposing trade unions but standing too against the excesses of industrialism and laissez-faire political economy. This combination of progressive aesthetic fashion and Tory paternalism reflected – in some degree – the views of Lockhart's father-in-law, Walter Scott. *Peter's Letters* expressed a similarly positive regard towards literary modernity and political disdain for those such as Whigs and Radicals who would too readily rip up the traditions of British society. In its reflections on the Enlightenment, *Peter's Letters* was well disposed to 'good worthy Dr Reid (honest man)' and to Adam Smith, but yet again is quick to point out the baneful influence of the Humean tradition. Morris attends a lecture by the Professor of Moral Philosophy at Edinburgh University, Thomas Brown (1778–1820).[30] Brown had argued that Hume's scepticism towards causality was not necessarily at odds with religious belief and this seems to be enough to have unleashed upon him and his students, Morris's – or rather Lockhart's – withering satire:

> Before the professor arrived I amused myself with surveying the well-covered rows of benches with which the large room

was occupied. I thought I could distinguish the various descriptions of speculative young men come thither from the different quarters of Scotland, fresh from the first zealous study of Hume, Berkeley and Locke, and quite sceptical whether the timber upon which they sat had any real existence, or whether there was such a thing as heat in the grate that was blazing before them.[31]

Notice that non-Scottish philosophers, such as Locke, and George Berkeley, a proponent of subjective idealism, join Hume the sceptic as foes of a common-sense view of reality; something which Lockhart saw as the everyday and the basis of a settled society. It is not so much the *Scottish* Enlightenment then to which Lockhart objected, but rather thrawn mystification which Lockhart aligned with Whiggish iconoclasm.

What ultimately underpinned Lockhart's antipathy to the *Edinburgh Review* was the spat that followed Henry Brougham's high-handed treatment in the *Review* of Lord Byron's 'Hours of Idleness' in 1807. Byron's response was famously to publish his *English Bards and Scotch Reviewers* (1809). Byron's poem was a huge success, indeed burnished the first flush of his fame. Crude and belly-laugh inducing, the text did much to install in popular parlance the crass ferocity of the *Review*. Really, a series of stereotypes about the dour, non-aesthetic (Calvinist, Whiggish) Scot, this was the template for Lockhart's portrait of Jeffrey and the Reviewer-Whigs in *Peter's Letters to His Kinsfolk*.

Although Byron's text also took sideswipes at his poetic contemporaries, Wordsworth and Coleridge, the *Edinburgh Review* was the focal point of his satire. Poets struggle uphill against the pronouncements of the *Review*: 'That, ere they reach the top, fall lumbering back again./With broken lyre, and cheek serenely pale' (ll. 417–18). The ancient Greek poet, Alcaeus, aristocratic and a lyric specialist (and so perhaps symbol of Byron himself), sees 'His hopes . . . perish'd by the northern blast: Nipp'd in the bud by Caledonian gales' (ll. 420–1). In rumbustious movement Jeffrey and his crew are 'northern wolves, that still in darkness prowl/A coward brood, which mangle as they prey.' Ferocious and ignorant, the reviewers next have their teeth drawn in bathetic description of an Edinburgh landscape overwhelmed ostensibly by the furore of a duel between Jeffrey and Thomas Moore. However, the magistrates prevented the event and pistols were found to be empty anyway, with the implication that the contest had all been an affected show. Instead of blood and flesh strewing the streets of the Scottish capital, what is witnessed is a different kind of furore, the literary endeavours of Jeffrey and his cabal in paper and ink:

> Strew'd were the streets around with milk-white reams,
> Flow'd all the Canongate with inky streams;
> This of his candour seem'd the sable dew,
> That of his valour show'd the bloodless hue;
> And all with justice deem'd the two combined
> The mingled emblems of his mighty mind.[32]

Here is the bluntly stereotypical image of Scottish intellectual life and criticism which long stuck in the consciousness of the literary mainstream.

Thanks to Byron, Lockhart, Buckle and Carlyle the Scottish Enlightenment – though, of course, not named as such – lived on in the nineteenth century as a crude stereotype, partly an expression of anti-Scottish bias, but more fully a manifestation of confessional and political prejudices found on both sides of the border. No longer, of course, does the Scottish Enlightenment attract pejorative comment of this sort. Nevertheless, we are only beginning to unpack the rich but largely ignored history of its post-eighteenth-century afterlives in polemic, satire and overdetermined certainties.

## Notes

1. Muriel Spark, *The Prime of Miss Jean Brodie* (1961: London, 2000), p. 33.
2. Spark, *Brodie*, p. 33.
3. Spark, *Brodie*, p. 43; in the highly successful film of Spark's novel, produced in 1969, this text from the omniscient narrator is altered and put into Brodie's mouth so that Hume and Boswell are cited as she reminds her girls, 'You are Europeans, not dowdy provincials.'
4. For the best introduction to this topic see John MacQueen, *The Rise of*

the Historical Novel: The Enlightenment and Scottish Literature Volume 2 (Edinburgh, 1989).
5. George Davie, The Democratic Intellect: Scotland and her Universities in the Nineteenth Century (Edinburgh, 1961), pp. 134–7.
6. Davie, Democratic Intellect, p. 274.
7. W. R. Scott, Francis Hutcheson (Cambridge, 1900).
8. Edwin Muir, Scott and Scotland: The Predicament of the Scottish Writer (1936: Edinburgh, 1982), pp. 36, 72.
9. David Craig, Scottish Literature and the Scottish People, 1680–1830 (London, 1961), p. 63.
10. Craig, Scottish Literature, p. 52.
11. David Daiches, The Paradox of Scottish Culture: The Eighteenth-Century Expérience (London, 1964), pp. 21–2.
12. Daiches, Paradox, pp. 21–2.
13. Such ideas are again powerfully reiterated in Kenneth Simpson, The Protean Scot: The Crisis of Identity in Eighteenth-Century Scottish Literature (Aberdeen, 1988).
14. Davie, Democratic Intellect, pp. 111, 149.
15. Davie, Democratic Intellect, p. 219.
16. For a good introduction to this recent critical terrain, see Murray Pittock, 'Nibbling at Adam Smith: A mouse's sma' request and the limits of justice in the Scottish Romanticism of Robert Burns', in Gerard Carruthers and Johnny Rodger (eds), Fickle Man: Robert Burns in the 21st Century (Dingwall, 2009), pp. 118–31.
17. Davie, Democratic Intellect, p. 190.
18. H. T. Buckle, On Scotland and the Scotch Intellect (Chicago and London, 1970), p. 235.
19. Buckle, On Scotland and the Scotch Intellect, p. 236.
20. The phrase 'democratic intellect' is cleverly appropriated from the conservative, politically unionist, culturally nationalist Walter Elliot.
21. Buckle, On Scotland and the Scotch Intellect, p. 255.
22. Buckle, On Scotland and the Scotch Intellect, p. 267.
23. 'The Social Significance of the Scottish Philosophy of Common Sense', in George Davie, The Scottish Enlightenment and other essays (Edinburgh, 1991), pp. 51–85.
24. Davie, 'Social Significance', p. 67.
25. Thomas Carlyle, 'Signs of the Times', in Scottish and Other Miscellanies (London, n.d.), p. 230.
26. John Gibson Lockhart, Peter's Letters to His Kinsfolk (1819: New York, 1820), p. 239.
27. Lockhart, Peter's Letters, p. 232.
28. Lockhart, Peter's Letters, p. 232.
29. In 1961, even amid his account of Scottish literary disability from the eighteenth-century onwards, Craig sought to bestow a crumb of comfort

on the Presbyterian-cradled (as he read it) sardonic utterance of poetry in Scots labelling this the 'reductive idiom', which is probably inspired by Lockhart's similar, less positively accented identification of Scotland's 'keen talent for sarcasm'. Craig, *Scottish Literature and the Scottish People, 1680–1830*, p. 95.
30. Lockhart, *Peter's Letters*, p. 428.
31. Lockhart, *Peter's Letters*, p. 93.
32. *Byron: Complete Poetical Works* (Oxford, 1970), pp. 113–27. Quotations are at lines 417–18, 420–1, 484–9.

# Index

Abdy, Edmund, 116
Aberdeen, 32
Abernethy, John, 153
Adam, Robert, 32
Affleck, James, 92–3, 94, 95, 102
Afghanistan, 118
afterlife, 98, 99
agnosticism, 3, 223, 229
agriculture, 40, 45–6
Alexander, Sir James
  *Discoveries in the Interior of Africa*, 119
Alison, W. P.
  *Observations on the Management of the Poor in Scotland*, 113
America *see* North America; United States of America
American Revolution, 22, 58, 73, 74
anarchy, 44, 74
anatomy, 99–100, 151–2, 153–4, 155, 157–8, 159
Anderson, John, 20
anthropology, 10, 14, 26, 152, 229–30
  and Lang, 209, 210
anti-Catholicism, 170–1
Antiburgher Seceders, 108
Antigua, 118

Archer, William, 3, 225–6, 227–8, 230, 232–3, 237
architecture, 31–2
aristocracy, 19, 38, 42, 44, 76–7
art, 26, 131–2
arts, the, 20, 24, 27–8
Ash, Marinell, 13, 29
astronomy, 92
atheism, 60, 82, 182, 223, 229
  and Glasgow, 96, 98
Athens, 126, 129
Australia, 2, 117, 118
Aytoun, James, 112

Backhouse, James, 117
Bailyn, Bernard, 13
Bain, Alexander, 26
Balfour, Arthur
  *Defence of Philosophic Doubt*, 236–7
ballads, 216–17
Barclay, John, 153, 154
Barrie, J. M., 217
Baxter, George, 131
Beattie, James, 246
Beccaria, Cesare, 40
benevolence, 172, 178, 180, 183
Bentham, Jeremy, 176, 190
  *An Introduction to the Principles of Morals and Legislation*, 196

Berkeley, George, 254
Bible, 12, 30, 162, 193, 230–2
  and Macindoe, 193, 196, 200
biololgical determinism, 152,
  159–60
birds *see* ornithology
birth control, 224, 228, 229
Black, Joseph, 235
Blackwood, William, 109
*Blackwood's Magazine* (magazine), 6,
  170, 253
  'The Chaldee Manuscript', 174
Blair, Hugh, 28
Blake, Charles Carter, 152, 163
blasphemy, 90
Blumenbach, Johann Friedrich, 159
Bombay Literary Society, 82
Bonaparte *see* Napoleon Bonaparte
Boswell, James, 242–3
Bradlaugh, Charles, 98, 225, 226,
  228
Braxfield, Lord, 62–3
Brewster, David, 92, 146, 147–8
Britain *see* British Empire; Great
  Britain
British Army, 109, 110, 153–4, 155
British Convention, 60
British Empire, 6, 23, 36, 118,
  245–6
  and Lang, 212, 216
  and wars, 71, 77
British Guiana, 118
Broadie, Alexander, 25–6, 126–7
Brougham, Henry, 38, 112, 113,
  118, 130, 254
  *Discourse of Natural Theology*, 91
Brown, S. J.
  *Thomas Chalmers and the Godly
  Commonwealth*, 9
Brown, Thomas, 197
Brown, William Laurence
  *Essay on the Existence of the
  Supreme Creator*, 91, 94
Bruce, John, 63

Bruce, Robert the, 18
Bryce, James, 31
Buchan, David Erskine, Earl of, 58
Buchanan, George, 77, 197
  *De Jure Regni Apud Scotus*, 193,
  194
Buckle, Henry, 234, 237
  *History of Civilization in England*,
  10–12, 19, 248–50, 255
Bulwer, Henry Lytton, 116
Burgess Oath, 108
Burke, Edmund, 61–2, 81, 83–4,
  171, 194, 197
  *Reflections on the Revolution in
  France*, 73–4, 75
  and regicide-peace letters, 77–80
Burke, William, 151–2, 154, 163,
  164
Burns, Robert, 18, 172–3, 181, 226,
  246
  and Davie, 248
  and Lang, 214
  and Muir, 244
  and Ross, 228
Bute, John Stuart, 3rd Earl of, 54
Butler, Samuel, 179
Byron, Lord, 249
  *Cain*, 94
  *English Bards and Scotch
  Reviewers*, 254–5

Caird, Edward, 214
Calderwood, Henry, 14
Calvin, John, 182
Calvinism, 31, 56–7, 89, 223, 245
  and Carlyle, 168, 172, 173
Cambridge University, 8, 13, 38
Cameronians *see* United Societies
Campbell, George Douglas, 148
Campbell, Ilay, 63
Campbell, John, 114
Campbell, Thomas, 73
Canada, 70, 84, 117, 118, 188
Cant, Ronald, 24

capitalism, 245–6
Carleton, William, 214
Carlyle, Alexander, 60
Carlyle, Jane, 133
Carlyle, Thomas, 3, 168–83, 228, 249
  *The French Revolution: A History*, 168–9, 172, 173, 177, 180, 183
  *Past and Present*, 169
  *Reminiscences*, 181
  *Sartor Resartus*, 173, 177
  'Signs of the Times', 173–4, 175–6, 177–8, 251, 255
Carnegie, Andrew, 30
Castlereagh, Viscount, 83
Catherine the Great, Empress of Russia, 78
Catholicism *see* Roman Catholicism
Catlin, George
  *Adventures among the North American Indians*, 117
Celts, 29
censorship, 230
Chadwick, Edwin
  *Report on the Sanitary Condition of the Labouring Population*, 113
Chalmers, Thomas, 25, 92, 113
Chambers, Robert
  *Vestiges of the Natural History of Creation*, 142, 145, 146, 147, 148
Chambers, W. & R., 6
Charles I of England, King, 187
Charles II of England, King, 47, 187
Chartism, 22, 112, 189
chemistry, 20
Church of Scotland *see* Kirk
Clarke, Adam, 114
Clarke, Samuel
  *Demonstration of the Being and Attributes of God*, 96, 97

class *see* aristocracy; elites; middle classes; working classes
classicism, 32
Clive, John, 13
Cobbett, William, 249
Cockburn, Lord, 39, 62
Cole, Thomas, 127, 132
Coleridge, Samuel Taylor, 73, 254
College of Physicians and Surgeons (Glasgow), 8
Collins, William, 6
Combe, George, 95, 100, 101
  *Constitution of Man*, 143–4, 145, 148
commerce *see* trade
Common Sense philosophy, 20, 24, 41, 72, 96, 243–4
communications, 6, 23
Confession of Faith, 12, 56, 57
Congress of Vienna, 72, 83
Constant, Benjamin, 72, 82
constitutionalism, 29, 39
Corelli, Marie, 218
  *The Silver Domino, or side whispers, social and literary*, 213, 215–16
Corn Laws, 113
Corsica, 79
*Cosmopolis* (journal), 213–14
*Cosmopolitan* (journal), 213–14
cosmopolitanism, 205–6, 208, 209, 210–18, 216
Covenanters, 172, 187–91, 199; *see also* Reformed Presbyterians
Craig, Cairns, 9, 14, 26
Craig, David
  *Scottish Literature and Scottish People, 1680–1830*, 245–6
Craik, Henry, 27
crime, 22
Crockett, S. R.
  *Cleg Kelly, Arab of the City*, 217–18

Cullen, William, 235
Cuvier, Georges, 157–8

Daiches, David
 *The Paradox of Scottish Culture: the Eighteenth Century Experience*, 246–7
Däniken, Erich von, 137
Darwin, Charles, 127, 132, 153
 *Origin of Species*, 148
Davie, George, 14, 15
 *The Democratic Intellect: Scotland and her Universities in the Nineteenth Century*, 24–5, 26, 29–30, 31, 243–4, 247–8, 249, 250
De Lolme, Louis, 75, 190, 194
De Quincey, Thomas, 111
degenerationism, 137–8, 139–43, 144–5, 146–8
deism, 93
democracy, 24, 29–31, 63, 195–6
Denmark, 83
Derham, William, 132
d'Holbach, Baron, 101
 *Système de la Nature*, 93
Dickens, Charles, 127, 128
 *Oliver Twist*, 129
Disruption of 1843, 2, 19–20, 22, 25, 31, 142
divine Providence, 139
Dobson, Austin, 216
Doig, David, 142
 *Letters on the Savage State, Addressed to the Late Lord Kaims*, 140, 141
Dostoevsky, Fyodor, 216
Downie, David, 63, 64
Dunbar, James, 138
Dundas, Henry, 57, 58, 59–60, 62, 66
 and treason, 63, 64
Dundas, Robert, 63
Dundee, 127–8

Dutch Republic, 79
Dwight, Timothy, 193

economics, 4–5, 6, 12, 21, 25
 and states, 70–2
 and universities, 28
 *see also* political economy
Économistes, 40–1
Edgeworth, Maria, 115
Edinburgh, 3, 4, 5, 13, 18
 and freethinking societies, 95–6, 100, 102
 and Johnstone, 110–11
 and Lockhart, 251–3
 and Mudie, 126, 128–9
 and New Town, 31–2, 246
 and publishing, 6–7
 and science, 9
 and Secession, 108
 and Watt execution, 64–5
 and West Port murders, 151–2, 154, 163, 164
*Edinburgh Review* (periodical), 5, 13, 26, 38, 97
 and Byron, 254–5
 and Carlyle, 173–4
 and Lockhart, 252–3
 and Mackintosh, 81–2
 and progressivism, 170
Edinburgh Secular Society, 226, 228, 237
Edinburgh University, 28, 32, 38–40, 46–7, 54, 65–6
education, 5–6, 8–9, 22, 30–1, 43–4
 and Johnstone, 107, 110, 112
 and Stewart, 37, 40, 48, 49
 *see also* universities
Education Act (1872), 30
Edward III of England, King, 64
egalitarianism, 30, 31, 41, 44, 107
Eliot, T. S., 245, 247
elites, 21, 23, 61
Elliot, Walter, 31
Ellis, Sarah, 115

*Encyclopaedia Britannica*, 6, 13, 127
England, 20, 23, 31, 63, 74–5
   and Church, 114, 187
   and poor relief, 46–7
   and Teutonic identity, 29
   *see also* Glorious Revolution (1688); London; Union of 1707
Enlightenment *see* European Enlightenment; Scottish Enlightenment
enthusiasm, 171–2, 174–5, 176–7
Erskine, Henry, 57, 58
Erskine, Thomas, 58
ethics, 19, 26
ethnology *see* race
Europe *see* cosmopolitanism; individual countries; states
European Englightenment, 19, 20
evangelicalism, 3, 5, 10, 11–12, 19, 25
   and degenerationism, 142–3, 144
   and Moderatism, 55, 57
   and revival, 148
   *see also* Popular Party
evil, 94, 95
evolution, 61

Fall, the, 142–3, 144, 148
Fascism, 241
feminism, 116, 228
Ferguson, Adam, 18, 20, 28 71, 194
   and Covenanters, 190
   *Essay on the History of Civil Society*, 138
   and Lang, 211
   and Robertson, 234, 235
   and Stewart, 38, 39, 47–8
Fergusson, Robert, 248
Ferrer, Francisco, 230
Ferrier, J. F., 243
Ferrier, Susan
   *Marriage*, 109
feudalism, 46, 58, 64, 74, 76–7

First World War, 1, 2
Fleming, John, 92, 146
Fletcher, Andrew, 77
Fox, Charles James, 73, 79, 83
Foxites, 57, 59, 60, 79
France, 19, 20, 27, 31, 38
   and Johnstone, 116
   and Knox, 157–8
   *see also* French Revolution; Napoleon Bonaparte
Frazer, Sir James, 1, 26, 224–5
   *The Golden Bough*, 10, 14, 225, 229
Free Church of Scotland, 12, 142, 199
*Free Review* (journal), 226
free trade, 28, 40, 45, 113, 211, 227
freethinking, 3, 10, 12, 223–5;
   *see also* Archer, William; Robertson, John Mackinnon; Ross, William Stewart
freethinking societies, 6, 89–90, 91, 92–103
French Revolution, 1, 2, 10, 12–13, 22
   and Britain, 36, 37, 42, 59
   and Burke, 73, 78–9
   and Carlyle, 168–9, 172, 173, 180
   and Irving, 181
   and Johnstone, 107
   and Mackintosh, 70, 74, 75, 76, 77–8, 80–2
   and Moderate Party, 60–2, 65
   and political economy, 48–9
   and principles, 39
   and Scotland, 54
   and Whigs, 175–6
Friends of the People, 60, 61
Froude, James Antony, 168–70

Gall, Franz Josef, 95
Galt, John, 242
   *Ringan Gilhaize*, 172

Gellner, Ernest, 23
Geneva, 79
geology, 92–4
George IV of Great Britain, King, 128
Germany, 19, 20, 27, 94–5
Gib, Adam, 108
Gibbon, Edward, 77
Gifford, Douglas
  *History of Scottish Literature*, 9
Gillespie, Thomas, 55–6
Gillespie, William Honyman, 102
  *The Argument, A Priori, For the Being and Attributes of God*, 95–6, 97, 98
Gladstone, William, 31
Glasgow, 20, 32, 96, 100–1
Glasgow Eclectic Society, 237
Glasgow University, 27, 28
Glen, Tam, 112–13
globalism, 44–5
Glorious Revolution (1688), 73, 74, 75–6, 81, 197
God *see* natural theology
Godwin, William, 36, 45, 46, 48, 49, 73
  *Enquiry Concerning Political Justice*, 37, 41–4
Goethe, Johann Wolfgang von, 210, 211, 214
Gore, Catherine, 114
Gosse, Edmund, 216
government *see* politics
Gowdie, John, 54
Graham, Henry Grey
  *Social Life of Scotland in the Eighteenth Century*, 20–1
Granville-Barker, Harley, 228
Great Britain, 4, 6, 7–8, 45, 58, 78
  and Carlyle, 180, 181
  and crisis, 36–7, 42, 71–2
  and French Revolution, 48–9, 59
  and Mackintosh, 76–7, 81, 84
  *see also* England; Scotland

Grotius, Hugo, 80
  *De Iure Belli ac Pacis*, 40

Hackney, William, 128
Hailes, Lord, 206–7
Hall, Robert, 114
Hamilton, Elizabeth, 110, 112
Hamilton, Sir William, 27, 38, 97, 243
Hancock, Graham, 137
happiness, 39, 47–8
Hardy, Thomas, 216
Hare, William, 151–2, 154, 163, 164
Harrington, James, 77
Harvey, Thomas
  *The West Indies in 1837*, 118
Henderson, Alexander, 187
Henley, William Ernest, 216
heresy trials, 12
hierology, 229–30
Highlands, 29, 109, 116
Hill, George, 59, 60, 65, 66
history, 4, 13–14, 18–19, 20–1
  and Carlyle, 179–81
  and Godwin, 42, 44
  and Stewart, 44–5
  and universities, 28–9
  *see also* degenerationism; progressivism; stadial history
Hodgkin, Thomas, 156
Hogg, James, 214
  *The Private Memoirs and Confessions of a Justified Sinner*, 172, 242
Holland, 19
Home, John
  *Douglas*, 235
Horner, Francis, 38, 41
housing, 22
Howitt, Mary, 114
Howitt, William, 114
  *Colonization and Christianity*, 117
Hudson, William Henry, 132

human nature, 40–1, 46–7, 80, 92, 103
Hume, David, 10, 11, 14, 18, 19, 223
   and British constitution, 71
   and Carlyle, 179–80
   and causation, 65
   and cosmopolitanism, 205, 206
   and Craig, 246
   and Davie, 243–4
   *Dialogues Concerning Natural Religion*, 94, 96
   'Essay on the Immortality of the Soul', 98–9, 101
   and freethinkers, 226
   and histories, 28, 45
   and influence, 26
   and Lang, 207
   and Lockhart, 252–4
   *Of Miracles*, 97–8, 209
   and Moderate Party, 57, 89
   and progress, 138
   and religion, 91, 93
   and Robertson, 234, 235, 236–7
   and scholarship, 21
   and sentiment, 169, 171
   and Spark, 242
   and Stewart, 38, 39, 40
Hume, Joseph, 112
Hume Brown, Peter
   *History of Scotland*, 20
Hunt, James, 152, 160, 163–4
Hutcheson, Francis, 20, 169, 183, 249, 250
Hutton, James, 235
hypocrisy, 181

Ibsen, Henrik, 227–8
imagination, 169–70, 175, 177
imperialism *see* British Empire
India, 70, 71, 72, 73, 117, 118
indigenous peoples, 117
Industrial Revolution, 31
industrialisation, 2, 20, 21–2

inequality, 42
intellectual life, 2–11
International Congress on the Enlightenment, 21
Interregnum, 187
Inverkeithing patronage case, 54–6
*Inverness Courier* (newspaper), 109
Ireland, 2, 70, 71, 72, 83
   and Burke, 73
   and Church, 114
   and Covenanting, 188
   and Johnstone, 109
irrationality, 174, 176, 178
irreligion, 3, 10, 171, 223, 225
Irving, Edward, 168
   *Signs of the Times*, 181
Italy, 20, 241

Jacobinism, 3, 22, 77, 188
Jamaica, 76
James, Henry, 216
James VI and I of Scotland and England, King, 47
James VII and II of Scotland and England, King, 187
Jameson, Anna
   *Winter Studies and Summer Rambles*, 117
Jeffrey, Francis, 38, 252, 254, 255
   and Carlyle, 173–4, 175, 181
Jewsbury, Geraldine, 133
Johnston, Archibald, 187
Johnstone, Christian Isobel, 107–19
   *Clan-Albin*, 109, 110
   *Cook and Housewife's Manual*, 109–10
   *Elizabeth de Bruce*, 110
   *Nights of the Round Table*, 110
   'The Sabbath Night's Supper', 114
   *The Saxon and the Gael*, 109
Johnstone, John, 108, 109, 110

## INDEX

*Johnstone's Edinburgh Magazine* (magazine), 110–11
justice, 41–4, 46, 49, 63

Kames, Henry Home, Lord, 57, 138, 211
   *Elements of Criticism*, 233
   *Sketches of the History of Man*, 140
Kant, Immanuel, 209–10, 211
Kelvin, Lord, 210
Kemp Smith, Norman, 243
Kipling, Rudyard, 216
Kirk, 47, 113, 148, 187; *see also* Covenanters; Moderate Party; Secession
Knight, Charles, 129
knowledge, 4–6, 43–4, 45, 193–4; *see also* education
Knowlton, Charles
   *The Fruits of Philosophy*, 228
Knox, John, 21, 30, 182, 206–7, 241, 242
Knox, Robert, 3, 151–64
   *Manual of Human Anatomy*, 158
   *The Races of Men: A Fragment*, 152, 155–7, 158, 159, 160–3

labour, 44, 46, 47
labouring classes *see* working classes
Laing, Samuel, 116
Lally-Tollendal, Marquis de, 76
Lamarck, Jean-Baptiste
   *Philosophie Zoologique*, 146
Lang, Andrew, 3, 205–18, 230
   *John Knox and the Reformation*, 206–7
   *The Making of Religion*, 209
   *Myth, Ritual and Religion*, 209
   *Short History of Scotland*, 205
Lang, John Dunmore, 118
Laurie, Thomas, 228
law, 8, 20, 39; *see also* legislation
law of nations, 80–1

Lawrance, Hannah, 115
Lawrence, William, 157
Lees, John, 226
legislation, 37, 48, 45
Leslie, John, 100
   *Experimental Enquiry into the Nature and Propagation of Heat*, 65–6
liberalism, 22–3, 62–3
liberty, 24, 36, 39, 63, 76–7, 83–4
libraries, 130
Linnean Society, 133
literacy, 30, 44
literary criticism, 225–6, 231–3, 244–8
literati, 11, 60, 61, 63, 146
literature, 4, 7, 8, 26
   and 'kailyard', 9–10, 207
   and Lang, 211–12, 213–18
   and travel, 116
   and universities, 28
Locke, John, 77, 193, 197, 254
Lockhart, John Gibson, 249
   *Life of Sir Walter Scott*, 113
   *Peter's Letters to his Kinsfolk*, 251–4, 255
London, 3, 6–7, 10, 13
   and freethinkers, 224, 225–6, 226, 227, 228–9, 238
   and Mudie, 128, 129, 134
Longman, F. W., 213
Lonsdale, Henry, 152, 155
Lorimer, James, 31
Louis XIV of France, King, 77
Louis XVI of France, King, 73
Louis XVIII of France, King, 82
lower orders *see* working classes
Lowlands, 29, 47
Luther, Martin, 182

Macaulay, Catherine, 116
Macaulay, Thomas, 174
   'Milton', 170
MacCall, William, 224

McCall Smith, Alexander
  *Isabel Dalhousie* novels, 89, 102
MacDiarmid, Hugh, 245
Macfarlane, Frederick, 108
Macindoe, Peter, 189, 199–200
  *The Application of Scriptural Principles to Political Government Essential to the Piety, Virtue, Order, Freedom, and Prosperity of Christian States*, 190–1, 192–8
Mackenzie, Henry, 107
Mackenzie, John Stuart, 224
Mackinnon, W. A.
  *The Rise, Progress, and Present State of Public Opinion*, 177–8
Mackintosh, Sir James, 61, 72–4, 78, 190, 197
  *A Discourse on the Law of Nature and Nations*, 79–83
  *Vindiciae Gallicae*, 62, 70, 74–7, 194, 195
Maclaren, Ian, 217
McLennan, J. F., 14, 26
McLeod, Alexander, 192, 193
MacLeod, Fiona, 218
Macmillan, John, 192
Malthus, Thomas
  *Essay on the Principles of Population*, 49
manufacturing, 40, 42
Marcet, Jane, 114
marriage, 37, 41, 44, 46, 49
Martin, Thomas Carlaw, 226
Martineau, Harriet, 132
  *Life in Demerara*, 114
Mary of Guise, 206–7
Mary Queen of Scots, 206, 208, 241, 242
Masson, David, 238
Maxwell, James Clerk, 14, 26
Mechanics' Institutes, 6, 7, 20, 112
medicine, 20, 23, 28; *see also* anatomy

Melbourne, William Lamb, Lord, 13
Meteyard, Eliza, 114
middle classes, 22, 23, 90
migration, 2
Mill, James, 26, 176
Mill, John Stuart, 26, 181–3
Millar, John, 13, 138
Miller, Hugh
  *Foot-prints of the Creator*, 146–7
Milton, John, 77
Mirabeau, Marquis de, 40
missionaries, 118–19
Mitford, Mary Russell, 114
mob violence, 36, 44, 60
Moderate Party, 19, 20, 21, 56–7, 235
  and decline, 89, 101
  and French Revolution, 60–2
  and Leslie, 65–6
  and natural theology, 90–1
  and Robertson, 54–5, 57–9
  and soul's immortality, 98–9
Moffat, Robert
  *Missionary Labours*, 119
Molyneux, James, 77
monarchy, 194–5
Monboddo, James Burnett, Lord, 138
  *Antient Metaphysics*, 139–40, 141
monotheism, 209, 230
Monro, Alexander, III, 153, 154
Montaigne, Michel de, 232
Montesquieu, 40, 77, 190
Moore, Alexander, 190
Moore, Thomas, 255
moral philosophy, 38–9, 43, 49
morality, 169, 170, 178–9, 180
Morgan, Lady
  *Woman and Her Master*, 115
Morley, John, 143
Mounier, Jean-Jacques, 76
Mudie, Robert, 3, 126–34
  *The Air*, 130

*Autumn*, 130
*Babylon the Great*, 129
*The Complete Governess*, 130
*Dundee Delineated*, 127
*The Earth*, 130
*The Feathered Tribes of the British Isles*, 130
*Glenfergus*, 127
*The Heavens*, 130
*A Historical Account of His Majesty's Visit to Scotland*, 128
'The Maid of Griban', 127
*Man, as a Moral and Accountable Being*, 132
*Man, in His Intellectual Faculties and Adaptations*, 132
*Man, in His Relations to Society*, 132
*Mental Philosophy*, 132
*The Modern Athens: a dissection and demonstration of men and things in the Scotch capital*, 126, 128–9
*The Natural History of Birds*, 130
*Natural History of Domestic and Wild Animals*, 132
*A Popular Guide to the Observation of Nature*, 130–2
*The Sea*, 130
*The Second Judgement of Babylon the Great*, 129
*Spring*, 130
*Summer*, 130
*Winter*, 130
Muir, Edwin
   *Scott and Scotland: The Predicament of the Scottish Writer*, 244–5
Muir, Thomas, 62–3
Munro, Neil, 217, 218
Murray, John, 100
Mussolini, Benito, 241
Mylne, James, 224

Nairn, Tom, 23
Napoleon Bonaparte, 36, 81, 82, 83
National Covenant, 187
*National Reformer* (periodical), 225, 226, 228
nationalism, 23–4
natural history, 130–2, 158–9
natural laws, 139
natural order, 45
natural sciences, 23, 191
natural theology, 56–7, 90–103
navigation, 45
neo-Hegelian idealism, 27
neo-Malthusianism, 228
New Lanark, 22
New Liberalism, 229
Nicholl, William Robertson, 10
Nicoll, Robert, 113
North America, 2, 71, 72, 74, 83; *see also* American Revolution; United States of America
Norway, 116

Opie, Amelia, 114
ornithology, 130–1, 133
orthodoxy, 3, 10–12, 56–7
Owen, Robert, 22
Oxford University, 8, 13, 27, 38

Paine, Thomas, 36, 43, 73
   *Age of Reason*, 95
   *Rights of Man*, 60
Paley, William, 190, 197
   *Natural Theology*, 91–2
Palmerston, Henry Temple, Viscount, 13, 38
Pardoe, Julia, 115
parish schools, 30
Parnassians, 216–17
patriarchalism, 22
patronage, 54–6, 61, 199
Peacock, Thomas Love
   *Crotchet Castle*, 31
Peltier, Jean, 81

perfectibility, 42, 45, 49
Perth, 32
Phillipson, Nicholas, 13, 38
philosophy *see* Common Sense philosophy; moral philosophy; Scottish Enlightenment
phrenology, 94–5, 100–1
Pike Plot, 63–5
Pitt the Younger, William, 59, 77
Plato, 137
Playfair, John, 13, 18, 134
Poland, 76, 78, 79, 82, 83
political economy, 12, 21, 28, 37–42, 44–9, 82
   and Johnstone, 107, 113, 114
politics, 12–13, 19, 21, 60–1
   and Dundas, 59–60
   and Godwin, 42–4
   and Johnstone, 110, 111–13
   and Macindoe, 192–8
   and Mackintosh, 72
   and Robertson, 227
   and universities, 28–9
   and Whigs, 26
   and women, 115
   *see also* liberalism; radicalism; Whigs
polygenesis, 152, 157, 160, 164
polytheism, 209
poor laws, 22, 37, 40, 47, 107, 113
Pope, Alexander
   *Essay on Man*, 139
popular culture, 211–12
Popular Party, 56, 60, 89, 99, 146
   and natural theology, 90, 91–2, 101
population growth, 37, 39, 40
Postans, Marianne
   *Cutch; or Random Sketches of Western India*, 117
poverty, 22, 43, 44
   and Stewart, 42, 46–7, 49
   *see also* poor laws

Presbyterianism, 5, 19, 187, 238, 249
   and Carlyle, 172, 180–1, 182–3
   and education, 30–1
   and Johnstone, 107
   and Lockhart, 252–3
   *see also* Kirk; Reformed Presbyterians
press *see* publishing
Price, Richard, 40, 77, 84
Prichard, James Cowles, 156, 157, 159, 161, 162
Priestley, Joseph, 250
printing press, 45
progressivism, 137, 138–9, 143–4, 145, 146–7, 148, 170
   and Carlyle, 176
property, 22, 43, 44, 195
   and Stewart, 37, 41, 46, 49
Protestantism, 19, 231
provincialisation, 3, 8, 10, 13–14
Prussia, 116
psychical research, 209, 210, 211, 215
publishing, 3, 5, 6–7, 23
   and Johnstone, 109–12, 113–14
   and Lang, 213
   and Mudie, 127, 128, 129–32
   and Ross, 228–9

Queensferry paper, 196
Quesnay, François, 40–1

race, 22, 29
   and Johnstone, 107, 116–17, 119
   and Knox, 151, 152, 154–7, 158–64
   *see also* slave trade
radicalism, 36–7, 42, 54, 57–60, 62–5
   and Carlyle, 182–3
   and Johnstone, 112–13
   and Robertson, 227
railways, 6, 7, 23

Rational Dissent, 43
rationalism, 19, 170, 171, 178
Ray, John, 132
Reform Act (1832), 22, 70, 189
Reformation, 18–19, 21, 30
   and Carlyle, 182
   and Davie, 244
   and Lang, 206–7
   and Robertson, 234–5
Reformed Presbyterians, 187–8,
   191–200, 194, 199
Regency Crisis, 73
Reid, Marion
   *A Plea for Woman*, 116
Reid, Thomas, 20, 71, 243, 250,
   253
   and Stewart, 38, 39
religion, 3, 8, 9, 10–12, 21
   and Knox, 162
   and Lang, 209
   and philosophy, 24–5, 26–7
   and Robertson, 229–30
   *see also* Bible; Disruption of 1843;
      irreligion; missionaries; natural
      theology; Presbyterianism;
      Reformation; secularism
republicanism, 194–5, 227
resistance, 197–8
Restoration, 187, 190
Revolution of 1688 *see* Glorious
   Revolution (1688)
riches *see* wealth
Rider Haggard, Henry, 209, 211
Rintoul, R. S., 127
Riqueti, Victor, 40
Robertson, John Mackinnon, 1, 3,
   225–7, 229, 232, 233, 238
   *The Perversion of Scotland*, 234–5
   *Rationalism*, 236–7
   *William Archer as Rationalist:*
      *A Collection of his Heterodox*
      *Writings*, 228
Robertson, William, 18, 19, 21, 28
   and cosmopolitanism, 206

*History of America*, 138
*History of Scotland*, 208
   and Lang, 207–8
   and liberty, 178
   and Macindoe, 197
   and Moderatism, 54–5, 56, 57–9,
      62
Robertson, William, Jr, 57, 58
Robertson Smith, William, 14, 26,
   224–5, 229
Roman Catholicism, 22, 57,
   58, 189, 207; *see also*
   anti-Catholicism
Romanticism, 9, 13, 25, 29, 252
   and Carlyle, 173, 251
   and Lang, 211, 212, 216
Ross, William Stewart, 225–6,
   228–9, 237
   *God and his Book*, 230–2
   *Woman: her Glory, her Shame*
      *and her God*, 231
Rothschild, Emma, 12
Roy, Rammohun, 114
Royal College of Physicians
   (Edinburgh), 8
Royal College of Surgeons of
   Edinburgh, 154
Royal Society (London), 7
Royal Society of Edinburgh, 5, 7,
   8
RP *see* Reformed Presbyterians
Russell, John, Lord, 13
Rutherford, Samuel, 190, 197

St Andrews University, 21, 59
Saint-Hilaire, Étienne Geoffroy,
   157, 158, 162
St James's Ornithological Society,
   133
Saintsbury, George, 214, 216
Saladin *see* Ross, William Stewart
Sale, Lady, 118
San People, 151
Schism Overture, 55

*Schoolmaster and Edinburgh Weekly Magazine, The* (magazine), 110, 111, 115
schools *see* education
science, 4, 7, 9, 20, 26
   and evangelicals, 146
   and universities, 28
   *see also* geology; natural history
Scotland, 4, 6, 8–9, 29, 31
   and Britain, 23–4
   and culture, 241–3, 244–7
   and education, 48
   and industrialisation, 21–2
   and military recruitment, 58
   and poor relief, 46–7
   and provincialisation, 13–14
   and rebellions, 74–5
   and Reformation, 234–5
   and Reformed Presbyterians, 191–2
   and religion, 10–12
   *see also* Dundee; Edinburgh; Glasgow; Scottish Enlightenment; Union of 1707
Scott, Clement, 227
Scott, Walter, 6, 9, 13, 18, 242
   and history, 29
   and Johnstone, 113
   and Lang, 207, 214
   *Letters on Demonology and Witchcraft addressed to J. G. Lockhart*, 209
   and Lockhart, 252, 253
   and Muir, 244
   *Old Mortality*, 172
   *Rob Roy*, 29
   *St Ronan's Well*, 109
   and supernatural, 210
   *Waverley*, 29, 109
Scott, W. R., 3, 205, 244
Scott, William, 20
   *The Harmony of Phrenology and Scripture*, 144–5

Scottish Enlightenment, 1–4, 10, 20–1, 22–3, 72
   and architecture, 31–2
   and Broadie, 25–6
   and Buckle, 248–50
   and Carlyle, 168, 169, 173–4
   and Covenanters, 190–1, 199–200
   and Craig, 245–6
   and Davie, 24–5, 243–4, 247–8
   and education, 30
   and freethinkers, 233–4, 235–8
   and French Revolution, 12–13
   and historiography, 18–19
   and Johnstone, 107
   and Lang, 205–6, 208–9, 210, 211
   and Lockhart, 252–4
   and Moderate Party, 56–7, 65
   and Mudie, 126–7, 129, 130, 132, 133
   and nostalgia, 207–8
   and progressivism, 138–9
   and religion, 11–12
   and Stewart, 26–7, 37, 38–9
   and sympathy concept, 171, 172–3, 174–5
Seceders, 108, 181, 187
Secession, 54, 55–6, 107, 108, 181
   and Johnstone, 110, 114
sectarianism, 22, 25, 170, 171
secularism, 19, 22, 225, 226, 228–9, 237
sentiment, 169, 170, 171
Shakespeare, William, 226, 232
Shields, Alexander, 190
Sidney, Algernon, 77
Simpson, George, 101–2
   *Refutation of the Argument A Priori*, 96–8
Simson, James H., 94
slave trade, 76–7, 114, 117–18
   and abolition, 199, 231
   and Covenanters, 188, 189

Smith, Adam, 11, 12, 14, 18, 20, 21
  and Buckle, 249–50
  and Covenanters, 190
  and Davie, 25
  and education, 48, 110
  and empire, 71
  and free trade, 211
  and histories, 28, 45
  and Johnstone, 107
  and Lang, 209
  and liberty, 178
  and Lockhart, 253
  and parish schools, 30
  and progress, 138, 139
  and Robertson, 234, 235
  and sentiment, 169
  and Stewart, 37, 38, 39, 40
  and sympathy, 242
  *Theory of Moral Sentiments*, 196, 248
Smith, Sydney, 38
Smollett, Tobias
  *The Expedition of Humphry Clinker*, 251
Smyth, Charles Piazzi, 148
Snell, W. E., 226
social science, 29
socialism, 212, 229
societies, 6, 7
society, 22–3, 40–1, 42–4, 44–9, 61
Society for the Diffusion of Useful Knowledge, 130, 133
Society of Antiquaries of Scotland, 8, 58
sociology, 4, 5, 26, 226
Solemn League and Covenant, 187, 189
Somerville, Thomas, 61–2
soul's immortality, 98–101, 102
South Africa, 116–17, 118, 119, 151, 154, 155–6
South America, 83
South Pacific, 119, 188
Spain, 11, 83, 109
Spark, Muriel
  *The Prime of Miss Jean Brodie*, 241–3
*Spectator, The* (magazine), 127, 133
spelling reform, 225, 228
Spurzheim, Johann Gaspar, 95
stadial history, 107, 116, 209
Stark, John
  'On the supposed Progress of Human Society from Savage to Civilized Life', 141–2, 143, 146
states, 70–2, 78–81, 83
Steuart, William Henry, 92, 93–4
Stevenson, Robert Louis, 211
  *Weir of Hermiston*, 214–15
Stevenson, William, 191
Stewart, Dugald, 13, 18, 26–7, 62, 196
  and Britain, 36
  and Covenanters, 190
  *The Elements of the Philosophy of the Human Mind*, 38, 39
  and history, 28
  and Johnstone, 107
  and Lang, 209
  and liberty, 178
  and Macindoe, 200
  and Mackintosh, 72
  *Outlines of Moral Philosophy*, 38
  and political economy, 37–42, 44–9
Stewart, House of, 206
Stewart, James
  *Jus Populi Vindicatum*, 197
Strickland, Agnes, 115
Stuart, Gilbert, 57–8
Sturge, Joseph, 112
  *The West Indies in 1837*, 118
suffrage, 107, 114, 189

supernatural, 209, 210
superstition, 19, 71, 76, 81, 171, 176
Sweden, 116
Swedenborg, Emanuel, 210
Swift, Jonathan, 177
Symington, William, 191
sympathy, 169, 171–3, 174–5, 177, 180, 242, 249–50

Tait, William, 110–11, 112
*Tait's Edinburgh Magazine* (magazine), 110, 111, 112–14, 115
technology, 45
telegraphs, 6, 23, 137
Teutons, 29, 31
theatre, 227–8, 230, 233
theology *see* natural theology
Thompson, D'Arcy, 4
Thompson, Perronet, 112
Thomson, Andrew, 198
Tolstoy, Leo, 216
trade, 6, 63, 70–2, 76, 77; *see also* free trade
transcendentalism, 157, 158
treason, 63–5
Trevor-Roper, Hugh, 21, 24
truth, 43
Tulloch, John, 235
Turgot, Anne-Robert-Jacques, 40
tyranny, 197–8
Tytler, Alexander Fraser, 28, 141

Union of 1707, 8, 23, 71, 72, 206, 208
United Irishmen, 36
United Societies, 187–8, 194, 199
United States of America (USA), 55, 38, 130, 132
and Covenanting, 188, 194
and freethinkers, 223–4
and indigenous peoples, 116, 117
*see also* American Revolution; North America
universities, 3, 5, 14, 20, 23
and curriculum, 27–9
and democracy, 24, 29–30
and secularisation, 22
and Stewart, 26–7
utilitarianism, 25, 176, 196
utopianism, 37, 41–4, 49

Vanuatu, 188
Vattel, Emer de, 78–9, 80
Vizetelly, Henry, 225
Voltaire, 170–1, 205

Wallace, William, 18
war, 44, 45
Watt, Robert, 63–5
Watts, Charles, 229
wealth, 39, 40
Webster, Grace, 113
West Port murders, 151–2, 154, 163, 164
Wheeler, Joseph Mazzini, 226
Whigs, 26, 29, 38, 73, 251–3
and Carlyle, 173–4, 175–7, 178–83
and Covenanters, 189
and Robertson, 57, 58
Whyte, Adam Gowans, 224
Williams, John, 119
Willis, Robert, 224
Witherspoon, John, 55
Wollstonecraft, Mary, 116
women, 22, 49, 114–16, 215–16
and Christianity, 231
and Covenanters, 189
and education, 5, 130
and freethinkers, 227, 228
*see also* Johnstone, Christian Isobel
Woolf, Virginia, 133
Wordsworth, William, 254

working classes, 5, 22, 107 112, 194, 195
   and education, 48
   and freethinking societies, 90
   and literacy, 130
Wright, Frances (Fanny), 223–4

Young, Arthur, 40
Young, R. M., 4–5

Zetetic societies, 90, 92, 93, 94, 96, 99, 100, 102
Zola, Émile, 216, 225

EU representative:
Easy Access System Europe
Mustamäe tee 50, 10621 Tallinn, Estonia
Gpsr.requests@easproject.com

www.ingramcontent.com/pod-product-compliance
Lightning Source LLC
Chambersburg PA
CBHW050210240426
43671CB00013B/2285